Praise for Meg Greenfield's *Washington*

"Greenfield had a great b.s. detector. . . . [she] is reporting what she knows, and pomposity, hypocrisy and self-delusion make wonderful targets."
                                        —Molly Ivins, *The San Francisco Chronicle*

"Quintessential Meg Greenfield: the detached observer who never missed a detail, the wit who specialized in irony and understatement, the remarkably smart woman who for thirty years persuaded, poked, scolded, and provoked the most powerful people in the world."
                                        —The Seattle Post-Intelligencer

"The brainy, classy *Washington Post* editor and *Newsweek* columnist. . . saw a whole lot, and her posthumously published study of when bad Beltway culture happens to good people—left and right, noble and numbskull—holds back nothing."
                                        —New York magazine

"Something very different from a traditional memoir . . . a new way of looking at a flawed Washington, one that is scathing in import if not in tone, a useful framework even to those who think of government people as more real, more human and even more truthful than she does."
                                        —Adam Clymer, *The New York Times Book Review*

"Offers a cultural dissection that would thrill anthropologist Margaret Mead. . ."
                                        —BusinessWeek

"Meg Greenfield . . . had professional and personal integrity and toughness I have never seen matched. . . . All amply demonstrated . . . in this remarkable, concise volume. If a better field guide to American political animals has been written, I can't think what it is. . . . For anybody with an ounce of political junkyism in their veins, this is a book of delight, of charm—of joy."
                                        —Michael Pakenham, *The Baltimore Sun*

"Like its author . . . the book has a foxy, confiding, come-into-my-parlor quality. . . . Part memoir, part zoology of Washington elites, with the former serving the scathing purposes of the latter."

—*National Journal*

"Much better than the stuffy old "Education of Henry Adams" that everybody swoons about and nobody reads. . . . A feast of Greenfield in a sweet and sour mood."

—*The Bridgewater Courier-News*

"What makes Greenfield's book appealing is a heart that reveals remorse, doubt and affection."

—*The Rocky Mountain News*

"Greenfield's prose is careful, quiet and diligent as she peels away all the high-gloss of power inside the nation's capital and shows us an elite world inhabited by men haunted by insecurity and women frequently frustrated in their efforts to carve out a place for themselves."

—*The Philadelphia Lawyer*

"Greenfield dissects Washington as well as novelist Tom Wolfe captured New York or Atlanta."

—*The Iowa City Gazette*

"A connoisseur's book with the bouquet of a well-aged vintage, the testament of a brilliant writer who learned hard truths about the defects of modern mass democracy and journalism, expressed them with surpassing originality, and longed with diminishing hope to set them right."

—Edwin M. Yoder Jr., *The Washington Times*

"With great intelligence and self-awareness, Greenfield dissects the culture of politics and life (are they different?) in the nation's capital. . . Her memoir leaves us better informed about her, her town and her times. Finish the book, and you'll wish you could sit down and keep the conversation going."

—*The Topeka Capital-Journal*

Meg Greenfield

Washington

PublicAffairs

NEW YORK

BOOK DESIGN BY JENNY DOSSIN.

Library of Congress Cataloging-in-Publication Data
Greenfield, Meg.
Washington / Meg Greenfield:
with a foreword by Katharine Graham and an afterword by Michael Beschloss.
p. cm.
ISBN 1-58648-118-5 (pbk.)
1. Washington (D.C.)—Social life and customs. 2. Capitol Hill (Washington, D.C.)—
Social life and customs. 3. Politicians—United States—Social life and customs. 4. Politicians—United States—Psychology. 5. Political culture—Washington (D.C.). 6. Political
culture—United States. 7. United States—Politics and government.
I. Title.
F201.G74 2001
975.3'041—dc21
00-045876

10 9 8 7 6 5 4 3 2 1

"Princes appear to me to be fools. Houses of Commons and Houses of Lords appear to me to be fools; they seem to me to be something Else besides Human Life."

—WILLIAM BLAKE

Contents

Foreword

BY KATHARINE GRAHAM

MEG GREENFIELD HAS LEFT US a fine book about Washington, journalism, and life. We get a vivid picture of Washington, but we have to read between the lines to learn more about Meg.

To me, Meg was a friend like no other. We were friends at work and play. I long to re-create her, but even to her handful of close friends, Meg remained largely hidden. In a way, no one ever really got to know Meg. Despite playing a huge and powerful role at the *Washington Post* and *Newsweek,* within Washington, and even in the larger world, she was a mysterious figure to many.

The outline of her biography fits neatly into a few paragraphs. Mary Ellen was born in Seattle in 1930 to Lewis and Lorraine Greenfield. Her father was an antiques dealer whose entertaining auctioneering was carried live on a Seattle radio station. Her mother died when she was eleven, a loss that affected her profoundly. She grew up more or less alone because her father was preoccupied with his work. She and her older brother brought each other up, insofar as one could tell. Meg adored both her father and her brother, who, like Meg, was very smart but undisciplined and wild, although in a happy kind of way. He got money from his father for four years of college at UCLA but never attended. His death several years later, while he was still a relatively young man, may have influenced her tendency to conceal her personality.

In high school the blue-jeaned Meg was popular and enjoyed dancing and singing but had no beaus or real romances. She did, however, have top grades and went on to Smith, where she studied English literature, graduating summa cum laude in 1952. On this her father commented, "Remember, that's not everything in life." After a not altogether happy experience in Cambridge on a Fulbright scholarship, she took herself to Rome, where she worked on a never-completed novel. When she'd had enough, she packed up and left for New York, where she settled into Greenwich Village and found some kindred spirits on the Adlai Stevenson campaign. She went to work as a researcher for the *Reporter,* a lively journal whose commentary and analysis were widely read. She moved up at the magazine before being sent to Washington in 1961 to fill in as the Washington editor. She never left. She became bureau chief–editor, writing a breakthrough piece on the language used by Richard Nixon.

When the *Reporter* folded in 1968, Phil Geyelin, then editorial page editor at the *Washington Post,* recruited Meg. Her writing quickly made an impact, and she became Phil's deputy. He described their work together as "two people playing chopsticks at the piano." I was puzzled at first when Phil asked to bring Meg along to our meetings. I soon realized why, when I saw how much she added.

Meg began writing a column for *Newsweek* in 1974, and her voice grew even stronger. She was awarded the Pulitzer Prize for editorial writing in 1978 and was named editorial page editor of the *Post* in 1979. She wrote for and oversaw the editorial and opinion pages right up until her death of cancer on May 13, 1999.

All of this is simple fact. To flesh out who Meg was, we have to dig deeper and ask some of the questions she resisted during her lifetime. Behind her humor and shimmering intellect was a point where she retreated into herself. There was some sort of lone fortress there into which one did not intrude. She was guarded and private and seemed to pull back from people in some ways, only reluctantly revealing glimpses of a personal Meg from time to time. Consequently, it is only by looking at how lots of others—her friends, her colleagues, her readers—saw her that we can even begin to come up with a fuller picture of who she was.

Physically, Meg was what some would have called diminutive; she would have said she was short. At one speech she delivered in the early 1990s, her first words on taking her place to speak were: "I never met a podium I could see over." Her friend Mary McGrory, a *Post* columnist whom Meg had guided to the newspaper in 1981 with the demise of the *Washington Star*, Mary's longtime home, wrote that Meg looked "strikingly like the Queen of England." Indeed, however short she may have been, she did have a presence. Mary's explanation was that, in part, Meg "had a grande dame streak in her, an awareness of the majesty of her position on a newspaper to which she gave her total allegiance and commitment."

Meg may have been small in stature, but she was a giant in impact and intellect. In fact, anyone who knew Meg or read her work was impressed by the strength of her mind. Although honorary degrees formally recognized the sharpness of her unique mind, *Post* executive editor Ben Bradlee cut to the quick when he exclaimed over "her goddam brain power." She was gifted, logical, reflective, fresh, and independent in her thinking. Sometimes you could almost see her thinking things through from the ground up.

Beyond being smart, Meg was wise. She was perceptive about people. As someone once said, Meg seemed to be able to "see around the corners of your mind." She was clearly an intellectual, but a far from purely academic one. Her sense of humanity and understanding of human nature and the human condition were reflected in her thoughts and actions.

Without psychologizing too much—because Meg first of all would have hated that—it is important to say that she had rock solid moral and ethical standards. At her core was this innate sense of what was right and what was wrong, and she took her bearings on what was right.

In many ways Meg seemed to have sprung full-blown, Minerva-like, from her mother's head. Her mother even called her "little lady," and she did give off an aura of having been formed early on. She changed remarkably little through time. The smart, short teenager seemed more grown-up than most of her contemporaries—which is not to say that Meg didn't have fun. She was full of mischief always. At one point in her younger life and when I first knew her, she enjoyed parties and could drink quite a lot—and did.

Everyone recognized her humor as one of her signature traits. She was a comic genius whose timing with a bon mot was perfect. She loved to hear and tell funny stories and jokes, and she made people laugh until they cried. She had a wonderful laugh that you always wanted to hear, mostly because you knew you'd be laughing, too. Ben Bradlee once said of Meg's laugh that it was the "greatest laugh ever . . . deep, dirty, husky, sensuous. . . . I feel better each time I hear it."

Her humor came through in her writing, where she artfully used her wit—droll, wry, sardonic—to great effect. One of so many examples of this is a column about new American hotels, which began by asking who decided to bring the lake into the lobby: "The undertow has followed me indoors," Meg wrote, "and upstairs as far as the mezzanine. . . . I have stayed in hotels with waterfalls, with rivers, with canals and with what looked to be, in Georgia, an attempt at re-creation of the elaborate irrigation system of early Sumeria."

Meg was also tough. She once joked, "I don't *have* stress; I *give* stress." It was not possible to push her around. I saw some of her toughness especially in the period when I traveled with her so much, going off on reporting trips around the world, along with Jim Hoagland, one of the *Post*'s longtime foreign correspondents. I think Jim got it completely right when he wrote a piece called "Don't Mess with Meg," published in the *Post* a few days after her death:

The adjective that popped up most frequently in her obituaries has been "tough," and she was that. Being described as tough helped her make her way in a male-dominated profession and capital. But it misses the essential point about Greenfield's willingness to grill dictators, to flay incompetent secretaries of state in editorials or to harp on what China's dictators had done at Tiananmen Square long after it became politically fashionable in Washington to suck up to those dictators.

What drove her was the determination to recognize and oppose human evil wherever it occurred and by whomever it was committed. She would not agree to explain evil away in the terms of the moral relativism that has infected the late 20th century or in the cause of diplomatic strategy. This was not mere toughness. This was existence and essence for Greenfield.

It's true. On these trips and close to home, I certainly witnessed Meg's toughness, as when she confronted Mikhail Gorbachev in Moscow in 1988 with the contradiction between his public protestations and his private policies. Jim cites another example, "the South Korean ruling general du jour who ignored the diminutive, slightly bookish-looking woman fidgeting a few chairs away from him as he droned on about how stable and wonderful his rule was. Greenfield cut to a simple, piercing question when he paused for breath: 'What had the general's brother-in-law done with the $3 million he was said to have stolen?'" Jim also recalls that "Nicolae Ceausescu sat upright in disbelief when challenged by the woman he assumed was a note-taker for the polite conversation he envisioned with a *Washington Post-Newsweek* 'delegation.' She sank her teeth into his ankle with detailed questions about the shoddy, cruel Romanian police state that was to collapse later in bloodshed and revolution."

Meg wrote about Ceausescu after his execution in 1989: "Ceausescu killed himself. He choked on his own arrogance, greed, and unimpeded ascent to what seemed and, for a while was, absolute power." Tough words—and she purposely chose every one of them.

So she was tough, but as evidenced by the first impressions of some of the world's leaders, she was old-fashioned and mannerly as well. Her manners were impeccable, and she liked to see good manners on display in others. Among the virtues she practiced and respected were modesty. Again, Jim Hoagland evoked a real picture of Meg in a letter he wrote to me, saying that "she didn't eagerly pocket praise. . . . I was always in awe of how Meg would respond to a compliment on a particularly brilliant piece; [she'd say:] 'Was that okay? You thought it worked?' She . . . used it to turn the thought or theme of the piece over one more time, to see if you really had anything to add or subtract."

She was also self-deprecating and fairly easily embarrassed at being recognized for her many great qualities. In a thank-you note to me, she once wrote, "Everything embarrasses me—including and especially being embarrassed."

When Meg was awarded an honorary doctor of humane letters from her alma mater, Smith College, she sent me the speech she'd given—which was unusual to begin with, since she was so unsentimental. She enclosed a little cover note, saying: "I have had the temerity and bad taste to include a Xerox of the citation attached to the degree because it was only the most marvelous thing that ever happened to me."

Meg had an incredible affinity for hard work. She was tireless and driven, working long hours daily and on weekends, too. She was endlessly curious and always a good student, not just as evidenced by her grades in her early school years but by her lifelong learning. She took up Latin again in middle age.

Meg was loyal—to people and places and things, including to me and my son Don; to Washington and Seattle; and to the *Washington Post* and *Newsweek*. She had just a handful of close friends and took a lively and caring interest in those friends and their children. She certainly was alone a lot and rarely paired up with a man. She never married and, from all appearances, did not seem to have many romances in her life.

Once in the mid-1970s she was asked about marriage and, as the reporter noticed, her words "became more measured and reflective." Meg replied, "I suppose I could tell you—not that I would—about how I didn't get married during two episodes of my life when it was a possible decision. But that's not the question. The question after all these years, is *why*, and my answer is: Damned if I know. I think it was an awful mistake."

Hendrik Hertzberg of the *New Yorker*, who read Meg when he was a teenager and came to know her better in the 1980s when he shared with her "some enjoyably gabby meals," recalled her being introduced to an audience as "one of those modern women who had elected not to get married and have children," to which Meg had responded, "I don't recall voting in that election." Hertzberg believed that her friends felt that she would have liked to marry and have children and "that it was a source of sadness to her that things didn't work out that way."

I've said that she was a friend to me like no other. She was supportive in so many ways. In the mid–1970s, during a long string of labor troubles at the *Post*, when my nerves were on edge, she wrote me a reassuring note, adding, "Maybe all this sounds like Norman Vincent Peale as summarized by Little Mary Sunshine." It helped.

Post columnist Charles Krauthammer told of another example of Meg's friendship and kindness: "She never emoted. But she always did the right thing, undemonstratively." When Charles's father died, he was, prior to a later burial in Israel, temporarily buried in Washington, where his father had known no one. As Charles recounted the story, "That meant a funeral lonely and sadly small for a man who had lived such a large, robust, friend-filled life. At the cemetery, there were just a few family and almost no one else—except Meg. She'd come to bury a man she'd never met simply because the son who loved him was her friend."

Meg herself knew that making and maintaining friends wasn't easy, especially in Washington. She once told a reporter,

> It takes a long time to create friendships that have some life apart from mutual, professional need. I mean a friend you can call up or who can call you up and say, "God, I feel lousy today" and not have to talk about what Kissinger is supposed to have told Sadat. Or someone you can go to the movies with on Sunday night. That's the hard part. Finding friendship and being good at it. Washington is a company town and what you do all day is what you talk about when you're out to dinner in the evening. Practically all human relationships are affected by this. . . . You become so consumed with politics and with secrets behind the official business that you stop seeing or responding to anything else. You think of yourself as some kind of a register. You don't see the flowers and, more important, you don't see the people. You see only in terms of how they're doing, are they in or out . . . or just sideways. So people become less than people and it's terribly destructive to one's self.

Her compassion, of course, wasn't limited to her friends, or even to those whom she knew personally. *Post* and *Newsweek* columnist George Will wrote, "It is a measure of Meg's personal generosity and intellectual self-confidence that she often went out of her way to help people . . . with whom her political disagreements were many and occasionally robust."

Maybe the first of the qualities that she liked and had in abundance was that she was responsible. Bill Pepper wrote in *Vogue* in 1974 that "the basic ethic, for Meg, is contained in being responsible toward one's self—and others." In an interview with Pepper, Meg said,

> We never used *words* like this at home, but I was taught that you
> could only be free and have dignity and self-respect if you were
> responsible for what you did. It was also assumed that you could
> do anything if you only applied yourself to doing it. Also, courtesy
> had nothing to do with what you learned out of a book or which
> fork to use. It depended more on how you treated other people.
> You couldn't get away with anything on the grounds that all the
> other kids did it, or because you were only eight years old and
> blameless. No excuses were accepted. Unless your temperature
> was 108, you went to school. As a result, I never dug those girls
> who complained about a grade, saying it was low because the pro-
> fessor didn't like them, or because they were Jewish. I can imag-
> ine myself taking off in a space capsule before I would say I didn't
> win because the game was rigged against me.

Meg applied these same principles to public officials—and she
often found that they came up wanting. She wouldn't have dreamed
of making excuses for her actions and hated it when others did. One
of her columns that appeared in the *Post* a half year before Richard
Nixon resigned gives some indication of this. The piece was called
"Adam and Eve and Watergate." In it, she suggested that the Bibli-
cal metaphor was useful in offering a way "to view our own responses to the present day Fall, the one that's in the papers":

> Adam and Eve abused their grant of authority; their firstborn
> child was a felon; and their principal adviser was a snake. So it's
> not as if we were without experience in these things. The first
> First Family, after all, blew their mandate . . . and they gave the
> concept of cover-up more than its rather earthy original meaning:

when called to account they first ran for cover, and then tried to lay it off on each other and the snake. . . . It remained for Cain, of course, to do a little plea bargaining with the Lord and also to perfect the evasive, diversionary answer—simple, flippant, aggressive and untrue. . . . Wise guy. The first, but not the last.

She went on to make some convincing comparisons between the "first First Family" and all the president's men, led by Nixon.

Meg's interests were myriad, but she had little time in her early working years to pursue them. She read voraciously, particularly classical and medieval history, which she said did "things to my imagination, especially Livy." During the Watergate scandal, she described reading Livy as "like taking a vacation. It has nothing to do with what Haldeman said to Magruder on the 23rd of some month." She loved a good mystery and was a self-described Nero Wolfe "freak." Meg needed to escape now and then, and she did that with a book.

She also loved language and the use of words. Some of her favorites were "goo," "hoo-ha," "skulduggery," and "bushwa." She was sometimes a secret source for William Safire's "On Language" column in the *New York Times Magazine* and shared with him an interest in arcane puns. After her death, Safire wrote that he had once used the title "That's My Baby" in an article about the Palestine Liberation Organization and its leader, all the while wondering "if someone, somewhere would catch the dim allusion." He reported that there was "Silence for a day. Then in came the call from Meg, singing in her sweetly rasping voice: 'Yassir, that's my baby. No sir, don't mean maybe.'"

Although she started out in Seattle and, especially in the last decade of her life, returned there as often as she could, and although she found intellectual energy in New York City, Meg derived a great deal of joy from living in Washington. This city was one of her great loves. Combining her interests and her attraction to the ridiculous and the sublime, Washington was the perfect place for her.

George Will wrote that when Meg moved to Washington in 1961, it "markedly increased the thoughtfulness of the nation's capital." Whatever her effect was on the city, the city clearly had an effect on her. It was a good match. She made Washington more fun. Ken Auchincloss of *Newsweek* found her "passionate about a city that rarely commands such devotion." At the same time as she poked her fun at the foibles, she never turned contemptuous or caustic. On the contrary, as Charles Krauthammer wrote, "She could expose the innards of the Washington game without ever losing her appreciation of its more noble possibilities."

Among the great loves of her life were her houses and gardens— both in Georgetown and, in the last years of her life, on Bainbridge Island, just across the water from her native Seattle. She would often withdraw to one place or another for a certain amount of solitude—"just an evening, or a Sunday alone, to kind of clear the head." Her gardens, which she tended with great pleasure, gave her much satisfaction, and she regularly consulted the *Post*'s gardening writer, Henry Mitchell. She once described her "gladiatorial pleasures" at her Georgetown house, saying her garden there was

> not the Grand Canyon, but just the right size. I planted a lot of things after people said: "Don't put that plant in, because it'll take over and you'll be out there fighting it." So I said: "I can't wait." My intention is to have something that in Georgetown terms would be a countergarden—not the sophisticated plot, with twelve shiny dark-green things and two azaleas, where you go to get plastered. That's not for me. I'm going for a garden that's considered physically impossible in Washington weather. A sort of English garden with Palermo-erotic and Seattle memories, full of

flowers, and so inappropriate to this style of life that my ultimate goal will be to get zoned out of the neighborhood, with the Citizens Association of Georgetown saying, "Honeysuckle and hollyhocks are the last straw . . . now you've gone too far!"

Meg also liked the movies, especially horror movies and movies geared to teenyboppers or featuring ninjas. Every now and then, at Meg's suggestion, we would play hooky from work, creeping out of the office in the late afternoon to see a movie. I was always a bit worried, but she advised me to just leave, saying "no one will know." Meg was so focused on the movies during a certain period when we were beginning to see many foreign leaders both in Washington and abroad that one day when I called her and asked if she wanted to see the French president, she paused ever so slightly and then asked where it was playing.

Meg liked food and drink, although bologna sandwiches on white bread with mayonnaise and bourbon were, at least until her later years, probably her favorites in each category.

She loved the excesses of American culture, never ceasing to be amazed at true-life stories. She once said, "There's no accounting for the way people get their kicks," and she found great joy in reading the tabloids and watching popular television series. She devoted many hours to following one of America's least intellectual television programs, *Dallas*. She was also fascinated by the doings of characters as disparate (and real) as the Menendez brothers, who murdered their parents; Lorena Bobbitt, who severed her husband's organ; and Tammy and Jim Bakker, the televangelists whose potential for major corruption she was among the first to spot—a happy result of her secret addiction to late-night TV.

Meg also had a passion for the latest skinny. Although she was discreet and circumspect when it came to the many secrets she knew and would never give away, she loved the juicy gossip or the tasty bit of scandal that surfaced from time to time.

Her adventurous spirit led her to kayaking in her later years, and she was quite proud of her sleek sea kayak, berthed at the side of her Bainbridge Island home. Despite her nonpenchant for mechanical devices of any kind (which Meg would say is one of the great understatements), she did learn to drive a speedboat, even though she basically didn't understand machines. As *Post* editorial writer Colby King said of her, she was "traumatized by technology."

At the memorial service celebrating Meg's life, Colby, one of many *Post* writers for whom Meg was a mentor and friend, said that while she may have been a master of the English language, she was completely baffled by a budget, and "numbers—simple arithmetical calculations—were beyond her comprehension." It's funny, although she was self-confident in giving off the idea that if she didn't know something, she could learn it, technologically speaking, as Colby said, "Meg was best suited for pre–World War II America. . . . Meg is the only person I know whose inability to remember how to access her computer finally forced our systems technicians to reduce her access instructions to simplicity itself. Meg's final password was 'password.'"

In addition to technological wonders, she had a hard time with decisions—or at least decisionmaking was not always easy for her. Everyone thought she somehow analyzed all of her options and then decided, but in fact she often (if indirectly) admitted to how she slid into one decision or another. For example, she once compared her life to a Charlie Chaplin film:

> You know, where Charlie catches a red danger flag falling off a construction truck, then is swept up in a passing anarchist parade, and finally arrested for leading it. That's me. I don't know about

other people's lives, but mine's been nine parts accident and one part indecision. One can decide a lot of things, but personal choices are harder. I tend to wait until one alternative is no longer available, then inform myself that I have chosen.

The things Meg didn't like also add up to a lengthy list, but they can mostly be fit under the heading of fakes and phonies. She didn't like self-serving people and those who cozied up to anyone for the wrong reasons. Those who were ingratiating only grated on her. Toadies were anathema to her. She brooked no hypocrisy, saw right through pomposity, hated condescension. George Will called her a "one-woman early-warning system for detecting nonsense."

Charles Krauthammer echoed that idea when he wrote:

> She had more antibodies to pap, flacks and fakes than anyone in Washington. She was immune. Indeed, one of her great talents in her own writing was her ability to cut through the fog produced by professional fog makers in this town—politicians and bureaucrats, journalists and publicists—to expose the ironies, the foibles, the vanities, the poses that inevitably attend the politics of a great capital. And yet she did it—and this was the distinct Greenfield touch—without condescension, without ever letting criticism turn into contempt.

She gained some notoriety in Washington in 1982 when she declared war on press agents who purported to be able to "deliver" the *Post*. She wrote a fiery internal memo lashing out against flacks and the very idea of public relations firms influence-peddling at the *Post* on behalf of various clients. "If people want to get to us . . . it's easy as pie, so long as they don't come in . . . via a flack firm. The reason for saying no to these wolves is plain and very strong. . . . Why should we be in their goddam memo traffic as exploitable or exploited 'resources'?"

Her rigid sense of right and wrong provided the benchmarks for many of her decisions and caused her to return even the smallest gift with alacrity and pleasure—preferably on the spot. The only exception I remember was in a foreign country, where Meg didn't think she could hand back the watch and gold-embroidered gown to the prince who was surrounded by 100 armed guards with bandoliers, guns, and daggers. Those gifts went to Goodwill.

She didn't like the idea of celebrity journalists either. When she won the Pulitzer Prize in 1978, she accepted only one interview request. That was from an in-house newsletter at the *Post*. Even then, she found herself more than a little embarrassed at being the object of attention, saying, "It's very uncomfortable to be interviewed on how you do your work. . . . You see, I use a number two pencil. . . . I work like everyone else—deadly chaos up until deadline. I think it's darn pretentious of journalists who see themselves as celebrities."

.   .   .

What does all of this add up to—or perhaps the better question is, who does all of this add up to? Meg was resistant to labels and couldn't be pigeonholed. How could she be a liberal if she was a hawk on foreign policy? How could she be a conservative if she opposed capital punishment? Conservatives claimed her as a friend, but so did liberals. When Phil Geyelin first found Meg, he asked her to talk to the news editor, Russ Wiggins, before signing on at the *Post*. Russ had been editorial page editor and was more hawkish about the war in Vietnam than some, including Geyelin. Russ concluded by saying, "You are making a mistake, my boy. She's on my side."

But, in fact, Meg was on *no* side and thought in *no* mold. She was not a partisan. She had a completely independent mind. Rick Hertzberg wrote of her after her death: "Every day, on its editorial page, the *Post* styles itself AN INDEPENDENT NEWSPAPER. Meg Greenfield made that slogan stick."

Meg's views of women's issues were certainly highly independent and individual. Fairly early on, she wrote me a memo saying: "I've been trying to work out a position—any position—on women's lib. Do you suppose there's a book one should read?" In her office hung a sign that read: "If liberated I will not serve." She insisted on the title "Miss" when "Ms." began to come into common usage, believing that "Ms." did not represent her or much of anybody else for that matter. Nonetheless, she reached out to women and to minorities. Above all, she wanted first-rate brains, and she had a short string for anyone who didn't measure up.

She was a trailblazer only in an objective sense—that is, she was among the first women in many rooms full of men. She certainly experienced something that most women didn't—that palpable discomfort at being not just the only woman in a roomful of men, but the one in charge. But she never felt that she was blazing a trail, nor did she intend to. She did not view herself as having purposely forged a career in a male-dominated profession. Instead, she said of her position and jobs, "It was all a series of accidents and non-decisions. . . . I was an English major who couldn't decide what to do. I wasn't trying to strike a blow for sisterhood."

Indeed, Meg was a self-labeled "wobbly spear-carrier in the feminist march." She did understand many of the claims of women and got, as she said, "a lot more sensitive to what's serious about the feminist movement" as the years passed. She knew that "women as a group have gotten the short end of the stick in economic, political and social life" and felt that in some ways it was more difficult for women in Washington. She said:

Washington especially is an abnormal place, a company town where government is the company. Wives are thrown over the side in the social contest . . . really pushed around. So, in many ways, I don't want to put the movement down. But I'm temperamentally alien to most of it. I'm afraid they regard me as an Aunt Jemima or something; but I can't imagine myself marching down the street with a great stick saying anything on it, especially in a group claiming to speak for womankind.

Also, I don't know what people mean when they say the 'woman's view'—except on certain issues. For instance, in the defense and strategic nuclear stuff I write about, Bella Abzug has a view that's not mine; Margaret Chase Smith, who used to be on the Armed Services Committee, has an opposite view that's not mine. The person closest to my view in the U.S. Senate happens to be a Black man from Massachusetts, Edward Brooke. . . .

Housewives in Silver Spring talk about liberation as escaping from the washing machine into the newsroom, while I have some vague sense that for me it would be going in the other direction. I think, "Gee, wouldn't it be great: three small children and a washing machine . . . and a fella."

Jim Hoagland quite accurately described why Meg couldn't be pigeonholed:

It was not the editorial writer's trick of being as critical of Republicans as of Democrats, of doves as well as hawks. It was not scorekeeping, or "balance." She had that marvelous capacity to make each judgment on its own, to reject the noxious idea that if you say or do x then you will be obliged to do y. No, she would say, I am capable of making that judgment when I have to on its own.

One of the best answers to anyone who tried to label her came from Meg herself, from the speech she gave at Smith College when she received an honorary degree. In essence, what she was talking about was truth and journalism. She began to talk about these "not two mutually exclusive subjects" by telling a story about George Washington's wooden false teeth and whether they ever had been on display at Mount Vernon. This example, she said, "reflects the factual situation in which the questing and generally confused journalist habitually walks." Her conclusion:

> "Truthfulness" in such a case does not necessarily repose solely with one party to the dispute. Nor does the truth usually lie . . . somewhere in between. Unfortunately, journalistic truth tends to lie all over the place. . . . There can be contradictory perceptions of the same set of events, each valid and truthful as far as those bearing witness are concerned. That is one of the elements that make our work interesting and accident-prone when it comes to remaining faithful to reality. The other is our necessary effort to reduce a mass of headbreaking material to manageable, column-sized truths.
>
> At a time when we have a national budget that cannot be read, a nuclear strategy that cannot be understood and social welfare, social security and health insurance programs that cannot be explained, it is hardly surprising that some attempt to grasp and communicate these things in a reductive way will be made. And it is even less surprising that we will, as a society, find ourselves, in consequence, in a continuous cranky dispute as to who distorted and deformed the truth, who quoted what out of context, who is misreporting whom.

She asserted "the overriding virtue of an honest, large, undoctrinaire, open and yes, principled approach to the way we organize our insight and experience." She concluded by telling the story of a book by the critic John Malcolm Brinnin about the Welsh poet Dylan Thomas that had stressed Thomas's last, dissolute days. Thomas's widow wrote letters to the author and engaged in a heated exchange in which she said, "I know a better truth than Brinnin's." Meg found this to be "so poignant and so right." She said: "A better truth—not necessarily a more positive or friendly or comfortable one, or even a contradictory truth, but one that is larger, roomier, more complex, and more authentic than the narrow version. That is what we are meant to pursue and it is also I think the central value of humane education . . ."

It was through her writing that Meg talked to the larger world. For more than thirty years, from 1968 until 1999, she helped create the institutional voice of the *Washington Post*. At the *Post* she managed a dozen or so people; ran the editorial page and the op-ed page, with its columns and freelance contributions; wrote editorials; and line-edited most of the two pages.

She found editorial writing to be a distinctive form of journalistic expression, one that had a different set of obligations from news writing and reporting. "You write in a way that ideally has some vitality to it, some personal feeling, so that a reader doesn't feel a computer did it. At the same time, it imposes a discipline and responsibility that's self-evident. You can't say one day you think price controls are yummy and the next day they are dumb, to use girls' school parlance. You become part of an institutional personality."

She saw editorials as different from a signed column "because you're taking the whole paper with you and have a certain responsibility to consistency and to the ideas, thoughts and sensibilities of the editorial group."

At the same time, Meg knew editorial opinion was not some sort of sermon. She thought we owed readers information about the big issues, like nuclear policy (including throw weights, about which she was an expert), as well as news about the child who had fallen down a well.

As editorial page editor, Meg lifted all of our thinking. She made sure that she and Don and I all understood that the best way for editors and publishers to work together is to have a constant conversation. Her sensitivity made everything both challenging and fun. But don't get the wrong idea about who made the final decisions on the editorial page. As Meg once wrote, "I don't believe in democracy, except as an extreme measure." Colby King said of her, "When it came to putting together those two editorial pages of the *Washington Post*, that's when Meg became sovereign, the warlord, the grand duchess all rolled into one."

Knowing that Mussolini had once been an editorial writer, she coined the term "Mussolini-ism" to describe what she called the "principal occupational hazard of editorial writers." In a chapter on the editorial page she prepared for a book about style for the *Washington Post* Writer's Group, she wrote: "There is a little Mussolini in every editorial writer . . . pompous, meddlesome, pretentious, a figure of fun to everyone but himself . . . issuing grandiose orders that have no effect on anything at all . . . to which an ungrateful nation will reply, 'Oh, knock it off.'" She both elaborated and enlightened by adding, "Shunning a shrieking editorial voice doesn't mean we don't want to be strong and clear."

Strong and clear she was. Although her words seemed as if they had come to her without effort, she didn't find writing easy, confiding once that "the actual sitting down to the typewriter . . . is something most of us in this racket will do anything to avoid." She said that, to her, writing was an "anxiety-making" activity, where she always had "this feeling that you'll sit down at the typewriter one morning and it'll all have gone away." Yet that was exactly what for her put the thrill into writing: "The anxiety is necessary. Whenever I've gotten complacent that's when I've had trouble."

She was a master craftsman in the world of words. What someone referred to as her "guff-free prose" helped illuminate issues of concern to those of us living in Washington and so far beyond its borders. Her own writing was informed by her wide-ranging reading, her unparalleled integrity, and her heightened sense of fairness.

In addition to being an inspired writer, Meg was also a great editor. She was a hands-on editor, a genius at pencil-editing with an unerring sense of what goes where, and I was the happy beneficiary of her editing skills. From the period when she first volunteered to help me write the speeches that I was beginning to give more and more—especially during the years of Watergate, about which she knew every detail—to the years when I was working on my memoir, *Personal History,* she helped me with my own writing. When I was writing the memoir, I was enamored of my experience with the Brandt Commission and wrote page after page describing in great detail the meetings and endless debates about the problems of developing and developed countries around the world. In the margin on the first page of this endless commentary, Meg wrote: "Three lines will do for this." Of course, she was right.

Meg was a leader, too, but often in her quietly influential way. Colby King answered the question of what it was like to work for Meg by saying, "She set the highest standards for everyone. And you knew it when you fell below her expectations. She didn't hesitate to pull you up short. And it was done within the true spirit of EEOC guidelines—without regard to race, creed, color, national origin, religion, or gender. She was an extraordinary teacher and mentor and journalistic drillmaster."

After her death, Jim Hoagland wrote me about what it was like to be her colleague. What he said was also true of being her friend:

> Working with Meg was what I would imagine working with a police detective partner would be for cops. You knew you could count on her to cover your back when you took chances. . . . You knew you could count on her to keep you honest, mostly by setting an example that you dare not betray. . . . You knew she would

not go on the journalistic stand and lie for you or anyone or anything else. You had better be as straight as she was, or get another partner. And you knew that in the work she would find not only reward and fulfillment but joy, of getting it right, of doing the right thing, of being nobody's fool.

Many of the words those of us who knew Meg use to describe her sound contradictory—tough and tender, rollicking and serious, humble and regal, formidable and friendly—but they all came together in Meg to make sense. They combined to create this unique character who was indeed fun-loving yet serious of purpose. So many of us—from the people who started *Newsweek* at the back to read her column, to those of us who loved her as a friend—have benefited from the pleasure of her company.

I miss Meg and am grateful that she has lengthened her time with us by leaving this book.

CHAPTER ONE

"Something Else Besides Human Life"

O VER THE YEARS I have earned my living writing about Washington politics. I got there from English literature, an early passion. What I, born in the Pacific Northwest and reared in a mixed culture of Depression and World War II–era Seattle and militantly Americanized Judaism, was doing immersed in English literature is something I wonder about. Nothing in my family's background—the nineteenth-century immigrant trek from eastern Europe to Ellis Island and the slums of the Atlantic coast, and then further west—and nothing in the salt air and Douglas fir environment of my own childhood spoke of Dickens and Dr. Johnson, of plum pudding and Tudor cottages with little leaded window panes, or of place-names like Threadneedle Street and Drury Lane.

Yet these were always the resting points of my imagination. From England came the past I conjured for myself and the destiny I felt would fulfill my life. It was as compelling as it was ludicrous. Not when first visiting the original American haven of my father's family, a much-romanticized and much-reminisced-about tenement in south Philadelphia, or finally seeing that part of Europe from which these determined relatives had come, did I feel the sense of homecoming and excitement I felt as a college sophomore on first viewing the grunge of dockside Liverpool from a rundown, soon-to-be-retired Cunard liner. It wasn't exactly Ann Hathaway's cottage or Westminster Abbey, but it would do. It was England, the motherland.

What was all this about? I think in the beginning it was merely the predictable inclination of any American child of the period who liked to read and write and had been recklessly encouraged to produce reams of grade-school poetry featuring words like "e'en" and "ere" and "o'er." After all, the body of writing once thought essential to and sufficient for an American education was pretty much English literature and history and myth. These defined our cultural universe, beginning in the nursery with Little Jack Horner and Little Bo Peep and Wee Willie Winkie and the rest. "Who killed Cock Robin?" my brother and I would somberly ask, as part of the perform-and-be-gone appearances we were compelled to make for the women who came to drink tea and play mah-jongg with our mother. A more realistic question might have been, "What is a 'Cock Robin' anyway, and why are we being made to stand here and recite this senseless thing?"

But there was more to the experience than just a protracted dunking in English folklore. As we got older and went from recitation to pens and inkwells, we learned that there were two basic modes of expression: Formal style, to which all writing must aspire, as distinct from plain, understandable talk, was what we respectfully thought of as "English." The other, idiomatic and vulgar, was for use, if at all, in messages that didn't matter. It was in the process of accommodating this thought that snobbery and retrogressive social climbing began.

For English, as it was being daily defined by our teachers and often by our parents as well, came to mean much more than a mere language or literature to us. It also meant being better brought up, more personally desirable, the accepted center as distinct from the tolerated fringe of the common culture. It wasn't ever said but it was known that social distances were measured in miles from that center, starting with the near-miss, much-invoked "Scotch-Irish" origins claimed (sometimes, I suspect, spuriously) by so many, and working outward toward the rare Mediterranean background or eastern European Jewish provenance such as my own. And no matter what we had been told in a fitful way at home about being proud of our real heritage, we were in truth under pressure from within and without to assume a second, overriding descent, which almost all of us, of every background, cheerfully did.

Thus the American colonial and revolutionary ancestors with whom we came to identify were exclusively the English. We were, out there in Seattle, a seaport that hadn't even existed until the late nineteenth century and one distinguished primarily by its sizable Scandinavian and Asian populations, fourth-graders unequivocally on the side of the British Crown in all of the seventeenth- and eighteenth-century settlement struggles we read about—save only the ultimate struggle, the American Revolution. The latter we saw as a family fight between the better Englishmen—us—and the worse Englishmen—them. (Except for two fearsome queens and Lady Godiva, there were, of course, no Englishwomen, although Britain, when perpetrating some particularly horrible crime, would invariably be referred to as "her" and "she" and occasionally as "Albion," but who knew what that was, let alone its sex?)

This distinction between the good and bad Englishmen made it possible for us, with our reverence for things English, to absorb the isolationist Britain-bashing prevalent in our classrooms in the 1930s, the stream of exasperated complaint from our teachers about how Britain had defaulted on her World War I debt and thought she was oh-so-mighty and so much better than we were and so forth. The premise was: My, how low the progeny of those who oppressed us and took the wrong side in our glorious Revolutionary War have sunk, but, then, what would you expect? Our faith in our false lineage, by now firmly rooted and something we fully believed in, was unaffected by what we took to be the motherland's appalling behavior from roughly 1776 on. We were the good Englishmen, descended from the right Englishmen.

It is interesting to me that more than half a century and a torrent of social change later, I can see the phenomenon stubbornly persisting elsewhere. In an influential part of the Washington, D.C., I now live in, better-bred, country-house English remains the stylistic model, the affectation of choice. Established in the misty past by the big guns of permanent, old guard political/social Washington, it has since been assiduously emulated by various newcomers to town—politicians, lobbyists, and press people who were assigned, appointed, or elected to some fixed-term job in the capital and eventually decided to stay on.

The look can take work. In pursuit of it some would go to extravagant lengths to acquire, for example, not just used oriental rugs, but downright threadbare ones, for the air these were thought to convey of old family, old money, and, above all, a self-assured, upper-class-Brit-like indifference to the ratty state of one's possessions. Clearly, just as there was more than poetry and prose involved in the adopted Englishisms of my childhood, so there is much more than household furnishing involved here. What is involved is impersonation: the appropriation of someone else's heritage, the donning of another identity.

To be sure, the Lord Plushbottom fantasy has seen better days in Washington. It was given a sound though far from fatal kick in the pants by a newfound preoccupation with race, roots, lineage, ethnicity, and a kind of scruffy "populist" pretense that goes in and out of fashion here. But both the ethnic and populist preoccupations, at least in their more opportunistic Washington form, often come across as merely a different type of role-playing, yet one more new persona, fashioned to meet the social and professional requirements of a changed political world. What both in fact reflect, along with the better-born British imposture they sometimes supplant, is a commonplace behavior in the capital that will concern me throughout this book. It is one I recognize and continually have to contend with in my own life and have seen played out a thousand times over in the lives of people I have tracked and written about as a journalist in Washington for more than three decades.

What I mean is how public people almost eagerly dehumanize themselves. They allow the markings of region, family, class, individual character, and, generally, personhood that they once possessed to be leached away. At the same time, they construct a new public self that often does terrible damage to what remains of the genuine person.

This phenomenon is increasingly present in our national politics as a whole. But it tends to be especially extreme and debilitating in Washington. That is not because people here are bad or set out in the first place to become phonies, but rather because high politics in the city seems to reward the transformation. It is regarded as a measure of competence and required as a condition of success. This is just as my betters fifty years ago managed to convey to me and my classmates the need to reconfigure our conception of who we were geographically eastward and socially upward.

This, I am convinced, is the principal tension of this city and the principal pressure that people who live and work here—people who are what others mean when they dourly say "Washington"—must contend with. This is the beast with which practically everyone who comes here sooner or later is obliged to wrestle. And the beast wins more than it loses. Still, and this is awfully important to me, it doesn't win every time. There is always a small but substantial company of people who manage to stay whole—the interesting, decent, strong ones, the ones who know what matters and what doesn't and what is serious and what is funny. I don't say the perfect ones, only those who manage to be effective participants in the political life of Washington without forfeiting their own better nature.

In an era in which only the dogs and cats among us fail to join the rest of the household in denouncing the capital and its pernicious habits, the point about such survivors needs to be stressed.

The Washington I have observed over the past thirty-plus years has been Republican-run and Democrat-run, Congress-dominated and executive-branch-dominated. The one constant has been that in each new phase there have been some good people who turned up, doing their best to do right by the government they work for and the public their actions affect. What they have resisted is the fatal, ever-present Washington temptation: disappearance into the abstract, bloodless, phony, self-inflating world of endless competitive image projection—at the expense of just about everything else. For the professional value system of political Washington entices those who come to it from elsewhere—bureaucrats, appointees, and elected officeholders—to mask, then deny, and finally misplace altogether their own identity and acquire another, fabricated one.

Among those who succumb, the most common result is neither fake English (now somewhat on the wane) nor ethnic firebrand nor gallus-snapping man of the people. It is self-re-creation as a walking, talking, person-shaped but otherwise not very human amalgam of "positions," that familiar, tirelessly striving figure interviewed on the evening news who resoundingly tells you what he is thinking—and you keep wondering whether you should believe a word of it. These are people who don't seem to live in the world so much as to inhabit some point on graph paper, whose coordinates are (sideways) the political spectrum and (up and down) the latest overnight poll figures.

Something similar may be said, of course, of that other figure on the evening television news, the one conducting the interview. For just as Washington political figures are in danger of being drawn into a kind of denaturing process, from which they eventually reemerge as improbable new life forms, so too are we of the press—not just the TV folks, either, but all of us. And just as the political figures may be rewarded for transforming themselves, so too may we. We are professionally admonished to freeze many of our ordinary human instincts, to distance ourselves from too much personal knowledge of or contact with the people we write about, lest we endanger our objectivity or adulterate our product with an excess of understanding of their behavior or, God forbid, sympathy.

Our unwritten code further ordains that we must ignore any animosity or revulsion we may feel along with any intellectual affinity or admiration. We are encouraged to bury our convictions in the backyard—or at least not bring them to the office with us in the morning or let them become too obvious in our after-hours lives. The working premise is that we are meant to be (or to be perceived as) uncontaminated vessels of truth and justice, if not necessarily of modesty. Our institutional propaganda frequently makes it sound as if we were that model jury the courts are always looking for in overpublicized criminal cases: wholly open; wholly disengaged; emotionally, politically, and ideologically blank—machines waiting to be imprinted for the first time.

The good news is that most journalists have to fake a lot of this. Our critics gleefully detect in us an inability to meet the impossible standards we have set for ourselves in thousands of terminally earnest conferences and printed exchanges on the subject. They are forever pointing out our egregious lapses: This one is guilty of secretly harboring views, that one of grinding an ax, another of actually liking or disliking a person being covered. In fact, they should be reassured by the inability of so many press people to manage the transformation that journalistic propriety is presumed to demand. For only the incorrigibly cold and arrogant, not to say the somewhat crazy, could authentically achieve the decreed ideal.

As with so many ideas people carry to absurdity, this one has its origin in an important and worthy purpose that ethical professionals can serve without becoming absurdities themselves. If the good news is that most journalists have to fake or at least learn this smug, dehumanized role, the bad news is that many of them do. Worse, they may become very efficient at it, a tad proud of their unconvincing new identity and even somewhat ruthless in promoting it as their image.

Such journalists, who profess to hate above all things being conned, will eventually con themselves into believing that they actually are self-abnegating, morally irreproachable foot soldiers of the First Amendment, and nothing more. They will admire themselves as paragons of detachment who never act out of a desire for, say, professional advancement or peer approval or money or in furtherance of their political leanings. Rather, as they see it, they are acting always out of an unending, dispassionate, magnanimous commitment to the people's right to know. Some among us carry the conceit to an insufferable degree. But I would say that all of us in the business display at least a touch of it.

The result can be that we in journalism become two of a kind with our subjects, neither of us credible in our self-presentation. Instead both of us are out there in full view, masked, swinging at each other with blunted wooden swords and disputing each other's version of a reality that those observing us from afar wisely conclude doesn't exist and never did. All of us have heard the following kind of televised interrogation:

> Senator, you still haven't answered my question. Why have you abandoned your effort to pass the Free-Everything-for-Every-body-All-Day-Long Bill? Some critics have said it is because you feel the need to move to the right to fight off a political challenge in your state, even though that means turning your back on a bill that was going to help the poor. Wouldn't the American people be justified in feeling even more disillusioned and cynical about Washington than they already do, since, in abandoning

FEFEADL, you have broken a major campaign promise and acted just like all the other insider politicians you were running against last fall?

Thus the question we put, ostensibly in earnest, to some senator we never doubted was a hopeless hack from the start and not the apolitical, reformist outsider he claimed to be, concerning a bill we know to be profoundly idiotic and without a single provision that is even borderline sane. To which there will of course come back the perfectly matched reply:

No, John, you've got that one all wrong. I won't deny that we may have had some temporary setbacks in the Senate—I'm a realist as well as an idealist—and we have had plenty of backstabbing from the bureaucracy too. But the American people know, even if you don't, John—heh, heh, heh—that this United States senator is not one of those political bait-and-switch, cut-and-run fellows. I will never give up the fight for FEFEADL.

What you need to remember is that deep down in the remaining brain cells that used to be this guy, he likely as not has the same low opinion of the legislation, which he nevertheless introduced, as the reporter. The two of them may even have earlier had a jocular chat to this effect while they were having their makeup put on. In the tel-evised action between them, neither remembers any such thing. To do so would undermine the role each is committed to playing.

Sometimes when I witness this kind of exchange—or, worse, par-ticipate in it—and find myself sounding for all the world like Jour-nalist John, I am reminded of my last two years at Smith College as the class of 1952's English major from hell. Many students back then venerated to a nonsensical extent the prevailing literary theory of the day. This was called "the New Criticism" (although it was already

much older than we were) and was a reaction against the undisciplined, kitchen-sink way of reading books that nineteenth-century
literary figures had established and bequeathed to later generations
of teachers, scholars, and critics.

The old critics had seemed more interested in the author's biography than in the author's work. Some, in fact, seemed mesmerized
by everything but the poem or novel before them, making what was
on the printed page seem almost incidental to the extraneous, sometimes purely fanciful material they dragged in. This might include
dubious clues they claimed to have uncovered about hitherto-
unknown episodes in the author's life, pointless speculations about
current events of the period in which the work had been written,
and even off-the-wall surmises about some kind of "life" the fictional
characters in a novel or play may have led off the page and apart
from the plot before the story began or after it ended. "How many
children had Lady Macbeth?" was the contemptuous way one of our
favorites among the rebellious New Critics summed up and disposed of this discredited practice. We 1950s students knew such old-
fashioned digressions were not merely irrelevant but could get in the
way of an intelligent reading of a book, concealing not just its shortcomings but also its very meaning in a haze of capricious chatter.

So we set about reading in a ferociously opposite way—Spartan,
bare-bones, no frills, no side trips—summarily ruling out of consideration the irrelevant, ancillary junk, rather as a scientist might do in
creating the conditions for a perfectly controlled laboratory experiment. We became ruthlessly clinical in our reading. We considered
only what was right there on the printed page. To stray beyond these
bounds was a corruption of the act of reading, an affront to purity
and integrity, a selling-out of the tough standard authors were required to meet to establish their literary worth with us. If a Ten-
nyson or Dryden or Trollope couldn't survive the test, well, tough.
Mind you, the really good New Critics did not go overboard like

this and indiscriminately rule out, as we did, not just the junk but also background information and insights that could be helpful in making sense of what was on the page. It was mainly we cocky kids and some of our instructors who did that. As a result, we paid a price in insight.

The contemporary Washington journalist is in danger of doing something comparable and, just as we fanatic English majors once did, feeling superior about it. Certainly, we in the news business developed our techniques and ethical standards largely as a reaction to discredited professional habits of the not-so-distant past. Partisan reporting on public figures was among them. But too many of us have moved on from establishing professional detachment to something different: a willful disconnectedness from the human reality that lies at the heart of the issues and stories we are covering.

Too often we don't report what we really see or share what we really know. We have taken instead to reading public figures as a hot-dog 1950s English major might read a great novel. Practically no elucidating or extenuating context is allowed. Public figures are described solely in terms of how well they live up to the impossible, ridiculous, and hypocritical postures they strike from the podium. "I am and will continue to be perfect," the public person says in the classic, age-old junkspeak that office-seekers everywhere have always indulged. "In a twelve-part series starting today," our newspapers will sooner or later gravely announce, "the *Daily Blast* evaluates the record of Congressman Jones and analyzes how well he has lived up to his campaign pledge to be perfect."

Guess who flunks? The congressman, of course, but also we in the media who forfeit just a little more of our credibility every time we become a willing and not quite straightforward partner in this silly game. "Of course he's not perfect," an increasingly exasperated readership says. "Who ever thought he was or could be? Why are you taking this guff seriously in the first place? Just so you can hang him with it? Why don't you tell us what is really going on? Why don't you judge him against a realistic standard? Who is he anyway? Why is he doing the things he does? It can't be out of an unrelieved desire to do wrong. Might he see it, not cynically but honestly, differently from what you have so sharply implied? And forgive the very thought of it, but might he, at least in some part of the presentation, have a point?" As an account of reality, our product too often rings false or empty or seems rigged.

I have spent a lot of my school and professional life first learning and then trying to unlearn such habits of mind and techniques of observing the world around me. As a result of the second of these labors—that of trying to unlearn—I now know that I am not descended from the Bradfords of Massachusetts, that you do not read a twentieth-century novel or a sixteenth-century poem the same way you might perform an appendectomy, and, most important for my purposes here, that understanding Washington means understanding that its denizens do not much resemble their poses.

The hardest part of a Washington journalist's job is to discover and comprehend what those real men and women are doing and why—not pretend "why" or posturing "why," but why. Oddly enough, that is still considered a heretical idea in some places.

And here is another even less reputable idea to which I also subscribe: You can't understand the "why" without considering the thought that maybe these big-deal Washington personages you hound and nitpick and trap and query—and describe and describe and describe—are fallible, two-legged, air-breathing, potato-chip-eating human beings. It doesn't mean you have to like them (though sometimes you may).

We recognize the conflicts and susceptibilities in others largely by imagining them in ourselves. Journalists who persist in regarding themselves as thoroughly clean and the world around them as thoroughly dirty are guilty of more than misplaced moral vanity. They are also in danger of rendering themselves incapable of plausibly explaining what they are covering—except as further implied evidence of their own virtue.

It's not just that we aren't better than our subjects or even all that different from them. It's that although we ought to do our damnedest to be truthful and fair, we can probably never be 100 percent disengaged from our subjects either, no matter how we try. I simply don't believe you can come to a place like Washington, as I did as a relatively young reporter, stay for your whole professional life, and then convincingly claim (though many with experience comparable to mine do) that you have remained a real-life version of the dysfunctionally dispassionate Sergeant Joe Friday, saying, "All I want are the facts, ma'am." It is self-deceptive to conceive of yourself as a perennially scandalized spectator/alien who has been peeking for years through the fence at the weird goings-on at the house next door.

At some level you are always personally engaged. That requires scrutiny and managing. Living and working in such an environment compels choices between the proprieties of journalism and those of ordinary human life. And—I freely concede—you don't always get it right. Sometimes your foot will slip, as mine surely has. You will lose the required detachment in one case. In another you will be pompously, priggishly, unfeelingly, and unnecessarily inaccessible, regarding yourself as exempted by the higher obligations of your trade from abiding by the most fundamental of obligations to a fellow human. If you can believe it, some argued over whether it was professionally proper for a press photographer to move in order to protect the handicapped Bob Dole's head from a four-foot fall when the Republican nominee crashed through a railing during the presidential campaign of 1996.

The too-close relationship is manifest in a less dramatic, insidious, easygoing "embuddiment" of the journalist with a public person that in time may fog the journalist's thinking about that person. Generally this embuddiment charge is made against those who hobnob with too many incumbent, establishment figures in Washington and let what were once press-to-subject relationships become something more like friendships. Although indignantly denied, the very same thing occurs among many of those who complain loudest about this establishment intermingling of press and public official: younger, antiestablishment journalists who enjoy precisely the same kind of relationship with less visible, dissenting young staff workers in government. These too are folks who should, by our standards, remain in the remote role of subjects and sources, personally treated without favor and kept at one remove, rather than getting special breaks, being allowed to guide coverage, and being accorded the status of friends.

But they aren't. Deny it to heaven though they may, they will develop their own personal stake in how they are themselves regarded within the community they may profess merely to be studying with such a cold, scientific eye.

What I am saying about inextricable involvement goes also for those who live by an unremittingly adversarial attitude toward what is official. There have also been useful scourges, gadflies, and mudrakers, from Tom Paine to Henry Adams to Drew Pearson to our own relentless contemporary Washington naysayers, investigators, and grouches—Ralph Nader, Irving Kristol, Charley Peters of the *Washington Monthly*—who make a career out of asking the snarly question and raising the unwarranted as well as the warranted suspicion of what the public person is up to. These people are an integral and, in some ways, complicit part of the society they denounce and deconstruct. They pay homage to that society by ultimately buying into its frame of reference; they certify its importance by their continuing attention; they elevate its status by taking seriously its pretensions, which they have devoted their whole professional lives to deflating.

Some of them develop a perceptible touch of self-satisfaction, perhaps bordering on grandiosity, about their roles as designated skunks. They will go soft on a few of their own sources and whistle-blower friends in government. Despite their injunctions against having favorites in public life, they will develop their own favorites. In short, they will become a part of the larger social-political organism in which they play an increasingly defined, expected, and accepted role. But how much of a threat can such dissenters be, how far outside the establishment castle, if they are the first choices of every major op-ed editor to write the ritual objection to whatever the common wisdom is that week?

In the end, they are proof that you don't spend a professional lifetime in Washington against your will or as a kind of joyless UN police force, no matter how assiduously you cultivate the image of crank. Whether you are incumbent or oppositionist at the moment, you end up inhaling the zeitgeist of the place, internalizing its idea of what matters.

You see this phenomenon at unending think-tank seminars on the ideological quibble of the moment, on the press plane, even in the exchange of set-piece surlinesses interspersed with easy, familial-type jokes in the White House briefing room. Each spring we go to big banquets, press and politicians all done up in formal dress, where everyone applauds the awarding of prizes to journalists who have exposed the crumminess of the political leaders sitting at the head table, joining in the ovation and fun. Lots of jokes are made. Lots of hands are shaken. It is a community affair. The community does not so much impose as insinuate its rules and ways (even the rules and ways of dissent and insurrection).

When I try to understand my creeping entanglement in this

Washington, in a career that took me from being a troublesome out-sider, a free-ranging kid reporter, to being an editorial-pronouncing, Sanhedrin-status heavy at the *Washington Post,* I have a hard time deciding how much I was attracted to the city because of the kind of person I already was, and how much the place itself grabbed hold of my life and exerted increasing influence.

I do know that even as a young newcomer who badmouthed and lampooned Washington from the moment I set foot here, I was also drawn to its mysteries. Even during my periods of greatest contempt for the city, I was still hooked on the challenge of trying to figure out why political surprises had happened. Another draw was a kind of predestination. You will read later in this book about how one kind of person tends to turn up and flourish in the Washington environ-ment. This is the often unbearable adult good child, a personality category into which I fall.

Whatever factors caused a self-assured, know-it-all, English lit graduate student, a politically liberal kid from Greenwich Village, by way of Seattle and Smith College, to choose to spend her life in the capital, the deed is done—and so is the damage. I have been Wash-ingtonized to the point where I can no longer write about my life without writing also about the Washington arguments and ideas and purposes with which it has been intertwined.

And I must also confess that it has become increasingly hard for me to write about any of that subject matter without conceding how very personal and idiosyncratic and human much of my observation is. This is true of my ideas about Washington and government and journalism and politics and liberalism. These are not just the topics but the realities that have loomed largest in my working life.

This book, therefore, is pretty much a mixed-bag endeavor: part memoir, part screed, and part my own attempt to figure out what has happened to Washington during the years I have spent here. It is also about what happened to me on the way to another life I had in mind for myself but never got around to living because I came to Washington and stayed.

When I got to Washington in September 1961, a preppyish, Adlai Stevenson Democrat who had spent a few postcollege years in Europe and New York City, taunting my Seattle family with my refusal to come home and pursue the conventional life they envisaged for me, I did not believe myself to be in search of a new identity. To be truthful, I thought I had a perfectly good one.

What struck me at the time as a life of daring and dissent was, from today's perspective, pussycat-mild. I believed that on the big, dangerous international conflicts of the day, my country was on the right side but that some of its actions were shortsighted and wrong. I thought that our system of government was noble in concept and workable in practice and that its shortcomings were due to the perversion of some of its rules by a small cabal of southern conservative politicians I abominated and too little federal money spent on its social problems. A lot of things needed to be fixed, but everything was fixable. Everything would be fixed with the proper political exertion. And that was that.

The Washington I came to generally saw life within that same framework. It too was perfectly content with its identity: newly engaged, post–World War II superpower and supplier of ideas and material help around the world. None of us could have imagined the assassinations and disorder that were about to come, the trashing of icons and upending of certitudes that would become routine and traumatic.

Now we are in the aftermath of the hell that broke loose. Those of us who were here earlier think differently—not just because we are older but because of all that has happened. A great deal in Washington that was unhealthy, unjust, or outmoded has been chucked out. Some of what has replaced it is at least as bad or worse. This much is indisputable: Both the city and those of us who spent our working lives chronicling it have ended up with a different set of assumptions about ourselves and about American government, politics, and society than we had when we arrived.

I begin this book by examining the political and personal transformation of those who come to Washington. This is essential to understanding the capital. As I have suggested, it is as if everyone who came to the place were put into the witness protection program, furnished with a complete new public identity, and left with much untended anxiety about the vestiges of the old one. We are, most of us, much of the time, in disguise. We present ourselves as we think we are meant to be. In Washington this is greatly in excess of the ordinary hypocrisies and dualities of public versus private conduct that exist everywhere else.

But it is surely one of the bad jokes of our time that none of these disguises, with the slipping masks and the unconvincing accents, seems to be doing us in Washington much good with a public whose confidence we crave. Rarely in American history has there been more suspicion of the intentions of Washington politicians or more complaint about the lack of credibility and fairness in the press.

My hunch is people may be not so much repelled by our political behavior as by our fake persona. The problem is more the easily discernible pretense than the reality. In my own professional lifetime here, something has happened, causing many Americans to look at Washington and see, as William Blake wrote of other governing figures two centuries ago, "something Else besides Human Life."

CHAPTER TWO

The Good Child, the Head Kid, the Prodigy, and the Protégé

*E*VERY DEROGATORY COMPARISON you can think of has been invoked to show how political Washington works and thus to explain its least endearing ways. The city and its inhabitants have been likened to a boring, elitist men's club; a recklessly run business; and a den of every known public and private vice, including lechery, larceny, pride, sloth, dissembling, and, above all, the lust for acquiring power and wielding it cruelly and carelessly.

I can understand what has given rise to each of these unflattering analogies. But I don't think any of them quite gets it right. The analogy I favor is to high school.

So far as I have been able to discover, nobody, regardless of station, gets over high school—ever. Not even the most swaggery, balloon-headed types in the capital: Get them on the subject of their high school years, and you will soon see the assertive bearing wilt, the smugness vanish. This will be true whether they were among the golden boys and girls or the nerdy social outcasts or the great throng in between. All will have carried into midlife and beyond their high school insecurities and dreads, enduring vanities about tiny teenage triumphs that they would find either amusing or pathetic in another adult, and at least a handful of social-life memories so excruciating they still cannot be recalled without a shifting of the feet.

High school is a preeminently nervous place. Never mind that high school students everywhere are known for adopting a pose of "What, me worry?" nonchalance so extreme as to border on an appearance of being dead. And why shouldn't high school be such a place? These are the years in which young people first encounter a make-or-break, peer-enforced social code that calculates worth as popularity and popularity as a capacity to please and be associated with the right people (no matter how undeserving they may be), as well as to impress and be admired by the vast, undifferentiated rest.

Even in today's most anarchic high schools, with cops and metal detectors, the basic social code and the imperatives to conform seem to be the same. Some version of these imperatives exists in other group settings as well, from kindergarten to the nursing home. But nowhere are they so intensely and continuously and unforgivingly present as in high school and Washington, D.C.

In saying this, I go against one fairly settled idea of the nation's capital as the quintessential company town. Under that reading, Washington is just one more of those familiar American settlements whose social as well as economic life is tightly organized around a single industry—in this case government, not cars or clothing or insurance.

The Washington I am talking about is not really a town at all, let alone an entire city. I am not thinking of the actual, physical District of Columbia, surrounded by Maryland and Virginia suburbs. The smaller, political/governmental Washington of which I write merely nests within that larger jurisdiction.

This other, lesser Washington is a relatively interconnected segment of the capital area's population, numbering only a few tens of thousands, there to manage, staff, study, lobby, or report on the federal government. Many of these people will have come to the city from somewhere else, some for a brief tour of duty, others for most of their working lives. They will have left behind the familiar, comforting landmarks and supports of their previous lives: the schools they attended, the churches, the friends, the parents and grandparents and cousins and rest of the extended family. They will create new lives from scratch in Washington without any of that automatic grounding or affirmation.

Practically all will still be vaguely planning to go back sometime to the place that was home, wherever it is, to be buried when the time comes. This will be true of some who have lived in the capital long enough to raise a family, buy a house, and pay off the mortgage. Although over long stretches of time they may be productively engaged and even happy, they are still only provisional citizens of the city or the region in which they live. Even as personal strangers, they tend to know a lot about one another. As individuals and groups who are often working politically at cross-purposes, they think of themselves nonetheless as a kind of shaggily coherent whole.

This population of long-term squatters is attuned to its own purposes, answers to its own code, administers its own rewards and punishments, and has its own distinctive conception of what constitutes winning and losing. On the basis of some unfathomable combination of all these factors, it maintains its own separate social and professional pecking order as well. More than any other pecking order on earth, I suspect, including the real kind, thought up in the barnyard by chickens, this one is given to continuous updating, downgrading, and overall revision of who or what ranks as the celebrity or urgency of the hour. For those who take the code seriously, it permits no rest. Gaming it is like trying to game the ooze of a lava lamp.

Now consider this settlement's profoundly high school nature. It is psychologically fenced off from the larger community within which it makes its home, free—like irresponsible youth—of all but the minimal obligations of citizenship to that community, and absorbed to the exclusion of all else in its own eccentric aims and competitions. And the high-school-like feel political/governmental Washington takes on by virtue of all of this is intensified by certain givens of its existence.

One is the only-passing-through nature of so much time spent here. I know that nowadays other cities also have more transient populations than they used to and that Americans as a whole have become remarkably mobile. I know too that other enterprises that employ large numbers of people have rigid hierarchies and fixed advancement schedules and a scale of increasing perks to mark the ascension to power and glory. But here in Washington—unlike in Detroit, say, or Hartford or Fort Worth—the entire experience tends to be structured and spoken of and often even thought about in ways strongly suggesting school.

Those other cities' reigning industries, for example, surely don't have "freshmen," as we do. Nor is this some semantic fluke: The words retain their conventional implications in Washington. "Freshman," for instance, is a congressional designation that is taken very seriously, entailing if not exactly hazing at least some initiation rites and put-downs by the big kids and expectations of deference to the elders while one is being tested and looked over and kept busy learning the place's protocols and taboos.

Note the astonishment that greeted newly installed Speaker Newt Gingrich's decision in 1995 to give a number of just-elected House freshmen seats on desirable committees. Traditionally, the most a congressional freshman could hope for in Washington was to eventually become a "sophomore," a second-termer, who is by custom accorded slightly more freedom of action, office space, and respect. The fact is that senators as well as representatives all consider themselves members of some class or other, dating from their election—the "class of 1972," they will say, for instance, or "the class of 1986." They establish a special relationship with their "classmates" across party lines and have "class" pictures taken.

In addition to classes, we have "terms," underscoring the fixed period of time for which people in both the legislative and executive branches have been sent to do their jobs. We also have Christmas, spring, and summer vacations, when a considerable part of the working population is out all at the same time and not, as in more normal adult working settings, on staggered personal vacation

schedules. During such periods, much of the workforce that is technically not on vacation is nevertheless vaguely off-duty too—or at
least partially idled and catching up on backlogged paperwork while
waiting for the unruly bunch to return and the next hellacious, se-
mester-like session to begin. For this Washington, in truth, conducts
its business on a political variation of the school year, which is created by a congressional calendar that manages to affect much more
than Congress. It largely determines the timetable and the working
metabolism of others in and all around the edges of the federal government.

Finally, and most important, since we have, effectively, under-
classmen, so too we have upperclassmen and thus the ultimate sadistic joys of seniority. When the Republicans retook Congress in 1994,
as with other previous upheavals like 1964 and 1974 and 1980, it was
said that this time seniority had been dealt a mortal blow, that the
young rebels who came to Congress were really going to break the
old-guy mystique now, once and for all.

A lot does change on these occasions, but don't be misled: A lot
also doesn't change. That is because too many Washington veterans
of both parties have too much vested in the status they have acquired
as a group. They have as well the advantage of knowing their way
around the mine-strewn terrain that is federal-government Washington much better than any upstart, would-be supplanters could.

Seniority in Washington means more than merely having managed to get elected for fifty increasingly authoritarian years on the
Hill, or having ascended the prescribed "grade-steps" in the career
civil and foreign service, or having hung around long enough to be
accorded among journalists the old-walrus-like honorific of "dean."
It means having acquired the sway and savvy and special privilege of
upperclassmen. And since not everybody leaves at the end of a few
congressional terms or an administrative tour of duty or a rotating

journalism assignment, some become more or less upperclassmen in perpetuity. They are hazers for life.

Traditionally the arbiters of the Washington scene are these big guys who set the rules. They select promising freshmen who are singled out for special advancement as protégés. These few lucky newcomers, on the basis of their talent and willingness to accept a period of apprenticeship and work within the peculiar spirit of the place, suddenly find themselves being mentioned everywhere as the freshmen "to watch."

The "seniors," it is true, can lose some altitude that they can't later regain when there is an upheaval by the voters. But they fight hard to retain their authority, and owing to the vast web of indebtedness and camaraderie they have spun and their known ability to inflict punishment when they are really angry, they have over the years been able to retain clout. This can even be true of big hitters who actually lose their jobs in Congress, the executive branch, or the press, for that matter. They may hang around in some new capacity, poshly headquartered in an office where they can show off their autographed power pictures and other evidence of recent glory, work their rich and bursting Rolodexes, and generally for much more pay than they ever got before, continue to influence public business—until those Rolodexes become pitifully out-of-date.

All this is, in the most cynical sense of the term, bipartisan. Even though the power of appointment and an ability to monopolize the agenda and the news belong to whichever party wins at the polls, there is a sense in which ideology, political party, and majority or minority status are irrelevant to the internal workings and power relationships of this Washington. And it is precisely these relationships that people start to cultivate, worry about, and protect when they have been here a while. Once within the confines of the Capitol complex, most people come to accept its standards, live by its rules, honor its imperatives, treat its freshmen as they themselves once were treated, and—a telltale sign of embattled, bipartisan solidarity—start referring to the rest of the country (without quite realizing what the term conveys) as "out there."

Those two words say it all. "Out there" is the near equivalent of the schoolkid's term "the real world." It means where everybody else is, where we have to go some day when this is over, where we'll have to settle down and take "out-there" kinds of jobs, becoming just like all the rest. Both terms connote a less rewarding and more onerous environment in which to live, even if you are feeling oppressed by your homework and your tests or by your political pressures or gargantuan departmental workload. Like "the real world," "out there" seems less sympathetic and less exciting.

Although not publicly espoused or usually even admitted, this attitude is implicitly shared by people throughout political/governmental Washington, in the news bureaus and lobbying suites as well as in the government offices, among those newly arrived and newly addicted to the city as well as those who have been around forever and want just one more term in the House or one more high federal agency job. When my friend the columnist and editor Michael Kinsley let it be known that he was leaving town after many years to take a job in the Pacific Northwest, I was struck that the first reaction I heard was that of people wondering not if he would miss his friends but if he would miss "the buzz."

Just as it is in high school, the inhabitants of Washington become wrapped up in the peculiar life of the place and can no longer imagine caring so much about any other. This is often amusingly true of those politicians who spend many hours on the airwaves condemning, for public consumption, the intolerable city. People here become friends across party and regional and institutional lines, feeling an unexpected comradeship that tends, if anything, to be strengthened by assaults from "out there" against Beltway culture. Their daily lives and personal dealings within the much-denounced enclave come to seem more real and important to them than the distant abstraction they have taken to calling "the American people," which is spread through the great, shapeless wilderness that has been designated "out there."

From time to time, someone who has voluntarily or even involuntarily moved away from the capital will come back for a visit and proclaim with great satisfaction (knowing full well the inner churning this will cause) the unthinkable proposition that "there is life after Washington." People will chuckle and nod, as if to say, "Well, of course." But few can imagine that this could actually be true. This is very much in the mode of the high schooler who spent four years desperately wishing to get older and more senior and to the top but who really doesn't want and is secretly afraid to leave when senior year is over. He just wants to go on being a high school big shot forever. But in Washington some people get that wish.

The outsider must be mystified that any mature, self-respecting adult would go along with the archaic and often degrading demands made on those who come to Washington—the schoolish, because-I-said-so rules, the layered-on customs and traditions that have something like the force of law and yet no longer seem related to the kind of subject matter they govern.

The answer begins with the particular nature of so many of the people who come here. Leave aside the demographics and the social science surveys and the analyses of median income, consumption habits, and religious background. The key index is this: Political/governmental Washington is an adult community made up largely of people who were extremely successful children. I don't say happy children or wealthy children or godly children. I mean only people who, as children, were good at being children.

Many of them continue to think of themselves as successful children and pursue their ambitions in the manner of the successful child. I'm not talking about the fabled "inner child" here but the "outer child" (if there can be such a term)—the invincibly pushy, precocious, overachieving-kid-like personas of a Clinton, a Gingrich, a Jack Kemp, for example, or the stylistically different personas of others who embody a different version of the childhood success story.

Such figures will have kept much of the outlook and mode of operating that served them so well in childhood. Why change an approach that from the beginning enabled them to flourish in a grown-up-imposed system that seemed to other kids pointless, unfair, and impossible to master or escape? We don't get many of the unsuccessful children here—almost none of the outright kid losers and not even all that big a population of the middling, muddle-through nondescript. On the contrary, what we tend to get are the hall monitors. In truth, we get many more than any one city should have to tolerate.

Washington also gets the teachers' pets; the most likely to succeed; the ones who got excellent grades; the ones who were especially good-looking in an old clothing-ad way; the ones who mowed the neighbor's lawn and were pronounced "fine young people"; the ones who got the Chamber of Commerce Boy or Girl of the Year Award; or the ones who figured out how to fake it and still make it—that whole range of smiling but empty-faced youth leaders who were universally admired, though no one could have told you for exactly what.

We get 4-H Club and Boy's Nation and Debating Society officers, along with some who made the all-star football team; we get the ingratiators and the operators and the grinds. And most notably, we get a small but steady stream of amazing prevailers, men and women who were able to overcome horrendous adversity of some kind in childhood to get here—the determined, express-train kids who knocked down all the obstacles and were the first in their families to do practically everything.

Adolescent troublemakers and weirdos, in contrast, do not as a rule aspire to come here, the national seat of authority. At least a famous few of them are likely to accomplish feats of imagination quite alien to Washington and well beyond the reach of the talents it normally prizes. These are the oddballs who might start a pathbreaking, billion-dollar business somewhere, bringing them eventually to the attention of people in Washington mainly as potential sources of campaign contributions and/or targets of antitrust litigation. Other youthful misfits might gravitate to New York or California and create highly acclaimed and, to our eye, gross, sensibility-rattling art that sooner or later will come before the hall monitors of Washington for government funding.

This is, of course, an oversimplified, impressionistic reading of who inhabits the governmental world of Washington and who, at least on occasion, inhabits the upper reaches of business and art. Still, it is childhood success stories that disproportionately dominate the population here. They may be very different from one another in lots of ways, including their varying tickets to success—good looks, good mind, pure grit. But from their early, formative experiences they will share one thing: They don't just like to prevail; they need to and expect to. Prevailing in this context means securing their place at the very top of whatever social collectivity it happens to be and becoming an influential, leading member of it, a praised person.

I don't mean to suggest that everyone in political/governmental Washington comes here as a queen bee and continues to function as one. Like most hives, this one owes plenty to its large complement of worker bees. But the people in Washington you've read about are likely to have come here at the end of a pretty well uninterrupted ascent to leadership of some kind that began, to much acclaim and gratification, in childhood. Partly because, to their consternation, they will unexpectedly find themselves surrounded in Washington by others who have followed the same trajectory and are equally accustomed to being number one, and partly because it is in the very nature of politics, there turns out to be no respite from the competition once they get here.

That is the big surprise. They are astonished to learn that they have not, after all, reached some triumphant resting place in their career where they can sit back and savor the rewards of their effort. On the contrary, they are immediately propelled into a way of life characterized by unremitting worry that some other aggressive, prize-winning mama's darling or some utterly unmanageable political catastrophe is about to overtake them. This turns out to be a daily consideration, never absent, always commanding some portion of their attention, and, by definition, never laid to rest. For as soon as they have disposed of one such anxiety, another will turn out to have been patiently waiting to take its place.

Here you have a defining horror of life in the capital. Its impact slowly dawns on those who come here. Like professional athletes, to whom they bear no other obvious resemblance, Washington political people are compelled to see themselves as holders of coveted jobs that are continuously at risk. They feel in constant danger not just of being suddenly tackled by an opponent—that much was to be expected—but of suddenly losing their title altogether or being benched for the rest of the season because someone better has turned up.

Washington figures are always, except for a privileged, ensconced, senior few, on professional probation. They feel driven to establish anew, every day of their working lives, their basic claim to be where they are. This they do through press leaks, self-promoting statements, grandstanding gestures, and subtle (of course, routinely denied) preemptive strikes at real, potential, and wholly imagined rivals.

Larry O'Brien, one of President Kennedy's "Irish Mafia" inner guard, who handled the political needs and complaints of members of Congress for JFK, once told me he had never met a congressman, senator, or other elected official who did not believe himself to be in imminent danger of political extinction. This was true, O'Brien said, both of people who actually were in jeopardy and of those who were so strong and safe that no serious candidate had dared oppose them for years. When he would say to one of the latter, "But you don't even have an opponent," the reply would always be the same: "No, no, Larry. You don't understand. It's really very bad."

This is not the prescription for a grounded, serene life, let alone an ethically irreproachable one. And it gets worse. Professional athletes can at least protect their position by doing what they get paid to do on the field. But for those in politics and government in Washington, this whole preoccupation is something that must be handled as an add-on to their day job. It's not what they are paid to do, not what most of them want to spend their time doing, and, worse, not the kind of concern they can easily confess to others. They must pretend that the grand and petty struggles for place, which consume so much of their attention, never happened.

They will, as a rule, respond to press inquiries or opposition attacks concerning such activities with an I-can't-imagine-what-you're-talking-about protestation of innocence, which nobody believes. But they are more or less obliged to keep up the fiction. Many are here, after all, for the purpose of conducting public business at taxpayer expense, and that, in the public's view, is meant to be about something other than their own personal political fortunes or their rising and falling rank within the hive.

Yet the only people who can function effectively in Washington are those who have figured out how to integrate these two concerns—that of doing the substantive job and that of staying politically vital, ahead or at least abreast of all the other Little Rollos. The two efforts cannot be separated but must be in some right relation to each other. Officials who spend the bulk of their time serving mainly the requirements of personal ambition clearly will not get much governmental work of substance done and will in any case lack the influence needed to bring others along on such work as they do, since people will sneer at them as full-time self-servers. But, equally, officials who are all substance and no political maneuver, who are either indifferent to or contemptuous of the need to keep up in the wearing rank-and-status and base-building game, will fare no better. They may have the best intentions and the greatest ideas in the world, but they will probably soon be speaking into dead telephones.

Whether or not it should be the case, it is true that maintaining one's standing in political/governmental Washington is a condition of getting anything to happen. The rare political kamikaze flight or unexpected, electrifying breakout from the pack in a tell-all speech or defiant vote can have a tremendous impact. But it is generally a onetime impact, and a onetime impact for which its perpetrator will be made to pay plenty by offended colleagues at a later date, when the TV cameras aren't running and the public is looking the other way. To be productive over the long haul in Washington jobs of consequence, government people must establish and maintain strong political positions inside the governing complex.

This cannot usually be done simply by dictate or compulsion or intimidation or other strong-arm methods. It also cannot be done strictly on merit, that is, simply by being very proficient at something. Neither superior force nor sheer excellence, in other words, is sufficient. This can be categorically stated as a law: All durable success in political/governmental Washington—all "winning," all achieving—is derivative and dependent.

For finally what a winner must win is not anything that can be mechanically scored, like the outcome of a bowling match or a pie-eating contest, or anything that can be achieved on one's own, like a perfect half-gainer from the thirty-two-foot board. What a winner must win is the consent of others, whether out of respect or admiration or political agreement or mere expediency, to get something done. To get the machinery going at all, it is necessary first to elicit the cooperation—active or passive, freely or grudgingly given—of many other players.

Without this, one can only make speeches or rack up minor victories—obstructing a bill or an appointment or the implementation of a policy, for example, strictly by virtue of the delaying powers that go with a job. Even these will almost always eventually be undone by the larger group, and they only add to the disfavor in which the obstructors are held. On the Hill, their influence will wane. In the executive branch, they will be isolated, circumvented, and generally made the subject of ghastly, "authoritative" press leaks that will weaken them and, in good time, probably force them out.

The point is that loners may be able to sell themselves electorally at home and perhaps even nationwide in today's television-driven personality politics. But they cannot win in Washington, no matter how bad or good they are. Winning here means winning people over—sometimes by argument, sometimes by craft, sometimes by obsequiousness and favors, sometimes by pressure, and sometimes by a chest-thumping, ape-type show of strength that makes it seem prudent to get with the ape's program.

Every couple of years, when the parties choose their new congressional leaders, or from time to time, when someone is summarily kicked out of government or another high Washington post and someone unexpected is installed, you will be able to see the principle at work. This is how a dour, unpersonable, but favor-doing fellow like Senator Bob Byrd of West Virginia could ace out a personable but then self-involved and inattentive Ted Kennedy for Senate Democratic whip in 1971.

This explains how Newt Gingrich worked his way into a hostile, resisting, more moderate House Republican leadership and eventually to the office of Speaker. It explains why some of the most dedicated and brilliant people who have come to the capital in recent years, like Senators Jacob Javits and Bill Bradley, may have engineered certain important pieces of legislation but were never really able to fulfill their awesome potential as powerful leaders in Congress. And the same principle explains how any number of seeming "stars" who have come to any number of presidential administrations wound up being axed in favor of the less talented, less celebrated, less charismatic souls backstage who were doing the greasing and making the trade-offs necessary to prevail.

One way or another, and no matter what else they may seem to be up to at any given moment, successful political people in Washington will be engaged in some form of this activity: Operation Make Them Love You, Operation Pay Them Off, Operation Watch Your Flank. It may not be attractive to behold, but it is not disreputable. On the contrary, it is indispensable to their work.

I divide those who are best at it into two broad classes. There are the ones who have gotten ahead by earning the trust and admiration and therefore the active patronage of a key senior person or two in Washington; and there are the ones who have gotten ahead by earning the approval and, ultimately, the gratitude of a large grouping of their peers, for whom they function as tribunes and whose lives they make better in various ways in return for some degree of submission and support. Reverting to the anthropology of the schoolyard, we are talking here about the good child and the head kid—that is, the teacher's pet and, depending upon the environment, either the class officer or the gang leader.

There have, of course, been successful Washington figures who combined, in different proportions, features of both types. Newt Gingrich would be one such hybrid. There are, in addition, people of rank and clout who got there by just sitting there—living proof that where tenure and seniority count, sheer longevity sometimes conquers all. And there are grown men and women in Washington who largely defy all typing, who prevailed because they were hard-working, of indisputably good character, and blessed with sound political instincts. But most of those who "make it" here exhibit the markings of one category or the other.

Washington head kids fulfill a role that is classic and familiar in political, civic, and social life everywhere. Once student-government leaders, they are now organizers of the caucus, chairmen of the committees, folks who know how to mobilize a bunch of peers, play people against each other, and get things to happen so that everyone is at least a little bit happy and they themselves remain in place. This can be done, of course, only with a healthy dose of trimming, dealing, and not quite leveling with everybody. But that is accepted, so long as it stays within bounds, since head kids are very useful to others. That is their strength.

In government these may be wonderfully entertaining rascals who alternately stun and revolt onlookers. Or they may be stupefyingly earnest Boy Scouts, often chosen as leaders in reaction to too long a period of domination by one of the governing rascals who has exceeded the accepted limits of subterfuge and cute dealing and forgotten how much his authority rests on the tacit consent of the gang. His earnest supplanter will have won support by promising open meetings, first-come-first-served consideration, and favors by lot instead of the autocratic manipulations of which people have grown tired.

Both kinds of leader will generally have been rising to the top of their particular heap in this fashion since youth. You know them. In Washington they personify the cyclical swings back and forth from reform to restoration, from disgust with the system to disappointment with the results of an idealistic effort to purify it. But whether rascally or self-righteous, these will be people familiar in every community: born to mobilize the group and lead it, successful at this (and aware of it) since the age of six.

The grown-up good child, in contrast, who has long played a prominent role in Washington life, will not be nearly so familiar in other realms of adult activity. But the workings of Washington cannot be understood without noting the predominance of such people here. Some probably got their start as model children, your basic, well-comported, miniature adults. But more appear to have laid claim to their virtue the competitive way—by being not merely virtuous but maddeningly more virtuous than their brothers and sisters in the parentally blessed categories: reliability, studiousness, manners.

You may take it as a rule of thumb that the children who came to Washington are not the ones who put the cat in the dryer, but the ones who tattled. They are also the ones in whom the parents reposed special pride and who gave them many a beaming hour in the school auditorium. I haven't done anything scientific to corroborate this, but it does seem to me that an awful lot of our national political leaders established their reputations for special moral worthiness and a sense of responsibility beyond their years precisely against the backdrop of that entirely different sibling who slept in the next bed—the defiant player-around, breaker of rules, and flunker-out, who, though often the more charming of the two, was always either in trouble or just about to be.

Let your mind range over the astonishing number of exhibitionists, rogues, and ne'er-do-wells who have turned up in the exalted role of First Brother, for instance—people like Sam Houston Johnson, Donald Nixon, Billy Carter, and Roger Clinton. Right along with their willingness to exploit their presidential brother's status, many have betrayed a smirking disdain for Mr. Goody Two-Shoes and a self-centered indifference to whether or not they caused him embarrassment with their kited checks and turbulent nights spent drying out in the local jail. Some seem, in fact, to harbor a positive desire to embarrass.

And isn't it also true that the presidents so embarrassed almost invariably respond not with anger but rather with guilt and patience and what appears to be an endless supply of mercy? "You must understand dear old Earl," they will tell us, when Earl the Bellicose turns up yet again in the tank, resisting arrest, yelling obscenities, and throwing around his august brother's name. "He is really a very decent, generous person, and I'm sure he didn't mean to do harm." You have a feeling you are watching some ancient, familial pattern, a kind of recurring psychodrama between these two. The designated achiever achieves and the designated failer fails, and the one who should be feeling remorseful isn't. The other one is. The wrong guy—or is it the right guy?—assumes the burden.

Can this pattern in our politics be an accident? I don't think so. Do such obstreperous, self-destructive siblings merely represent a fair statistical sample of the population as a whole? Let us hope not. No, I think there is a method of relating to authority and achieving success that the good child repeats over and over again in his or her ascent to office and consolidation of authority once there.

I know this subject firsthand, because I recognize in my own office behavior and outlook over the years both what is professionally advantageous and what is kind of awful in the type. Books have been written about how the family is replicated in the workplace, people who are merely nine-to-five coworkers inevitably becoming each other's proxy mothers and fathers and brothers and sisters and husbands and wives and even in-laws and "steps" and "halfs." As was the case, I suspect, with many of the people I write about in government, the role of being the wondrously industrious young one came easily to me in professional life because I had grown up that way—second-born sibling, the child who got her rewards for being good at what parents want you to be good at, a little wiser and bookier than the rest of the crowd in the sandbox, nothing if not reliable, and, in fact, sometimes seeming to have been fifty years old at birth.

Further following the pattern, all this played out in the companionship of a funny and much-beloved brother who was fully as smart—probably smarter—but whose trademark was that he wouldn't do anything right by my parents' standards if he could possibly find another way. Jimmy wasn't close to being in the class of the legendary and occasionally slobbish political brothers of our time, but he did fulfill the good child's need for a more charming and magnetic and rebellious sibling in relation to whom the role of responsible one could be played.

The brash child gets elected and wins popularity contests; the good child, like an obedient dog, gets her kicks from the appreciative pat on the head or the marveling glance exchanged between adult admirers, which seems to say: "Isn't she something!" Isn't-she-somethingism, expressed by those in authority, was to become a motivating force in my office life. For years, I saw myself as the special young one, well beyond the time when "young" was a realistic description. It became a kind of inner understanding of my role, even into the days when new White House assistants (incomprehensibly, in my opinion) began addressing me as "ma'am." They would be half my age, but I still somehow thought of them as older people who needed to be impressed by my diligence and precocity.

In the context of government, this breed tends to be made up of people who come to town with reputations as awesome homework doers, dependable types who, at least until very recent times, did not at all mind accepting a protracted period of, as it might be described in the workings of the capital, protégé-hood. In no time at all, they seem to achieve the same relationship to their professional contemporaries that they once had to their siblings and are being given the same kind of limited but special responsibility by their political seniors that was once conferred on them by parents and teachers.

More than a few of these actually become quasi-permanent protégés, big-hitters-in-waiting for most of the length of their careers. This can be, although it doesn't sound it, a truly enviable position.

The very juniorness and sense of only "becoming," as distinct from already being a formally installed leader, leaves such select individuals gloriously free of blame for the things that irk or go wrong, while at the same time investing them with a great deal of borrowed authority as people known to be agents of those really running the show, not to mention heirs presumptive.

It's not a bad job description, when you get right down to it. There have been a few among the protégé class in Washington who kept the role into advancing age and accumulating seniority not just because their patrons perversely refused either to die or retire, but because they actually liked it. Some, of course, are blocked by contemporaries or classmates from moving up after their patrons have finally been called home by the Lord or, more mundanely, by the voters.

When I came to Washington in the Kennedy years, the savvy, youngish Democratic congressman from Missouri, Richard Bolling, was a famous protégé. A witty, genuine insider, he was a man we reporters were always trying to interview because he really knew what was what, and anything he said counted. We all knew that he had been a confidant of Sam Rayburn, the aging, Zeus-class Speaker of the House. Rayburn's previously best-known protégé had been a young Congressman Lyndon Johnson many years before. It was now generally supposed that Rayburn had anointed Bolling as the leader for the next generation.

Such a role would be significant now, but nowhere near as significant as it was then. For Bolling got his protégé status at a time when a secure, cohesive, interlocking Senate-House Democratic leadership, made up largely of senior southerners, still exercised its collective will pretty much as it pleased. Its members worked in tandem with their equally senior and equally conservative ranking Republican colleagues from the Midwest and a few states elsewhere. The result was that those legislators who frontally challenged this leadership—mainly frustrated liberals and almost-liberals from the rest of the country—were squashed. You could get concessions from the leaders and a bit of movement in a different political direction only by working with them, and this a strong-minded, clever, but respectful junior congressman like Dick Bolling was able to do.

Such anointings of promising younger colleagues—Bolling is a good example—were practically never capricious exercises in favoritism toward some undeserving junior who merely met the elders' patronage needs by being politically well connected or serving as a full-time toady. The protégés were usually people of high intelligence who, from their earliest days, resisted the temptation to coast on that gift. Your basic protégés were known for being willing to do the ghastly, painstaking work; to know down to the last, mind-numbing detail what they were talking about before they took the floor; to earn their rewards rather than grab for them.

Such a disposition is in fact the common characteristic of any number of prominent Washington figures who, although different from one another in many ways, seem to me to have reached prominence and used their accruing power as they rose pretty much in the good-child mode. That means dutifully, carefully, and, at least as measured by conventional behavior in politics, relatively self-effacingly. It is true that the power of protégé-hood no longer is what it was when people in high office (not just on the Hill but throughout government and private industry) were much more able to name their successors and lead by decree without fear of being thrown out, reversed, or even ridiculed. But in weakened form the protégé route to leadership endures.

For example, former senator Sam Nunn, the Georgia Democrat, was elected in 1972 at the age of thirty-four, defeating a man who had been temporarily appointed to fill the Senate seat left vacant by the death of the formidable hierarch Richard Russell. Nunn's model was his late great-uncle Carl Vinson, who had long presided over the House Armed Services Committee. It didn't take long for this young Georgian with the stellar political bloodline and sober bearing to get a seat on the Senate Armed Services Committee. He soon became known around Washington on two counts. He had taken the trouble to steep himself in all aspects of defense policy. And he had become the protégé of committee chairman John Stennis of Mississippi. He had the ear and the respect of the old boy, and, characteristic of any protégé worth his salt, he was known to be more open and responsive than Stennis.

This early word on Nunn was very like the early word on Democrat Tom Foley of Washington almost a decade before, when Foley, another good-child public figure, came to Congress as a politically well connected, professionally impressive protégé. Foley had gotten his start in the capital as a young staff assistant to Senator Henry (Scoop) Jackson.

Although Foley and Nunn hailed from diagonally opposite corners of the country, with very different political cultures, they had much in common. Both were believed to be more "modern," progressive, and sympathetic to change than the constituencies they represented. Foley came from a conservative Republican congressional district in the West, Nunn from a Deep South state where unashamed white resistance to the integration of blacks was only gradually dying out. Each man had entered politics with an instinct for walking the politically precarious line between deference to the views of an established order and a genuine but circumspect demonstration of independence from those views.

Typically, the Washington protégé must be able to offer his benefactor two delicately balanced assurances. First, he must show that he has the capacity to accomplish and a mind of his own, who will thus be perceived as a legitimate representative of his generation and not just some stooge or clone of the elders. Then too, he must show that he has no intention of going out and blowing up the power station tomorrow morning, since he aspires to inherit the thing intact. Probably there will be some sensible structural alterations when he takes over, the assumption goes, and a few willful, old time-servers on the staff who think they own the place will be pensioned off. But that will be all.

The protégé will soon be established as the go-between and man to see. He will be the one people approach to make a pitch to the Big Guy, and he will in turn be the one through whom Big Guy communicates with the young and the restless. Just as the protégé can maybe persuade the elders to give a bit here and there, so he can maybe also persuade the juniors to be a bit less impatient, impetuous, and contemptuous of "the system."

The protégé will never—meaning truly never, not Washington "never"—breathe down the neck of the beloved patron/benefactor while he is still ensconced, participate in anyone else's insurrection against him, or suggest by even the tiniest, subtlest gesture that he is thinking, somewhere deep down in the most secluded recesses of his decorous soul, that it's really time for Old Bones to move on. In this and some other respects, the protégé is required to behave in ways we have come to associate with vice presidents.

Outside of Congress, whose method of organizations lends itself to the creation of a privileged protégé class, you will find just as many good-child public figures who stand in some variation of this quasi-filial relationship to their bosses and to the presiding order in general. But the form it takes will be somewhat different. Although various strains of the noncongressional breed do tend to be mixed in each individual case, there are two main subtypes. One is the good child as almost insufferably rectitudinous son or daughter (Janet Reno, Al Gore), the kind that parents are always holding up before their own errant offspring in sentences that begin "Why can't you be more like . . . "

Their reputation for unrelenting probity and their apparently inexhaustible desire to honor their fathers and mothers persists even in the face of evidence that these perceived Eagle Scouts and mother's little helpers of public office are, in their offstage behavior, not necessarily like the earnest, funless, charmless son and daughter figures they have come to personify. This difference between a stern, stuffy public persona and a private self that is often exuberant, irreverent, jokey, or downright salacious is a core feature of Washington political life and does not appear only in figures who project a dutiful-offspring image on air. In both Hubert Humphrey and his own onetime protégé, Walter Mondale, for instance, it reached almost mythic proportions. As I later write, this two-track persona, which is partly learned and partly instinctive in politicians, may be seen as either hypocrisy or a requirement of the business.

The other noncongressional variant is more common than the public prig and, to my mind, much more interesting. This is the good child less as protégé than as prodigy. The key relationship is still a junior one, dependent on the sponsorship of a highly placed boss from whom the prodigy's importance flows. But unlike the designated protégé/heir or the dutiful offspring, it is more freewheeling, more self-starting, and, in notable instances, more dangerous to the patron/benefactor, who had better watch his back. I have in mind your basic baby wonk or whiz, Washington's functional equivalent of those thirteen-year-olds you occasionally read about who graduate from MIT or the freaky toddler violinist who stands right up there in short pants or puffed sleeves and knocks them dead in Carnegie Hall.

In Washington this prodigy figure will be someone a little bit down the organizational ladder from Madam or Mr. Secretary, a number two or, more likely, three or four or five in an agency, who becomes known for precocity and for being the "real brains" behind the boss, the one "you really ought to talk to." The same, it is true, is often said of the dutiful congressional apprentice/heir. But somehow the executive branch prodigy figures tend to acquire more glittery personal reputations than their good-boy and good-girl counterparts in Congress. "Dazzling" is the term most often conferred upon them after they have delivered one of their frequent background briefings or quiet luncheon-table expositions of policy. If only their principals could think and talk this way, we say.

Like their good-child kin, these prodigy figures are continually being marveled at for a sagacity and mastery of the system well beyond that of both their peers and their supposed betters. And like them too, they are continually publicly reasserting their loyalty and devotion to the boss. Thus while everyone else in town is saying it's a damn shame they aren't running the show instead of Madam or Mr. Secretary, they will be protesting that this is a grossly unfair point of view, telling you (voice rising slightly) how underappreciated the boss really is, and swearing their devotion to this revered person whom they nevertheless can't quite seem to help showing up on a regular basis with their discreet, not-for-attribution policy musings. Their impassioned declarations of loyalty will, of course, only further convince others that they are virtuous as well as brilliant (imagine!) and that they should definitely replace the big fools they report to.

Well, we weren't all born yesterday. Many of these wizards are obviously into low-grade treachery, inflating their own reputations at the boss's expense, all the while assuming this choirboy pose of humility. But others of their general breed are genuine straight arrows. It is a continuing challenge to those of us who write about such people in Washington to figure out which is which. Sometimes those who fall into this overall category will actually be known as "whiz kids," one of the city's enduring designations for grown men and women who may be only a little bit younger but are thought to be a whole lot smarter than their bosses.

There is just a whiff of mistrust and ridicule in the phrase, but by and large it is meant to convey awe. Whiz kids abounded in the Kennedy and Johnson administrations and were so called. They were also conspicuous before that, by other names, in Franklin Roosevelt's and other administrations. From Harry Truman's White House came one of the most celebrated of all, the young Clark Clifford. In more recent times there have been figures like Bobby Inman, once the brilliant staffer to see at the Central Intelligence Agency, and R. James Woolsey, another legendarily wise top national security operative who eventually became Clinton's first CIA director. Henry Kissinger, special assistant to Nelson Rockefeller, started out as such a junior prodigy and retained certain characteristics of one until the day he left office as secretary of state. Richard Darman, professional young Republican guru before he became George Bush's* director of the Office of Management and Budget, had the label that many of these people end up with: "brilliant but abrasive."

Among the best-known good-child prodigy figures of the 1960s was Bill Moyers, once Lyndon Johnson's press secretary and later the prominent television interviewer and essayist. Moyers was presumed to have a father-son relationship with Johnson. It was intense, tumultuous, and periodically poisonous. But Moyers, in addition to his public good-son image, was regarded even more as the child prodigy of the Johnson White House, known for his exceptional brightness.

He enjoyed one of those useful, dual reputations that the clever younger associate invariably acquires: He was an extremely important person in Washington because he was so close to the president but also because he managed always to project a certain measured detachment from Johnson. It is that familiar, small, but significant margin of separateness that, whether in a Hill apprentice or executive branch prodigy assistant or other type of good-child public ser-

*The forty-first president.—Ed.

vant, always spares the junior partner any share of the condemnation that is regularly heaped on the boss.

The result was that Moyers, who derived all of his authority from association with Johnson and was known to be in the innermost circle, was never dirtied or even slightly smudged by the things Johnson did wrong. On the contrary, it was repeatedly said what a bright, responsible, wise-beyond-his-years young fellow this former divinity student was. Wasn't Johnson lucky to have him around? And wasn't it obvious that Moyers could not possibly have supported the unspeakable thing, whatever it was that week, that his employer/patron/dad had just done?

Neither Moyers nor anyone else who ever fell under the general good-child heading could come in anything but a distant second to the purebred of them all, that other former divinity student and quintessential Washington prodigy, David Stockman. There is no contest here: When you're talking toddler violinists, you're talking David Stockman—underage Republican doctrinal wizard, underage congressman from Michigan, underage Reagan cabinet officer. This was the eternally boyish-looking man whom an awestruck Ronald Reagan put in charge of that gigantic octopus, the Office of Management and Budget. From this position Stockman serenely instructed people old enough to be his grandparents on how to run their affairs and, with a kind of frigid good cheer, did what he could (which was considerable in the early Reagan years) to punish or reverse them when they failed to comply.

Stockman had burst upon the Washington scene as the mysterious author—who was he?—of a long, erudite, much-talked-about article in *Public Interest,* arguing that many of LBJ's Great Society programs had long since lost all connection to their original mission and degenerated into dispensaries of political pork. He went on to sketch an elaborate programmatic and philosophical justification for Republican, free-market alternatives. Along with others, I supposed that such a tour de force could only have been produced by some crotchety, old Edmund-Burke-spouting scholar, one who had been amassing his material and fine-tuning his argument for years.

This supposition was firmly fixed in my mind the day I went to meet Stockman for a luncheon interview I had politely requested. His uninspired choice of eating place, the Capitol Hill Republican Club, only reinforced my preconception of whom I was about to meet. I remember rushing when I realized I was a little late, because I didn't think it would be proper to keep the old gent waiting— especially an old gent who sounded, in his writing, as unobliging and self-certain as this one. God only knew what kind of testy thing he might say.

I dashed, a bit breathless, into the front hall, looking around for my venerable luncheon companion, and had this little boy hail me and introduce himself. We had met before, Stockman smilingly re- minded me. He had been the resident babysitter in Cambridge for my old friends Pat and Liz Moynihan when they were at Harvard many years back.

After my initial surprise, like many another Washingtonian who encountered Stockman in that period, I was amazed at the range and detail of his knowledge. In time he wrote articles for the op-ed page I edited. I followed his unsurprising success in toppling a non- descript Republican incumbent and winning a seat in the House. There I watched him extend his sway and burnish his reputation.

He became the resident Hill expert in energy, which was then at the center of domestic policy arguments. He could, like another pre- cocious, conservative young know-it-all of an earlier generation, William F. Buckley Jr., debate most of his complacent liberal elders right into the wall. To them, he was a little, wrongheaded, Republi- can punk and smart-ass.

Stockman was an arrogant brat if you were on one side of the po- litical divide, an inspired baby genius if you were on the other. It says something about this durable sense of Stockman's youthfulness that when he got into big trouble for an act that often afflicts the breed—talking too much to a sympathetic reporter in a way that redounded to his own credit at the expense of the boss—Ronald Reagan spoke of having taken him "to the woodshed." The woodshed! You could not conceive of Reagan's using those words to express the anger he felt at other cabinet members—Alexander Haig or Donald Regan. The whack-on-the-bottom, naughty-kid language is as oddly forgiving as it is patronizing.

Prodigy pols like Stockman, no matter how old they may grow in office or out, almost never cease to be their youthful, intellectually bratty selves in the Washington imagination. Even when they have advanced sufficiently in years and rank to be considered normal adult achievers holding normal adult achievers' political jobs, they often are not regarded as such. Many are destined instead to be forever marked as grown-up child stars, political Norma Desmonds—known to the public as well as to their colleagues mainly for their stints as legendarily gifted junior advisers.

In my decades in Washington, I have seen many of these people, from administrations going back to FDR's, tottering around town and still being revered as that breathtaking White House kid of yore. Although they may come to lead lives of substantial new accomplishment, such latter-day accomplishment will turn up only in the last sentences of their obituaries. While living they generally suffer the fate of the late Robert Maynard Hutchins, who, as a preternaturally intelligent young man, made over the University of Chicago and created a distinctive, new intellectual life there, to be tagged ever after with the dreadful epithet of "aging boy wonder."

Still, there is one thing worse. However debilitating it may be for others to continue thinking of them this way, it can be far more debilitating that so many prodigies keep thinking of themselves this way too. As I've suggested in my own case, the young-achiever self-image and the mode of operation that grows out of it die hard, and these are graver offenses to the youthful achiever's self-image than merely being addressed as "ma'am."

Back in the winter of 1962–1963, after Edward Kennedy, barely thirty and inexperienced, had been vaulted into a Massachusetts Senate seat by the family machine, he made the rounds of Senate moguls, carefully primed on what to say in order to deflect their known resentment about his silver-spoon ascent. To Richard Russell, arguably the most powerful person in the place, Kennedy noted that Russell had come to the Senate at more or less the same age. It was a nice try. Russell, an alert guardian of his own credentials as the paramount boy wonder of Washington, replied that it was true: "But by then, of course, I had already been governor."

Russell is one of the few people I can think of who traversed the psychic distance from boy wonder to village patriarch and seemed entirely comfortable in the latter incarnation. Many more have no such luck. That is because the role they have become accustomed to playing since real childhood has in certain ways wrecked them for the role they are supposed to play when they finally assume full responsibility.

When they take over, though they have been in the thick of Washington battles for years, they may still be novices at open, direct personal combat and survival techniques that are quite different from those required in the quiet backstage knife play and maneuver at which they may excel. That is because, except for the occasional Washington column inveighing against their alleged Rasputin-like powers, they will never have been held publicly accountable for the foul-ups in their area of concern. They will never have had to make and remain responsible for (as distinct from merely brilliantly describing to a columnist over lunch) the brutal choice between truly awful policy alternatives, and do it by three that afternoon. Yet all these dread nevers come to pass almost immediately with elevation to visible top office. That elevation is often the death knell for what the good children had simply reflexively assumed were their eternally charmed lives.

This is true of protégés, prodigies, and all other brands of good-child politicians in Washington. Their elevation to the number-one jobs, if it comes, all too often seems, both to them and to those they are expected to lead, an anticlimax and disappointment, a kind of long, slow hissing of the air out of the tires.

There are plenty of reasons why. One is that over the years good children will not have developed the thick skins of head kids like Congressmen John Dingell and Dan Rostenkowski or Senator Bob Dole, who have been issuing the orders and taking the heat for years.

They will have developed instead the mediating-between-generations way of doing business, protecting the boss and appeasing contemporaries by telling them how much can be extracted from the boss. With that prop gone, newly elevated figures are expected to act boldly, to direct, to deliver, to have the brass to themselves utter the decisive words "yes" or "no"—not to negotiate, Moses-like, with God for limited concessions.

What may also now come out is much pent-up resentment from sibling-type contemporaries who do not enjoy the good child's new authority and frankly never have accepted the justice of his having been designated teacher's pet or chairman's agent in the first place. Years of exercising derivative power in a defensive, backstairs, unaccountable way have also unfitted the poor protégé/prodigy for the elementary requirements of his new role—the direct statement, the assertion of will or position, and, above all, the concomitant acceptance of the murderous criticism that being in charge inevitably generates.

This last is the toughest and most incomprehensible part for the good-child politician. For years, he has been accustomed to giving sage advice, receiving great respect, and never paying a price when things went wrong. His boss had the title and the big-time salary but also took the hit. Now overnight he has become fair game. When he does something well, people don't say, "Gosh, wasn't that brilliant? Too bad he isn't boss." He is boss, and so they say, "It could have been better," or, "It took too long," or, "It's fake," or, "It's only a small part of what needs to be done." When he does things badly, and often even when he does not, he will suddenly find himself unprotected by his former golden haze, by his great underground reputation, which, it will turn out, was only an instrument others were using anyway to belittle his boss by comparison.

Worse, probably for the first time in his life, going all the way back to the playpen, he will find himself accused not just of insufficient accomplishments but also of moral shortcomings—embarrassing vanities, possible felonies, and even mortal sins. How can this be? Surely, he will think, this is a case of mistaken identity.

When you hear his inevitable, keening complaint rising up to heaven—at a press conference or in a speech or even in emphatic, obsessive after-hours conversation in which he just can't seem to get away from the subject, you will in truth be hearing something primal. For the Washington good-child politician, ascended to high office, fully in charge and fully accountable at last, is utterly unaccustomed to being called anything except an outstanding young person of exceptional promise—no matter what his age.

CHAPTER THREE

Mavericks
and Image-Makers

*T*HE STUNTED, HIGH-SCHOOLISH social structure and the kinds of people I have been describing will not be features of life in Washington forever. The familiar types of political winners are endangered species, and their institutional habitat is under heavy assault. "So what?" you say. "None of it sounds all that hot to me anyway."

True. But here is another truth: Lamentable as the eccentric community I have been describing may sound, what is displacing it is something considerably less attractive. This new culture is also redolent of high school, but high school at its most dangerously deranged.

You can say this for the probably doomed Washington order: It has at least required public people to be in some actual, vital relationship with one another during their working day. Their success depends on other living, breathing persons whom they have to persuade or outsmart and to whom they are therefore in some way answerable.

Whether it is the chairman of the committee or the director of the agency or the competitor for the protégé role or the members of the caucus or "class" one aspires to represent as leader, there are flesh-and-blood others of one's professional life to mix it up with every day. It may be a strange society, overly hierarchic and frequently sophomoric. But those obliged to work in it have worked under relatively healthy social constraints.

They have had to maintain a modicum of consistency and veracity in their statements to those they have dealt with. They have had to prove virtue of different kinds to those they intended to lead or from whom they were seeking promotions, favors, deals, patience, or understanding. It may all look nuts to those on the outside, but the old system does provide a constant if modest reality check.

What is overtaking Washington is what has overtaken so many sectors of American society: an all but total weakening of the authority of those who used to wield it, the evaporation of the leaders' ability to punish or reward, the disinclination of individuals to submit to any kind of group discipline, and the fragmentation of the parties, delegations, lobbies, institutions, agencies, and even branches of government.

Since about the mid–1960s, Washington has gradually become more and more a colony of political independent contractors, loners, and freelancers. It is still true that the lone-wolf practitioner cannot get much done in a policy or programmatic sense. But in an era when getting things to happen may have less political value than merely seeming to be on the right side, this doesn't bother nearly as many people in the capital as it should. People market themselves; policy and program become stage props.

The explosion of new communications technologies—mass e-mail, blast faxes, Web sites, cable channels of all varieties—has accelerated the change, as have institutional reforms. Political people can now deal directly with their audiences of choice. They need not depend so much on party organizations. Individuals do their own hustling, run their own campaigns, and make their own deals, as do special interest caucuses and lobbies. They feel less bound to stay in tune with their group or its leaders. They often feel more bound to stay in tune with the antiauthority ethic of what has become a kind of electronic national conversation—part gripe session, part political bathing-suit contest—from which they increasingly take their cues.

Of course the proud, often arrogant possessors of seniority throughout establishment Washington still have plenty of special advantages. But they find it harder by the day to work their will as before. They cannot simply name their protégés and main agents and count on others to respect their choices. And the would-be, head-kid leaders of every kind of organization find that no one especially wants to be led. Fewer and fewer will consent to be. The upshot is that they themselves can no longer promise to deliver this or put a stop to that with anything like their former reliability.

In the old days, for example, a freshman senator from a small, not very populous western or northern state would quietly be asked by the Southern Directorate of Congress to vote its way on famous Rule XXII (making it hard to break anti-civil-rights filibusters) and he would get good assignments and other good stuff for his state. Don't vote with us, the corollary went, and you get zilch, plus a little kicking around. With most people it worked.

Today, if one of the ensconced party leaders quietly put forward a comparable proposition, likely as not that would be the last quiet thing that happened. We would probably see some or all of the following: The newly elected senator, undaunted and utterly uninterested in assuming the humble, silent, know-your-place role of traditional freshman, would go on CNN, MSNBC, and the Fox News Channel and e-mail his constituents, denouncing the ensconced one to hell and back for trying to intimidate him, for flirting with criminal conspiracy, and who knows what else.

He would make a very big deal of his defiance of the corrupt system. The question of how we all felt about this would be put to an immediate referendum of cable TV watchers and radio call-in show listeners. A horde of press would start investigating the big shot senator who had tried to put the arm on the freshman. Two unauthorized girlfriends (at least) and one disgruntled paving contractor would step forward from the offending senior senator's home state with tales to tell on a tabloid television program. The dirt would fly. In the court of public opinion—and this cliché phrase is the key to understanding what has happened—the novice senator would come out way ahead, and the would-be senate strongman who had been trying to bribe/browbeat him into compliance in the timeless fashion would be the big loser.

Clearly the kind of system being supplanted in this little tale is indefensible. It represents much of what I found so infuriating about Washington when I came here and to which I have never been reconciled. My point is merely that it is too bad that such a system is not falling to a more worthy inheritor. For while the basic high-schoolish order of political/governmental Washington has been in the process of disintegrating and the old pattern of relationships is changing too, along with the type of person most likely to gravitate to the capital, the sorry truth is that what is taking their place is no bargain.

Do not suppose that we are witnessing some kind of wonderful liberation of our previously hidebound, unresponsive instruments of government, some miraculous reincarnation of the nation's capital as in-touch city. On the contrary, the new, atomized life emerging is, if anything, even more unmoored from reality and more remote from the way business is ordinarily conducted among human beings. For it is preponderantly virtual life—simulated life, fabricated life—that is coming to the fore.

Virtual life is one prolonged encounter not between the public person and his colleagues or constituents (never mind how weird those relationships might be) but between the public person's image and that image's supposed audience "out there." What the latter kind of encounter increasingly requires of such people is not that they find ways to work with or around a variety of fellow human toilers in the public vineyard. It is that they find ways continuously to create and re-create their public presentation of themselves, with the aim of winning approval from an all-important, profoundly capricious, and (as they see it) life-sustaining Blob.

The great Opinion of Unseen, Unknown Others Blob is the

Loch Ness monster of American public life. In truth, like Nessie, it can neither be sighted nor even quite authenticated. Does it really exist? What does it want now? The same thing it wanted two hours ago? Three hours ago? People in public life can only surmise that it is always attentively there and try with what they take to be ever more foolproof technologies to measure its whims and foretell its responses.

It is fortunate that bright people in Washington no longer feel they must follow absolutely the dictate of some second-rate political or bureaucratic overlord, if that's who happens to be in charge. Nevertheless, too many of them have concluded that, instead, they must perform nonstop in ways that will catch and hold the Blob's attention and eventually make the Blob fall in love with them. They have to do this even though they are not at all certain of much of anything about the Blob from moment to moment and live in constant apprehension of a summary, unexplained, Dear John rejection by it.

When you add this harrowing preoccupation to the enormous dose of anxiety that already characterized the daily lives of so many people in public life, you may not sympathize with them, but you will begin to understand what accounts for the unseemly rise of their self-pity in recent years to record-breaking levels. You will also begin to understand what accounts for much of the exodus from public life of men and women who had learned to operate under a wholly different set of rules.

The reason I say this turn of events is reminiscent of high school at its most deranged is that it represents total, crazy-making engulfment by concern with one thing, image, to the progressive denial and neglect of practically all else. I want to be fair to high school here. Washington is by far the more egregious of the two.

High school is the time when people first contrive to have an image at all, by which I mean the kind of image that is self-invented and requires tending. It is the moment when kids begin consciously to fantasize, project, and finally inhabit an attractive, enviable, highly edited picture of themselves that they are all too aware may not entirely comport with reality. "This is who I am, what I like, what I do," the image says. It is doubtless not the first lie the adolescent ever told, but it is different in kind from the "I didn't do it" lie he has long since grown accustomed to dishing up to wrathful authority, and also from the tall tales he told in the schoolyard. That is because the image-lie is more than a lie; it is a program. There is nothing ad hoc about it. It is not intended merely to get him out of a temporary pickle or help him prevail in a childish, one-shot bragging contest. It is an attempt to fabricate a whole second persona for public consumption, a greatly improved, nonexistent new self that will always be on view, generating admiration and applause, while the actual person furtively looks on from some hidden vantage point within.

Acute image-consciousness is somehow always transparent. You see it in high school kids when they affect that peculiar, fake-oblivious saunter that pretends to be unaware of anyone's watching and yet manages, despite itself, to betray exactly the opposite: an all-consuming interest in whether there are watchers and, if so, whether they are properly impressed. There is an increasing temptation in these years too, one that is rarely resisted, to daydream about oneself in the third person doing wonderful things, looking fabulous, being a much-sought-after and altogether dazzling person by the standards of William Henry Harrison High.

To my own eternal discomfort, I can even remember in that period of life being for a time entranced by the mystery and romance I believed had accrued to my own image in the eyes of my classmates as a result of my mother's death when I was eleven. I felt ashamed of this, but a stirring picture of myself would nevertheless flicker in and out of the shadows at the edge of my grief. In it I was the object not so much of sympathy as of curiosity, romance, and awe: "Look at her"; "There she goes—her mother died. What can that be like?"; "What do you think she's thinking? It's so mysterious."

Third-personism runs riot through these years. It is a time of compulsive self-description and much-fretted-over description by others. I recall the anxious concern we kids used to have over what those succinct bios of us in the yearbook would say. And never do I recall that concern more vividly than when I get into yet another hassle (they are unending) with some Washington big shot over what the tiny, three-line identification of him at the bottom of a *Washington Post* op-ed page article he has written will say. There are public figures who will fuss infinitely more about the wording of this minuscule account of who they are than they will about the draconian editing you may have visited on the article itself. Grown, influential people, people who more or less have class-A pushing-around rights in Washington and who you would think had long since stopped worrying about such things, will carry on like banshees, sometimes almost in tears, to get one two-word phrase listing an accomplishment reinstated.

Similarly, I often recall that classic, fake-oblivious teenager's saunter when I observe Washington newsmakers feigning indifference to how they look in their quite self-conscious comings and goings—getting off the plane, arriving in the auditorium, emerging from the hearing room—in short, being watched. Their affectation of obliviousness is pure high school: unconvincing and comic but also, in their case, somehow embarrassing and sad.

It was not all that long ago that the word "image," when used to describe a politician's effort to impress, was regularly imprisoned in a cage of disparaging quotation marks. "He is concerned with his 'image,'" we would write. (We could even say it aloud with an inflection that put the quotation marks there.) What we were implying by those quotation marks was, first, that there was something discreditable about such concern and, second, that there was in reality no such thing as an image anyway. It was a falsity, a will-o'-the-wisp, a no-good concoction intended to deceive.

Back then an image was something your average political person would never admit to having, let alone cultivating. I am talking about the 1950s and early 1960s, when someone such as Murray Chotiner, Congressman Richard Nixon's behind-the-scenes operative since his earliest days in California politics, could be publicly savaged when his image-doctoring plan for the candidate somehow leaked to the press. In those days reputation, in the sense of one's good name, was what most public figures professed anyway to be protecting and promoting in their day-to-day work. It was reputation, not image, that people worried would be damaged in the wars over Joseph McCarthy's anti-Communist jihad. You didn't consider that somebody's "image" was being impaired by his being called disloyal. Image was fluff and fabricated. Reputation was solid and earned.

Now, in ever more quarters, concern with the first has overwhelmed concern with the second. And far from being covert, as they once were, in ministering to the presumed image-needs of people in public life, a flourishing industry of campaign consultants, technicians, poll takers, statisticians, and demographers has thrust itself into the spotlight, publishing newsletters, forming professional guilds, and rehashing one another's triumphs and failures on televised panels, as if it were they, not the candidates, who counted in the elections.

Of course, in this they might be right. For these days it's not just politicians who seek professional help in image creation and projection. It is also college presidents, businesspeople, figures from every part of the entertainment industry, and even some journalists, among many, many others. Moreover, professional help of this sort is thought to be not just desirable or essential but even a universal "right."

Whenever a public relations company is given grief for taking a fee to improve the image in this country of some particularly loathsome foreign tyrant, the firm piously states that Colonel Gizzard has just as much right to advice on image as anyone else, just as all criminal defendants under our glorious Constitution have a right to legal counsel. Some part of all this is about money: prettying oneself up to win a grant from Congress or forestall a cut in aid, if you happen to be Colonel Gizzard.

If you're a homegrown client, perhaps you have public relations advisers to increase your speaking fees or land a very big job. Some part of it is about exhibitionism and lust for celebrity: the validation of a person's very existence in accord with the newly revised Cartesian maxim, "I've been on *Larry King,* therefore I am." But for political people in general and Washington players in particular, the image obsession is no mere buck-raking enterprise or optional indulgence of a yen to be famous. To their way of thinking, it is a question of self-preservation. More and more of them have come to believe they must keep reinventing themselves in newly sophisticated ways merely to stay in the game.

I say "newly sophisticated" because at least since Yankee Doodle tried his scam, Americans have been engaged in the business of personally reinventing themselves—enthusiastically, with varying degrees of fraudulence (or ingenuity, if you prefer), and often to perfectly good purpose. I think at once of my dad, the first American-born son of poor, steerage-class Russian immigrants. He had himself driven around England in a grand touring car, conducting himself as he believed a well-bred British gent would as he visited his insufferable daughter, who was studying poetry at Cambridge University.

If my father wasn't reinvented from his days of scrapping and swiping his way out of a south Philadelphia slum, nobody ever was. You could say the whole immigrant assimilation process of our history has been in part a labor of personal self-reinvention. Americans came from everywhere and fanned out into a vast land where there was always someplace to appear and start anew, pretending, as they felt necessary, to be a better-born somebody else or not to have failed in some earlier enterprise or otherwise creating a not-quite-on-the-up-and-up life story. Our history is crammed with entertaining frauds in the mold of the "duke" and the "king" Huck Finn encountered in his travels—people who, unlike Mark Twain's two scoundrels, however, made it big in business and society and civic life, keeping their sometimes bizarre origins a secret.

Before self-reinvention became, as it has in our age, a matter of either electronic, political dissembling or self-obsessed psychological reconstruction (all that how-to stuff on the best-seller list), this is more or less what it meant. So the impulse is anything but new, and the same may be said, of course, of the habit of politicians to say one thing and do or think another and to portray themselves untruthfully—or at least only half-truthfully—to the constituents on whom their livelihoods depend.

But a couple of things are new and different in this picture—radically so. The first is that for today's anxious, image-driven pol, there is no end to the subterfuge and hocus-pocus, no resting place, no designated, reachable destination, as there was for your basic impostor of yore. Nor is there some single new, assumed identity (for example, heavily bankrolled investor from the East, virtuous female of marriageable age, godly itinerant pastor) to perfect for the purpose of reaching a single desired destination, like becoming rich, marrying well, or finding a sinecure.

Protecting one's secrets, if one had in fact been lying about such personal history, would admittedly be nerve-wracking. Modern-day practitioners of this old-fashioned form of scam, like the congressman with an invented military record or the surgeon sawing away without benefit of medical school education—or Janet Cooke, who invented an awesome résumé along with her infamous fictional news story for the *Washington Post*—may be supposed to have had their what-if-I'm-found-out jitters along the way.

But this kind of classic imposture, in my view, would be nowhere near as nerve-wracking as the more frequent current kind: darting ceaselessly from identity to identity, political hairdo to political hairdo, reinvention to reinvention, as so many of today's public figures feel they must, in a frenzied effort to keep the insatiable Blob-god happy. What this effort requires of them they dutifully seek to find out from the consultants, poll takers, and others thought to have special, priestly powers of divining the Blob's mysterious will.

Compliant public figures are never 100 percent sure what they are supposed to be, only that it is some unambiguously praiseworthy approximation of a human being that is pretty different from the one they really are in their own well-intended but messy natures.

The contemporary Washington public figure tends increasingly to forget who his alternative self is and who he is. The new, improved self starts to take over the actual one; to speak for it in stultifying, proclamatory prose on occasions that used to be personal and for kidding around; to behave in informal relationships and gatherings as if it were on camera in an open hearing; and to convert what would once have been relaxed, unguarded moments into stiflingly rectitudinous proceedings.

There's not a one of us who has lived for a long stretch of time in the capital, I believe, who has not experienced that awful moment of realization that a friend or acquaintance with some public responsibility is losing the gift of normal discourse. He will have begun to address us over a casual drink or at the supermarket as if he were orating at the United Nations. One of the most frequently uttered prescriptions one hears for a politically prosperous life in Washington is, "I never say anything I wouldn't want to see in the papers tomorrow morning." Think of it: self-installed monitors continually at work in the brain. What a way to live!

We journalists, of course, bear much of the responsibility for this phenomenon. Modern technology makes us an ever-present, all-seeing eye on public life. There is not a precinct beyond instant camera range anymore or the text of a craven statement, flipping away from a previously sworn-to flop, that we can't access on our laptops or Palm Pilots as soon as it is uttered. Once the flip-flopping politician was safe from our depredations while gassing off out in Podunk. Now there is no place to hide.

Just as important, the rules of journalistic engagement have changed. Much that we once considered off-limits because it was private, unofficial, or irrelevant is now routinely reported. Winston Churchill, at his 1943 Casablanca conference with FDR, ran into the traveling press corps one morning, clad only in his red dressing gown and black slippers. When photographers raised their cameras, he cried, "You can't do this to me!" They didn't.

Some two decades after that, the same principle still was in force in Washington. I remember sitting in the Senate Press Gallery with a bunch of colleagues from big newspapers in the mid–1960s and observing the raving drunk Senate floor manager of the bill under consideration having to be helped out of the chamber by another senator and an aide. He wasn't exactly carried, but he sure as hell wasn't walking either. Each of the two helpers had an arm under one of his arms, raising his feet a couple of inches off the floor and whisking him up the aisle and through the exit. None of us wrote about it except indirectly, with coy hints like "high-spirited."

What we consider private, unofficial, and irrelevant has clearly changed. The drunken-senator episode would be fully covered in the media today, as I think it should be. But Churchill's undignified, bathrobe photo would be there too, blown up on the front pages of the tabs, zoomed in on for television, everywhere. We say we judge material by the standard of whether it is relevant to the conduct of public business by the figure in question. And we do. But somehow, under this standard, we are always able to fit some juicy item into our papers or onto our screens.

The point is that public personages in Washington—a category that has come to include more and more people in and out of government who have acquired modest celebrity—now understand that there is practically nothing so intimate, unofficial, or even trivial in their daily lives that it may not turn up, to their mortification, in the news. Add this emerging worry about round-the-clock surveillance to (1) the basic, built-in, traditional anxieties of competitive Washington life and (2) the new compulsion to strike poses and take positions that satisfy the nonnegotiable demands of an all-powerful but hopelessly mercurial public opinion god, and you get the dimension of the problem.

People in Washington react in a few classic ways to the challenge all this presents. They may defy the challenge, they may try to play it out with two separate personalities (one for show and one for real), or they may surrender to it unconditionally and permit themselves to be transformed into something else. Each of these general approaches to the contradictory demands of Washington life existed long before those demands became as acute and frightening for people as they are now. Each represents a timeworn response to pressures to go along with political phony-baloney people neither believe in nor especially like but that in some irreducible amount is deemed necessary for their own or their organization's survival.

The defiers are rare and admirable people who, most of the time and where it counts, just say no. These folks are the class of Washington. I don't mean the lone wolves or the people who strike holier-than-thou poses. I mean the civil servants and legislators and administration appointees who manage to be effective at what they do for a living in Washington while retaining the natural identity they brought to town.

They may turn up at any point on the left-to-right political spectrum. I don't say they are perfect or that the true identity they brought to town is in every case appetizing. Nor are they virginal strangers to politics. They are, after all, political people. I say simply that they are people of unusual temperament and decency who know where the lines have to be drawn and who have remained unassuming and untempted by the eternally beckoning trapdoors of political life.

The late liberal Democratic senator Philip Hart of Michigan, undeservedly obscure these days, would be a model. He was a smart, dogged, honorable fighter for his side in the heyday of innovative Democratic legislation, a man of minimal vanity who got vast amounts accomplished (for which others have routinely taken credit ever since). Hart was who he said he was, almost always. More recently, I would put a senator like Republican Nancy Landon Kassebaum of Kansas in that category. She is a straightforward woman of catholic interests, humor, and no pretension. Senator John McCain has similar qualities.

The Senate is far from the single place where people like this may be found. There are and have been plenty of remarkable, often unsung others in political/governmental Washington. But the intensified pressures of public life probably mean there will be proportionally fewer with the passage of time.

Here is my test for identifying such people: Take some shameless, demagogic political speech you have heard, and see if you can imagine a particular public figure giving it. You will be surprised how many of those you really admire could plausibly deliver the awful thing (and afterward explain why they had to do it and how it will really help the right cause in the end because it will enable them to be more effective in other fights).

The kind of people I am talking about should not be confused with what Washington calls "mavericks." "Maverick," like "whiz kid," is one of those terms meant here as part compliment, part put-down. It is more often something people are called or call themselves than something anyone really is. As a put-down it is a word an irritated leader will use to disparage a legislator, agency head, or cabinet head who has just refused to go along with his policy: "Well, you know Margaret. She's always been something of a maverick." Margaret's action is thereby reduced from one of principle to one of idiosyncrasy. The policy is fine, the leader is saying, but Margaret is a nut.

When used as a compliment, the term refers to those who habitually think for themselves. Usually mavericks seem impossible to predict, except to say that they cannot be taken for granted as safe votes for their party or as silent observers when someone is doing something they really dislike. The late Oregon senator Wayne Morse—Republican, then Democrat and, as Democrat, early absolute nemesis of Lyndon Johnson on Vietnam—was the nearest thing to a pure, lifelong maverick in my time.

But there aren't that many real ones. Often the term "maverick" is applied to people who defy their party on a single hobbyhorse issue, while going along with tomfoolery on almost everything else. For some it is just another impersonation, one of many Washington affectations of cranky, down-home candor by people who are really something else. "I'm just an ole cracker-barrel country judge," their manner says, or maybe a "plainspoken cowboy" from the West, "and I just tell the truth as I see it. Cain't help it, I s'pose." We always have a supply of these. Odds are that like Tennessee senator Estes Kefauver in his coonskin cap, they have a degree from Yale Law School.

These impersonators belong to a different species and a far larger one: Washington people who try to handle the pressures of the place by constantly slipping in and out of dual selves. The public, blah-blah-blah-I'm-glad-you-asked-that-question person lives in the same skin with the other one, who acknowledges in a hundred different ways to a multiplicity of large and small Washington audiences every day what a crock he knows the blah-blah-blah to be.

I am not talking about a handful of unusually jaded pols here. Far from it. This kind of two-track existence has been a hallmark of Washington life as long as I can remember. It is actually celebrated in some of our most famous tribal rituals, such as the annual Gridiron Club dinner in March. At this white-tie event, about six hundred people, including the president, vice president, cabinet members, chairman of the joint chiefs, a couple of Supreme Court justices, the congressional leadership, and hundreds more from government, business, the military, and the press watch some of their leaders and representatives deliver speeches or participate in skits that mildly incinerate what they have been doing and saying all year for the public record.

The feeling of inside-the-Beltway solidarity this betrays is bolstered by the idea (naturally, not very successfully enforced) that the mammoth gathering is "off the record." The proceedings, which can sometimes be hilarious, are meant, in other words, as a fun secret to be shared and kept by the throng present who truly understand the two-track life because, in truth, we all live it. The very term "off the record," when you think about it (along with "off the record's" kin, such as "background," "deep background," and "not for attribution"), is evidence of an institutionalized way of life in which we have one gear for speaking what we think and another for speaking what we *really* think. The most frequently used phrase with which sentences begin in political/governmental Washington is probably: "Don't quote me on this, but . . . "

Many people outside Washington are repelled by the custom. Within the place, however, it has become so automatic and effortless that it can even be managed by fall-down drunks. When I first came to Washington, I was astounded when a TV correspondent friend told me that legislators came to the press gallery for scheduled broadcast interviews who were absolutely slobbery incoherent with booze.

But, he said, the problem didn't alarm him as much as it had the first time. Again and again, he had seen these fellows jerk into simulated sobriety when the little red on-the-air light flashed, vent the well-articulated gravities they wished to share with the American people, and then, when the light went out again, sink back into slurred nonsense and stagger out the gallery doors.

I should not have been so surprised. The two-track conversation is as close as the capital comes to having its own language. In time and with daily immersion, as with any language, you become adept in its subtleties. In most of the rooms where Washington people spend their working and relaxing time, its rules are understood. From time to time there will be an uprising. A newspaper or other media organization will declare that it will no longer take off-the-record or unattributable comments. But in time it relents because it decides it cannot function competitively while using only the disingenuous boilerplate dished up by official spokespeople.

Likewise, anti-Washington administrations that come to town determined to keep their distance from the compromised capital types who talk and live this way almost immediately backtrack. They increasingly yearn to tell the journalist who is covering them or the congressman who controls their spending what they really intend but feel they cannot quite yet own up to publicly. Before they know it, they are up to their eyes in the twofold way of doing business.

When there is a flap over one of these private Washington exchanges, it generally concerns charges that one side or the other broke the rules. Secretary of State Dean Rusk, holding his regular Friday evening drinks-and-background seance with a group of reporters, once famously got sore at a Vietnam question put to him by ABC's John Scali and snapped, "Whose side are you on?" When this exchange got out, there was a lot of talk about how Rusk was losing it. There was also much talk about whether the circuitous way the remark got into print was a journalistic breach of contract (it was published by someone not present who got an account of the episode secondhand—and thus was not bound by the rules).

But there was not much talk at all about the propriety of having the twenty or so of us chosen ones sitting together in a State Department reception room with the secretary every Friday evening, sipping scotch and being told things we agreed not to disclose that he had said. The practice was simply embedded by then.

When David Stockman, as Reagan's budget director in 1981, got into trouble for telling the writer William Greider at great length how thoroughly he disagreed with much of his president's program and how little he respected it (Greider wrote of this for the *Atlantic*), there was a firestorm. Many Washington people were less concerned with Stockman's apparent treachery and/or stupidity than whether the rules governing secret discourse had been broken. Maybe Stockman hadn't thought his outpouring was going to be published, the worry went. If so, an understanding had been violated. Again, it wasn't thought strange that such a not-for-publication conversation, taped over many months' time, should have been going on in the first place.

The practice has been so thoroughly internalized throughout Washington that it even has its insider parodists, people who like to highlight the gulf between public and private pronouncements for their own and others' entertainment. By the time he was Senate minority leader, the encrusted old Illinois Republican Everett Dirksen had become master of this. He took some things seriously. But he also loved to deliver send-ups of the tiresome oratory for which he and his colleagues in Congress were known. Periodically he would give a Senate floor speech nominating the marigold for national flower. These were near-perfect, line-by-line satires of the dreary rhetoric that had just been heard in the Senate chamber and would resume as soon as he finished.

I once sat in Dirksen's office getting his unvarnished, disgusted reaction to Republican senator Barry Goldwater's opposition to the Civil Rights Act of 1964. Dirksen had cooperated with the Democrats on the landmark bill and regarded its enactment in some part as his own personal achievement, not to mention a ticket to hosannas from history.

As the 1964 Republican convention approached, Goldwater, the certain nominee, was taking an ever harder anti-civil-rights line. The furious Dirksen denounced Goldwater to me. The interview was interrupted when his assistant, Glee Gomien, came in and announced that a Girl Scout troop from Urbana, Illinois, had arrived.

Dirksen kept fulminating about Goldwater as we headed toward the big double doors that led from his office. When they were opened and the little girls in their green uniforms appeared, a whole new self dropped over him. Glower gone, Dirksen adopted the quasi-silly look he favored for such occasions and the famously syrupy public voice, so unlike the one in which he had been speaking only moments before: "Welcome, my pretties! What lovely little ladies you are!" Naturally this made them giggle, as intended. Even then, I remember thinking that I had caught a rare snapshot of the Washington political molt as it happened.

Michael Kinsley once pointed out that in most of the notorious Washington public "gaffe" incidents of recent years, the gaffe itself was merely the expression of forbidden truths—for instance, that we can never have 100 percent full employment or that people on Social Security are going to have to take some punishment.

In such flaps the perpetrator is called upon to abase himself and make amends. The fiction is reasserted as reality (we *can* have 100 percent full employment). People in Washington are then free to resume speaking the truth to each other in private and throw pandering nonsense at everyone else in public. Life goes on.

But this is getting a little chancier every day. The old cozy, closed relationships are under strain and under attack. A huge press corps that cannot be counted on to honor all those obsolescent customs; a public, like the press corps, that has become more suspicious in the wake of so many scandals and revelations; an embittered political environment in which neither side can be trusted to pull its punches on certain subjects as both once did; a fed-up electorate that likes nothing better than to punish the hypocrisies of a governing elite it regards as spoiled and corrupt—all this has made it ever more dangerous for the Washington mover and shaker, no matter how adept, to speak copious blarney in public and hard-edged truth in private.

It would be nice if this caused those people to start speaking more truth in public. But I fear the tendency has been the opposite: Now they speak less truth in private because they are less confident of their interlocutors. More and more now you are seeing people in the public arena in Washington surrendering to the pressure and more or less moving into the phony images that they once were able to don and doff, Dirksen-like, at will.

Here the true Washington transformation—the public figures' eventual acquiescence in what they see as the imposed necessity of being someone else—takes hold. And it is from this unfortunate process that so much misery unfolds, both for the way public business gets conducted in the capital and, not incidentally, for the poor public people involved.

For what people find out in time is that the false self they are inhabiting isn't much of a friend after all. Nor is it any great shakes as a refuge or consolation. They begin to live lives of pantomime, in which gesture is all. They spend more and more time attending social functions with "friends" they don't much like, smiling when they want to frown or yell or tell someone off.

But life inside the image doesn't leave all that much time for real pals, in any event, because the image requires continuous care, feeding, and, above all, protection. That is the worst of it. Merely contemplate having to pretend twenty-four hours a day that you are a single-minded, perfectly comported, morally unimpeachable, endlessly motivated toiler for the public good. It's like never being able to get undressed. People who take this course will become increasingly lifeless.

And although they may believe they are acting to protect themselves, they are not. For it soon will have become the phony "self" that urgently needs the protecting—first as a means of staying in office or in favor with public opinion and shortly thereafter so as not to be found out as a fraud, as a figure far different from the paragon one has been pretending to be. Each new imposture, each new deception along the way has carried with it a new burden to be seen ever after as living up to it, however nonsensical or implausible the claim might be.

Finally all else will be made to yield to the urgency of preserving the false picture. The family and personal life that were once a haven for the beleaguered public figure have been shoved onstage too, and turned into something different. In truth, those who fall into the image-as-reality trap develop a kind of deadening Midas touch. It turns everything not to gold but to the equally lifeless cardboard of public presentation.

The spouse, the kids, religious belief and practice, and the lifestyle—right down to the allegedly favored recipes and spectator sports—get dolled up, revised, cheapened. They reappear in newly idealized and totally unrecognizable public form. We in journalism, I fear, go along with the gag. We used to call our rare dips into these people's domestic lives "color," meaning the odd item about workshop-type hobbies and tastes in breakfast food. Such touches were meant to make an article more readable and its subject more humanly understandable but were usually stilted caricatures, no truer than the rest of the person's public presentation. And this is still the case, even though we are writing less apologetically now about the so-called private side of public persons.

I say "so-called" because it is so often hoked-up private life and, as such, no more convincing than the professional self-presentation it is meant to complement. We don't really, deep down believe them, of course, but we nonetheless hold them to the standards they have so recklessly adopted for themselves. It is our schtick. We are, as a profession, ever less willing to let them get away with doing one thing and saying another—at least in our presence. We have become much more skittish about letting them function in the old, cozy, two-track way.

Thus our reporting on them appears to assume that, contrary to all human history, these people in public life can actually be expected to function as the bloodless, thoroughly consistent incarnations of political ideas and principles they profess to be. Then, when they fail, we let them have it. But until that moment of exposure when they are caught out, we behave as if we really thought that through their waking days and dreaming nights they could be first, last, and only, let us say, practicing neoconservatives or Christian populists or moderate liberals or pro-choice activists or some two-word tag like that—full-time, human captions.

The growing tendency of people in public life to take refuge in such pretense is what has gotten so many of them into big trouble. Real life won't be thwarted forever. So they become, in different degrees, sneaky indulgers of lusts, ambitions, and tastes they have renounced before the world. They take backstage actions they are not proud of to make the tableau on stage come out looking right.

It is by now a commonplace that practically all scandal these days, of which there is such a plenitude, is cover-up—less about what someone did in the first place than about the frantic, insane steps he took to preserve Mr. Image. But once things have taken a bad turn, there is nothing in the tinselly value system he has made his own that can save him. The bolstering vanities and affectations collapse, the hard-bought and much-treasured perks of power are taken away. Most important, the phony friends and supposed allies and fickle worshipers are out the door. The hapless, once-proud public figure, stripped of his false covering and of any residual dignity as well, stands before us, naked and discarded.

This humiliating moment often evokes a cry of pain from the real person. But one of the monstrous ironies of the situation is that the rest of us in Washington, still mercifully unhusked and wrapped in our own images and conceits, are unable or unwilling to recognize it as true pain. Our Washington receptors can only discern more sham, more posturing, more artful dodging, because we are still living happily in the pretend world and find it hard even to imagine the other life anymore, let alone to credit it when it appears.

I thought I saw something like this the morning of Nixon's resignation from the presidency in August 1974, when the disgraced leader delivered that long, rambling meditation on his mother and father and what they had dreamt for him. I speak as one who will likely be the last unreconstructed Nixon critic on earth. But to me it seemed most natural that at a moment of such unendurable shame, one's thoughts would go back to one's parents, to one's anxieties about how they would view the spectacle, to indirect pleas for their forbearance and love. Anyway, that's how I reacted as I listened on my car radio.

But I live in the other Washington. So I was only mildly surprised, on getting to the office, to find that no one else I knew was willing to entertain the thought or even quite grasped what I was getting at. Live by the image, die by the image. They saw Nixon's speech merely as evidence of further faking: "Did you hear that performance? Would you believe he's still trying that stuff? Yecch!"

I thought this reaction said something not about Nixon, but about us.

CHAPTER FOUR

A Night at the Opera

*T*HE GREAT CHANGE IN Washington began in the late 1960s. It had started with the defeat of the southern coalition in Congress on the Civil Rights Bill of 1964. People were startled to find that they could violate old cultural and political rules and the world wouldn't end.

With rising protest against the war in Vietnam, the same thing was happening around the country. From Congress to the cities and universities, diverse forms of dissent, from personal gesture to political demonstration, were being accommodated and accorded a measure of grudging acceptance—in time, even respect. Increasingly the breakers of the rules were to find that they had sympathizers in high places, in unexpected institutions and segments of the population.

"Thinking the unthinkable" was what defense analysts used to call the process of doping out the grisly details of nuclear war. Now the phrase took on a different meaning. Unthinkable thoughts were gaining currency. Unthinkable actions were becoming daily events. But they had nothing to do with war games. They were thoughts and actions that challenged the legitimacy of an establishment that had been bopping along with hardly a peep of interference since World War II.

Of course there had been bitter political disagreements in the capital—for instance, over McCarthyism and Korea. But what was happening now was a direct assault on the most time-honored ways of doing things in Washington. The sacred protocols of the ruling hierarchs were being openly challenged. All the you-can't-say-that things were being said.

It is hard now to remember the tentative, anxious quality with which the first expressions of dissent were made. And it is even harder to remember how readily scandalized we were. It is like the early Beatles, who by modern standards were well barbered and behaved but who were seen at the time as more likely from hell than Liverpool. It is embarrassing to recall how the 1963 March on Washington, a model of middle-class, middle-aged decorum, prompted many members of Congress to leave town in fright.

The same was true of the early questioning of both the Vietnam War and the first perplexing events that grew into Watergate. The skepticism expressed about those responsible, which struck people as so audacious at the time, looks awfully mild in retrospect. You would find most of the initial grumbling about the war almost courtly. The dissent that was enough to get Undersecretary of State George Ball charged with the unspeakable crime of "breaking ranks" was on the whole so supportive and understanding of official policy that no one would pay a whit of attention to it today.

Remember that it was still considered downright insurrectionary for a congressional committee chairman publicly to take on a president in matters of foreign policy or for a committee member to take on a chairman. And who would have supposed that the inhabitants of the august White House, consumed as they claimed they were with the incalculable gravities of superpower affairs, could be running a bunch of squalid little criminals committing squalid crimes. Opposition existed, but it knew its limits and its place. So, pretty much, did the rest of the country.

In the beginning, when some critics failed to honor this imperative, their sanity and patriotism were questioned. For a time after the congressional directorate's stranglehold on Washington's daily business was broken, the controlling mystique of the federal establishment remained. It was the shattering of this mystique that marked the arrival of a new age. It was like the end of the Wizard of Oz. A lot of snapping Totos kept tugging at the curtain. When they pulled

it down, they found behind it this infinitely fallible little fellow looking chagrined.

The mystique had decreed that the people in charge in Washington knew best. They could make things happen if they wanted to.
Almost all of them were acting in good faith. And they were entitled to both privacy and discretion to do what they judged necessary
for the nation's well-being.

Practically no one believes this anymore. Moreover, practically no
one admits to ever having believed it—which is a bald-faced lie for
hundreds or thousands of people in Washington. So I'll confess: I
believed it. My approach to the public people I covered was that they
were basically honest, competent, and usually effective.

It sounds so fatuous now I almost hate to say it, but I thought
most of the people I encountered were entitled to be respected for
what they were doing—and that we should allow them such tax-
payer-provided comforts of life as might help them do their jobs
without distraction. We did not wonder, as I find myself doing these
days, whether a single word government people told us was true or
whether they knew anything at all about what they were holding
forth on so self-confidently. We didn't wonder whether their stuffy
self-presentation might be a cover for thievery or some raunchy private lifestyle.

When the mystique crashed, it took with it everyone, not just a
guilty few or a handful of displaced southern oligarchs. We in Washington and most Americans changed our conception of both the
competence and the character, as a class, of the people who were
running the show.

One reason the mystique had existed was the history of the world
after World War II. Thanks to our leaders in Washington, the
thinking went, we had conquered the Great Depression, won the
war, resisted the Soviets. Then, with John Kennedy's failure to retake
Cuba at the Bay of Pigs, the surely-they-know-what-they're-doing

assumption took its first major hit. Other hits followed in Vietnam. So did urban riots, antiwar demonstrations, and assassination, bringing a widespread sense of frustration. The cranky old southern gents, the gracefully aging if too cocky Yale boys at the CIA, the Depression-seasoned Democratic pols seemed clueless.

I remember how this feeling stirred in me on the drizzly Saturday afternoon following President Kennedy's death. We White House reporters were invited to walk with White House staff through the East Room past the president's flag-draped coffin, guarded by four inhumanly still military guards. At word of JFK's murder the day before, most of us had torn off to deal with the emergency for our publications, without time for reflection. I had passed that next twenty-four hours in a frenzy of revising copy, trying to keep my New York office up-to-date by often-jammed long-distance lines, prodding sources deep in their own befuddlement and grief.

As I passed by, only inches from the closed coffin, I was seized by a vivid mental image of the jesting, press-conference Kennedy. I thought, "He can't be in there. It's a dream." I was overcome by a strange feeling of pathos. Here were these gorgeous trappings of office: Do we know how to do pageantry, or what? And yet all this was useless to prevent the murder of a president. It only accentuated the poignancy of his death, the vulnerability of the whole marble show of power to a bullet through soft tissue. Every detail of the surroundings said: "Look! We are mighty!" But everything else cried out: "We are forever unprotectable and exposed."

The mystique was also victim of the onslaught of deflating disclosures about the players themselves. The whole post-Kennedy era might be seen as a movie shown in continuous loop called *Honey, We Shrunk the Political Leadership*, a saga of wrongheadedness, cowardice under pressure, mendacity, and mindless improvisation put forward under the guise of carefully thought-out policy.

The chasm between the public majesty of the leader and the old coot's tawdry reality has been memorialized through the ages. It was part of Homer's insight that when the Olympian gods were not causing epochal storms, catastrophes, and last-minute rescues, they were bickering among themselves in a hopelessly petty way. Thanks to memoirs and historical documents, we know lots about the jealousies, physical infirmities, and homely habits of practically everyone who had a commanding role in history, from Adolf Hitler's strange addiction to June Allyson movies to T. S. Eliot's bowel troubles.

What is different about our time is that most of the protective veils have been ripped off while the performers are still on stage. None of their predilections and afflictions is deemed too demeaning or irrelevant to be unmasked—just when they were hoping to inspire a little awe or terror. The historian Gordon Wood writes of how the real American Revolution, which made the fought-out, political revolution inevitable, was the gradual transformation of the people's image of themselves in contrast to their presumed "betters." The concepts of fealty, subservience, and fixed place evaporated in colonial America, shattering the relationships of indentured servant to master, commoner to noble, noble to king.

Something similar has happened in our attitude toward political authority. We have figuratively stormed the palace. We are going through the closets and medicine chests with great guffaws. The nondeferential among us include not just a roughneck press but also a public that begrudges its leaders the perks of state, that is willing to accord them less power and privacy and honor. Even members of governments themselves join in this cutting down to size. They reveal in their press backgrounders while in office (and their hastily published memoirs once they are out) the most degrading and embarrassing behavior they have seen in their colleagues.

How and why did it come to this? Given the decline of political, civil, religious, and traditional family authority, would our leaders have lost their perceived entitlement to deference without any help from us? Or were we responsible for tearing them down? What I witnessed—and took part in—was circular and self-reinforcing. A press, newly brash in its pursuit of governmental quarry, would hang out evidence of official misfeasance, kinky high living, or stupidity. The reaction of the unmasked would be humanly familiar: cover-up, blaming subordinates, further misfeasance, multiple lies. These too would then inevitably be unmasked.

Some innocent politicians were victimized. Some guilty ones got away, even turned the assault to advantage. But all were under a new kind of surveillance. They were required to prove their probity over and over again in an age when it was no longer presumed. In 1973 Nixon's FBI director, L. Patrick Gray, was asked at a congressional hearing into the Watergate affair why he had not challenged an improper request from the Nixon White House. He replied that in dealing with the White House he had still been operating on a "presumption of regularity."

I think that phrase speaks volumes about our politics today. What has disappeared from our public relationships is the presumption that the people we are dealing with are on the up-and-up. It has been a long time since we actually even thought of right conduct as being "regular" and dubbed misconduct "irregular," as in the by now wholly quaint, "Say, might there have been some irregularities here?"

People bemoan the low regard in which Washington and government are now held by so many Americans. Democrats blame establishment-bashing Republicans. Republicans blame spendthrift, libertine Democrats. Officials of both parties blame the press. All of them are right. People seem to spend half their time lamenting the startling absence of confidence in any kind of authority. They spend the other half venting exactly the same kind of animosity and suspicion they find so destructive when expressed by others.

Some part of the original impulse in fact seems healthy to me. We, especially some of us in the journalism business, were much too gullible and complaisant in the old days. Just as a matter of republican principle, the hushed, reverential behavior (Quiet! Policy is being made here!) had gotten out of hand. It encouraged public servants to believe that they could get away with anything—and they did.

Since the 1960s, we have endured a series of jolts. Before the following things became known, I would have sworn to you that they were impossible: that a vice president (Spiro Agnew) would collect envelopes containing cash pay-offs in his office; that a White House (Nixon's) would authorize a break-in to a foe's psychiatrist's office; that an FBI director—even the weird and vindictive J. Edgar Hoover—would harass Martin Luther King by causing strange missives proposing suicide to be sent to him; that a president (Kennedy) would share a girlfriend with a Mafia murderer whom his administration had retained to kill Fidel Castro; that another president (Nixon again) would encourage aides to break into the apartment of a criminal suspect (George Wallace's accused gunman Arthur Bremer) to strew opposition literature around in order to tar the other party; that the number-three guy in the Justice Department (Clinton's friend Webb Hubbell) would do time for stealing from partners and clients; that a chairman of the House Ways and Means Committee (Dan Rostenkowski) would go to federal prison for fraud. These are just a few highlights of the Niagara that helped to erode our inhibitions about pursuing such stories.

Even if people around the country were embarrassed by officials they may have supported, they did not experience the additional chagrin so many of us in my business felt at having been snookered. We were entitled to feel that our affectation of tough-guy, cynical journalists had been rendered ridiculous. We, after all, were the ones who had been disseminating the accepted version of reality now being shattered like plate glass.

Remember that in the early days of Watergate, the big hitters on the national staff at the *Washington Post* were among the most disdainful about the bloodhoundlike pursuit of the story by those two young fellows on the Metro staff, Bob Woodward and Carl Bernstein. Like innumerable others savvy in Washington and its ways, they believed the hypothesis of active White House involvement in the scandal was preposterous.

By now we have become wary and self-protective. We no longer assume anything, especially ethical behavior. We entertain the plausibility of endless bizarre rumors that we once would have dismissed. We feel the nagging need to check out almost anything short of a tip that a public figure has been sexually molested by space aliens.

Thus what began as a challenge to received wisdom and heavy-handed authority ended up by the 1990s as the kind of political and cultural nihilism you see in the Left and Right today. With the loss of their mystique, Washington political figures have a much harder time getting anything done.

Nevertheless, to these reduced and often reviled figures clings the popular illusion of power—the notion that much of the world is run by some secretive, small group in the U.S. capital. This notion found its classic form in the romantic depiction of JFK's Executive Committee—"Ex Comm"—during the Cuban missile crisis of 1962. Ex Comm was the small group of top Kennedy advisers who from hour to hour decided what to do about the sudden presence of Soviet missiles in Cuba. Ever since, it has been the mind's-eye model of power in Washington for many in the press and others around the country.

Even though we in Washington especially should know better, we are still tempted to make all high-tension governmental drama conform to that scenario. "Lights burning late at the State Department" has long been one of our pet journalistic clichés because of the idea it rests on—the tense meeting of an anxious, grim, omnipotent few in a hidden room somewhere, making life-or-death decisions. The

Awesome Burden (which I have always imagined looking like a huge, gravel-filled waterbed) hangs menacingly overhead. For us in Washington, this is still our preferred picture of our government at work under stress.

Any crisis setting including all the people who by rank are entitled to be there is practically never the one where the actual decisions get made. Ex Comm excluded perhaps more than half of such people. But even so, the toughest decisions were made someplace else in a kind of Ex Comm of Ex Comm that included, say, the president, his brother Robert, Secretary of Defense Robert McNamara, and national security adviser McGeorge Bundy.

I began learning this truth as long ago as my first paid job, in 1956, working at the Adlai Stevenson for President headquarters in New York City. I observed what a physicist might call the law of the infinitely receding back room. This holds that as decisions are secretly made in a small room someplace, there will be ever more pressure from people desperate to gain admittance. When, because of such pressure, the size of the meeting has been expanded, the original little group will recede to a further back room for its quiet, secret meetings, while continuing the larger one for show. But word of the new back room will get out. (There will always be one person too vain not to let it be known that he is part of the innermost group.) Then the process will be repeated and repeated.

These days the handful of people responsible for any decision in Washington tend to keep trying to remove themselves to ever more inaccessible rooms. And although the undertaking of so much important governmental activity in private hideaways feeds the image of absolute power being wielded by some tiny, unaccountable elite, the reality may more nearly be the opposite.

This is because what starts out furtive can so readily become— precisely because of the furtiveness—feeble, misguided, frenetic, and entrapped. For in receding to privacy, public people can cut themselves off from specialists who might help them avoid monumental mistakes. Yet they are irresistibly drawn to the private huddle.

An inveterate private-huddler in the national security apparatus of several administrations once told me that part of the reason for the attraction is that after you have been inside the innermost club, speaking to others in the language of highly classified information, you can't help becoming scornful of those not in the know. Since the outsiders inhabit an ignorant, lesser universe, they can't possibly be helpful. From the moment that thought takes hold, it is only a matter of time before someone is on a plane taking a cake to the Ayatollah Khomeini.

Another impetus is that we increasingly attempt to bathe in sunshine practically everything people in Washington do. Greater visibility has prompted—predictably—ever more determined efforts to hide, just as the proven ability of journalists, scholars, and congressional investigators to compel the disclosure of notes has resulted in less and less being written down.

Various postscandal reforms required open meetings and publication of once confidential proceedings. But tradition has changed to much greater effect than all the statutory requirements put together. The press has reconsidered its once extensive restraints on what should be covered and reported. More consequential has been that participants in what were once considered privileged deliberations are now sometimes the first to go public with government secrets, to boast, expose, assail, and self-justify.

Nowadays this is often hailed as evidence that these government bandits decided to heed their consciences and tell the truth—even when what is offered is so often a patently self-interested, cooked version of what went on. They may do so out of pique, to show off, to ingratiate themselves with a reporter, or to inform the public of some covered-up stupidity. Or they may do it—and until fairly recently this alternative would have been unimaginable—out of desire to sell a book while the colleagues it is about are still in office.

The new Washington dynamic is "If you're going to get out your version of what happened at that meeting, I sure as hell am going to get out mine." For a public official, every day it is more of a crapshoot as to which confidence will and which won't hold. The media, not unreasonably, note that since these high officers of government publish commercially salable revelations the second they get out of office, they could not have been keeping them secret out of any worthy motive. Thus we have become even less receptive to the government's contemporaneous assertion of the need for secrecy in much of what it does.

Even in our more trusting days, we had at least a healthy skepticism about the pulling down of the shades by government document classifiers. I was once informed by a press officer of the Arms Control and Disarmament Agency that he could not let me have a list of the agency's advisory commission members on grounds of "executive privilege." I reminded him that the list appeared in the back of the agency's public annual report. (He relented.) The classified material we have acquired at the *Washington Post* has included clippings of newspaper stories stamped "secret."

Those in government making decisions have come to feel positively hounded, frantic, unfairly denied the most elementary privacy and freedom of action. They fear that having to conduct so much business in the open effectively renders them almost powerless. The problem is that the loss of freedom and of the ability to manage events is even greater once they have gone furtive. For they will at once have sharply reduced the already limited options available to them and raised the cost of being exposed.

Rather like the politician entrapped in his own false image as Mr. Perfect, so too these fellows need to do ever more to protect the clandestine activity, whatever it is. There is a difference between this secret conduct and what used to occur on Capitol Hill and in the executive branch. It is the difference between meeting in acknowledged executive session and hiding out and pretending you didn't meet at all. In the sunshine era, we do not expect so many closed-door meetings to take place.

Government people have gone from being unashamedly secret about some of their deliberations to being secretly secret, thereby adding a whole new layer of duplicity to their lives, creating an aura of illegitimacy about their acts. They tend to recreate themselves as double-dealers and fugitives who are not so much invoking a grant of privacy for their meetings as acting on the sly. For as we know, some of them don't just meet in secret to hash out a choice. Often they will try to keep a policy choice they have made—surely the public's business—as secret as the method by which they made it.

Lyndon Johnson's decision to go underground with his actual early planning for the Vietnam War was a classic, tragic example of the perils of trying to conduct supremely important public business on the sly. LBJ in 1965 and 1966 was just beginning to see Great Society programs, of which he was so proud, put into place, needing vast public funds and public support to get them going. Unable to face up to the impossibility of meeting the costs of both those programs and a war without a drastic increase in revenues, he tried to fake it, hoping that the war could be wound up fast. This brought the whistle-blowers out of the agencies, turned the press terminally disrespectful, and finally closed down his freedom, his choices, and his power. He had destroyed his freedom of action by trying to save it.

In later years various governments and public officials have tried to keep secret everything from Nixon's bombing of Cambodia to the financing of the Nicaraguan contras by Reagan officials to the voting of government pay raises. When Bill Clinton retained his much distrusted ex-consultant Dick Morris after his 1994 congressional defeat, he tried to hide from the White House staff that almost hourly working relationship, secretly whisking Morris in and out of the building and addressing him on the telephone as "Charlie."

For government leaders, this kind of thing is demeaning. And it is yet another way in which Washington figures' power has declined. By their refusal to own up to what they are doing, they convey the idea that there is something wrong with it. By claiming to be not of government at all, but rather critics of it like their constituents, they manage to validate the charges against government.

With their power diluted by the dispersion of authority throughout the bureaucracy, the development of "attitude" among civil servants, and the diffusion of power in Congress, Washington figures might be forgiven for feeling like what Nixon called "pitiful, helpless giants." No longer can they make a binding deal with a couple of titans on the Hill. They must deal there with new and continuously reconfigured coalitions, issue by issue. Combined with the mounting aggressiveness of the press, increased freelancing by colleagues and confidants, and their own heightened furtiveness, apologetics, and sham, they were right to feel crimped.

The myth of swaggeringly wielded great power in Washington has died hard. But read the books, memoirs, diaries, confessions, and (in the worst cases) court testimony and hearing transcripts of recent decades. What you will often see is a gulf between the picture of surefooted authority piped out to the public and the frightened, hapless scrambling that actually took place.

It is easy to be impressed that we may be talking about people who have access to nuclear war codes, who by uttering a sentence or two can cause thousands to lose their jobs. But none of this got them around the bases and back to homeplate in Vietnam. It didn't help them kick out Castro or punish OPEC or get the hostages out of Iran until Khomeini was good and ready or prevent the slaughter of the marines stationed by Reagan in Beirut or the bloodbaths of the 1990s in the Balkans.

On the contrary, their actual position of power may impede their flexibility. Like late medieval knights encumbered with heavy armor that limits their capacity for maneuver—including that to get up off their metal encased bottoms after a tumble—modern-day leaders are often pinned down by the trappings of office.

Exhibit A: the Nixon White House tapes. Publication of the first White House–edited version in the spring of 1974 was a landmark event in Washington. Lines of would-be readers, stretching for blocks, formed early at the Government Printing Office. Political-enclave Washington seemed to fall silent for days. People pored over the volumes, stopping only to call one another and trade revelations: "Have you got to April 13 yet? . . . Wait till you read April 22—you won't believe it!"

No matter where the increasingly agitated Watergate conspirators turn, they cannot take steps that even ordinary citizens might. The tapes are a saga of political impotence. The men recurrently worry to no avail. Can they communicate with this one? How can they contrive to do something without seeming to be doing it? That these men had to resort to a disreputable, black-bag operation conducted by delusional mercenaries shows how little absolute power they had to work their will, not how much.

My favorite moment is when the president and his top aides are trying to figure out how, without seeming interested, they can learn what Henry Peterson, a career prosecutor in the Justice Department, plans to do about Watergate. "We need to have someone talk to Henry Peterson, who can say to Henry, 'What does this mean in criminal justice? What kind of a case could be made on this? What kind of sentences would evolve out of that?'" says John Dean.

But who and how? They cook up the idea that H. R. Haldeman will call Peterson and pretend to have "a brother-in-law in school" or "a friend" who needs "a wild scenario" because, as Haldeman inventively suggests, "My friend is writing a play, and he wants to see how . . ." His words are cut off there, as these supposedly all but omnipotent men discard yet another transparent plan for finding out what is going on in the Justice Department, of which they are, in theory, in charge.

Even when you understand that the participants are scared, rightly mistrustful of one another, and trying to cover up crimes, you can't help but be struck by the scarcity of means available to them to achieve even the most measly of their purposes. This was just as in the Iran-contra scandal, when agents of President Reagan flapped around Europe and the Middle East trying to get information from scuzzy con men.

Another example was when President Carter's chief of staff Hamilton Jordan was sent to Europe to try to win the freedom of American hostages in Iran. He could not be sure of the legitimacy, or even the true identity, of the bizarre characters he was secretly dealing with. He even traveled in disguise—a small token of the circumscription of freedom that government prominence may bring. Jordan tells in his memoirs of meeting the CIA makeup artist in the White House barber shop after hours. Just like in the movies, the nameless man said out of the darkness, "Mr. Jordan?" At the end of the session, the man murmured, "I am leaving now. Count to sixty before you go out."

Since the early 1970s, "backstage" in high-level Washington has often become synonymous with "backstage" in *A Night at the Opera*—swinging ropes, collapsing sets, klutzy stagehands, affrighted sopranos crashing into each other behind the velvet drop curtain under the mischievous guidance of the Marx Brothers. I'm not saying that all government is managed by a dingbat squad. I'm saying that much in Washington that the public imagines to be muscle is really flab. The decision of so many lawmakers and appointees to get out of politics and out of town is in part a result of this new reality.

Another sign is the cavalcade of peculiar military celebrations of recent years. From Gerald Ford's exultation at the bloody military recapture of the U.S. merchant ship *Mayaguez* in 1975 to the Clinton hurrahs over the retrieval of downed air force captain Scott O'-Grady in Bosnia, these events, exalted as American victories, were actually cases of successful evacuation, repatriation, recapture, escape, or release. They were certainly to be welcomed, but they weren't exactly V-E Day.

Why do some Americans cling to the notion of the all-powerful Washington figure? It is useful to the wannabes and groupies who are thrilled by the idea of a thriving center of such people. They want to have dinner there and get their picture taken doing so. That same motivation underlies all those sycophantic, irremediably ignorant "hundred most powerful" pieces about Washington movers and shakers. People here know what bull it is. Nonetheless they buy the magazines the minute they hit the newsstands, in hopes of finding themselves on the list and, more important, their enemies off it.

The illusion is also useful to other Americans who are looking for something to hate, a ruthless oppressor to jump-start their politics and rationalize their defeats. Being a victim has become the rage during the past few decades. And one kind of victim is the powerless pawn of the mighty—the villainous Washington, tone-deaf siphon of taxes and enforcer of irrational decrees. This Washington must seem to be populated by superpowerful enforcers of its will. Dread of just such a capital, with its despised bureaucrats, elitists, and lifetime politicians, was what Newt Gingrich used to win the 1994 congressional elections.

Presumption of a diabolical ruling apparatus, controlling the levers of power, offers an explanation for the world's woes and, by implication, a relatively easy way to cure those woes: Throw the rascals out. The corollary to this conviction is that the entrenched order cannot be defeated because it is so strong. For many of those who believe this, the worth of their cause is, oddly, premised on the certainty of their losing and recertified each time they do.

If they succeed, they will feel not so much vindicated as bereaved. The oppressors won't be in charge anymore to provide a handy explanation for everything that has gone wrong in the society. Darth Vader is of no conceivable use to a crusader once he is dead or defeated—or even worse, as in the movie, maundering on to Luke about how he made a terrible mistake in joining up with the evil empire in the first place.

The Republicans' self-avowed revolution, begun in November 1994, went through this progression with the predictability of a cuckoo clock. First there was jubilation and promises of a quick, dramatic reversal of the loathsome trends generated by the gang they had ousted. This was followed by the crash of disappointment on learning that it didn't work that way. Then came the inevitable fracturing of the movement into those who wished to take a slower, more politically conventional route versus those disgusted by these accommodationists, vowing to rescue the revolution. The latter were luckier because they had an instant, new corrupt oppressor to blame.

None of this surprised me. I had been part of liberal and other insurgencies while young. After the first glow of victory, it had always seemed to come out the same way. As a reformer living in Greenwich Village in the 1950s, I was part of a movement made up mostly of people much like me. We were trying to topple the Democratic Tammany Hall machine and its head man, Carmine de Sapio. You couldn't have asked for a more suitable oppressor. But as I look back on him, de Sapio wasn't nearly as ruthless or commanding a figure as we thought. His take-no-prisoners predecessors found him far too accommodating to us, a kind of doomed, third-generation wimp.

But for campaign after campaign, we canvassed and poll-watched and protested and organized, tromping up and down the five flights of brownstone stairs in the unbearable New York City August heat. We recorded names, kept tabs on our voters, and rushed them to the September primary, challenging endless voting "irregularities," all with the self-certain fervor of the just. Then this weird, disconcerting thing happened: We won!

As it turned out, life was not transformed. But the even bigger shock was not being insurgents anymore. Now we had to trade moral self-certainty and freedom from responsibility for the gruesome daily headache of governing, the deals and the second-bests required to get anything to happen. Soon our elected leaders were being blamed for the absence of miracles. They were denounced as power junkies and sellouts for doing the most basic things that were part of incumbency. Once in our clubhouse, when the elderly gentleman reformer Herbert Lehman, former governor of New York, sought to speak, a bunch of my clubmates angrily chanted, "Bossism! Bossism! Bossism!" and kept the poor man silent.

This sort of thing drove me and other onetime red-hots away from that movement. Still, back in those "Madly for Adlai" Stevenson days, I took pride in our defeats, which I saw as proof that the world was just not good enough for my political kind. I knew I was leaving this behind when some of my buddies begged for Stevenson to run in 1960—even after JFK had been nominated—and pathetically manned card tables in the Village to hand out literature.

It was plain to me that the principal objection of my die-hard Stevenson friends was that Kennedy meant to win and might even do it. In our funny little world, this was subliminally thought to be disreputable and untrustworthy. I see that now as a kind of mild personal political disorder. When I hear people today attributing despotic power to the largely insecure, scrambling, diminished figures in Washington, I know that there's some of that still going around.

The myth of august Washington power is sustained by folks who consistently confuse clout with something else: status, rank, proximity to the boss, celebrity, access to certain keys, codes, clearances, meetings, internal paperwork that not everybody has. But these are merely the Tinkertoys of power.

Outsiders may be forgiven for being confused about the difference since so many insiders are confused themselves. They assume strutting rights by virtue of being able to accomplish tiny feats of exclusion, one-upmanship, and rudeness without generating a peep of protest. They can, say, keep grand hostesses waiting for hours to serve dinner until all the rest of the distinguished guests get drunk or cranky. They assume that lateness for a business or social engagement by anything less than seventy-five minutes requires no acknowledgment, let alone an apology.

This swaggering can happen anywhere in Washington, but it is most common among newly installed White House aides. Bureaucrats, journalists, and social figures who feel they need to make a first useful connection with a new White House flatter these people to death and put up with any amount of their imperious guff. So their heads begins to turn—big-time. Such people don't realize how cynically they are being used, generally by old hands who fully expect them in time to crash into irrelevance or disgrace and will enjoy the spectacle when it happens.

In the name of "the White House," they can order up all sorts of instant amenities and can, within limits, also see to it that those who have displeased are dropped from the invitation list, denied the special transport, left to make do with the second- or third- or fourth-best everything from parking spaces to briefers to seats. Others abuse their jobs, as in Watergate, Iran-contra, and some of the Clinton scandals. This is not power but petty crime. It is no more a sign of genuine influence over events than the little vengeances and self-inflations of the baby pashas.

I can't think of a White House in which such confusion of power with lesser capacities to make things happen didn't occur. Under Kennedy there were the famous arrogant kids. My friend Ward Just and I once even did a two-piece package on them. His was called "All the Bright Young Men." Mine was "Why Are You Calling Me, Son?" My title was taken from the witheringly dismissive question put by a big-deal senator to one of the stupid White House minions "threatening" him with not painting a post office in the senator's state if the senator did not buckle on some vote.

I also recall the young woman who over dinner with some of us one night boasted how she had "punished" a Pennsylvania Republican congressman. In the name of the White House, she had seen to it that this marine veteran, who had no family in Washington, had his tickets revoked to the Friday night marine drill, which was his single off-hours diversion.

Although not much older or more Washington-schooled at that moment than the people doing these things, I knew they were over-reaching. Having seen it with every new government that comes to town, I have become almost maternal about it, in a resigned, head-shaking, vaguely disgusted way.

I saw less of it in the Johnson administration, probably because it was full of Washington habitués—and because everyone who worked for him was so scared of Lyndon Johnson. I can imagine what LBJ might have done to, say, some of the more callow whippersnappers of the early Carter years; or to Bush's* chief of staff John Sununu, defiantly ordering up White House cars and planes to take him to ski slopes, dental appointments, and postage stamp sales, even after his custom had been revealed; or to the kid in the Clinton administration who told reporters that it didn't matter what the Democratic chairman of the crucial Senate Finance Committee, Pat Moynihan, thought on the eve of the health care debate because

*The forty-first president.—Ed.

they were going to work around him and whip his butt. Johnson would have dismembered the aide on the spot, and in the presence of plenty of witnesses on whom no part of the message would have been lost.

Wherever people in Washington mistake for actual power mere sycophancy and a newfound authority to press a few restricted buttons, you have entered the culture of people who are content to be seen as powerful and don't know that that is not the same thing as acquiring and using power.

The emblem of this is the power picture. What are these blank-faced official photos, autographed in the most noncommittally possible "friendly" way and hanging on the office or living-room wall for all to see? I used to have them up all over my study at home. One day I became embarrassed about them and stuffed them into a closet. Maybe my heirs can get $1.75 apiece for them if they find them in the mess: "To Meg Greenfield, with best wishes from President Whatshisname," the one everyone thought was a particular turkey.

This kind of thing betrays weakness, not strength—utter dependence on the regard of others. You exist only in relation to their perception of you. I dwell on this because it brings us to the real demarcation between the tiny number of those who seek, get, and use power in Washington and practically everybody else. The dilettantes and dabblers and self-deluders I have been talking about are hoarders of pennies, interested only in building a conspicuous "power" bank account into which they never dip. Their opposites are the riskers of big bucks. The first try to maintain their reputations; the second try to make things happen.

Those long-gone geezers of the once mighty southern coalition succeeded in imposing their will for so long, even in their shrinking numbers, because they knew what they wanted and they knew how to organize power. Their daily turnings on and off of everyone else's most important faucets bore no resemblance to the isolated punishments that newly installed White House aides liked to brag about. Theirs were not random or capricious little demonstrations. On the contrary, they were all part of a deliberate program to accomplish an unswerving end. And they didn't care what it cost. We could also be talking about saints here, not departed, reactionary senators, or hugely outnumbered but eventually triumphant freedom fighters who bring down imposing fortresses with little more than the sheer force of their commitment.

Among Washington figures I think of people who had little in common regarding style, purpose, personality, or ideology but had this quality of commitment: Hubert Humphrey, Philip Hart, Lyndon Johnson, Ronald Reagan, Richard Russell, Federal Reserve Chairmen Alan Greenspan and Paul Volcker, Oliver North of the Reagan NSC, Bobby Kennedy, and William Casey, director of Reagan's CIA. I think of others who were not associated with anyone or any collection of big things but who were willing to use power for causes they considered important, like Senators Nancy Kassebaum and William Cohen.

I think also of more workaday power users who knew how and wanted to get things done: Bush* budget director Richard Darman, Carter's secretary of health, education, and welfare Joseph Califano, Clinton's health and human services secretary Donna Shalala, Secretaries of State James Baker and Henry Kissinger, Nixon's defense secretary Melvin Laird. These were cabinet officers who ate everyone else's lunch and, though they wickedly enjoyed the hell out of doing it, were actually more interested in the substantive end they were pursuing. And that was why they prevailed.

*The forty-first president.—Ed.

CHAPTER FIVE

Women and Children

A LONG TIME AGO IN Seattle, when I had just turned twenty, my estranged maternal grandparents arrived separately from out of town for the wedding of my brother, Jimmy. Since their divorce many years before, the antagonism of these two had not lessened but actually grown worse.

There was no discourse between them, no gesture or facial expression even acknowledging the other's presence, and no eye contact at all, although my grandfather would sneak the occasional, furtive glance when my grandmother was looking the other way. Heavy stuff, and as you would suppose, it didn't do a whole lot for the festivities. But even so, something did happen between them that was so startling to me, and so emotionally revealing, that its memory has lasted long after their discomfiture was demoted to bittersweet family joke.

That week, at a small gathering of visiting relatives, where my late mother was being warmly remembered, my grandfather, always histrionic and self-indulgent, went from a few understandable tears to a full-scale, Metropolitan Opera–style performance—great wails and sobs and lamentations without apparent hope of any end. It just went on and on, and none of us knew what to do. We would murmur something we took to be consoling and he would shriek all the more inconsolably. It was awful.

And then, suddenly, we heard another sound, a wholly unexpected one. It was my grandmother, addressing my grandfather by name for the first time in fifteen years and, for the first time that I could remember, looking him directly in the eye. She did not sound angry or especially concerned about him or moved or forgiving, but strangely sure of her jurisdiction. "Reuben," she said crisply, in a voice that somehow conveyed the intimacy of all their years together and bore the authority that was its consequence, *"Stop it."* He did. Silence.

I sometimes think of that voice and its power when I contemplate how much people of inflated stature in Washington finally remain vulnerable to the gut claims on them of parent, spouse, or kid. You may think of them in the larger-than-life third person they so tirelessly project on the public screen. They may often even have begun to think of themselves that way.

And in furtherance of anything from image to insatiable ambition to what they actually conceive of as the public good, they may have taken to living personal lives of such abnormal absorption in career as to rule out the possibility of practically every grace, courtesy, and consideration for others that people regard as the minimal requirements of family and communal life. But whether it is Nixon's dead mother at once seeming to comfort and reproach him from the grave or the midlevel Pentagon official's very live teenager becoming genuinely distraught about a war that his dad is enthusiastically prosecuting or the fed-up congressional wife of many years who's not going to take it anymore, these are the voices that tend to get through when no others can.

They may be plaints or calls to obedience, tantrums or importunings, reassurances or threats. But whatever their nature, unlike all else, they often have at least a capacity to penetrate the shell, brush aside the image-impostor standing in their way, and reach the real person. This is power, but it is not the kind of power we most often talk about in Washington commentary, the kind provided by some constitutionally authorized check or balance, the ex officio right to sit in on committee proceedings, the much-sought-after appointment at long last to the big-deal commission. It is real power.

It derives, as it did in my grandmother's moment of sudden control over a man for whom she had long had no use and who had long had no use for her, from some powerful old emotional reality that may be only an echo by now but that is still vital and still heeded and cannot be explained in terms of political arrangements. Nor does it have anything to do with the cardboard family served up as a photo-op to the public or with so much of what is cynical blather out of Washington on the subject of family values. And it usually also is un-related to the sidebar trivia we journalists like to produce under the headings of "color" and, alternatively, "human interest."

These involvements and the priorities they create account for much more than is usually apparent or acknowledged in Washing-ton life. It's not just that they often constitute the most important limitations and influences on a public person's conduct in office. It is that, by and large, such relationships, not the surveys of what care-fully chosen demographic groups "out there" think, are the link with reality.

The relationship among them that is easiest to understand and in its way least complex is that of public figures with their parents. It is, of course, the case that many people in politics succumb to the temptation to re-create their parents—not just themselves—as phony images, rendering the poor old progenitors "cute" and engag-ing in endless cutenesses themselves about how the eighty-seven-year-old mum, bless her, really chewed them out for this vote or that on the phone yesterday (ha, ha, ha).

They also slide rather easily into what has by now become a po-litical/parental cliché about how "my mother was a saint and always had faith in me and told me I could be anything I wanted. . . . We had nothing, but we had everything that mattered." Dad often emerges in this retrospective as the guy who hit the kids with a chain from time to time but only for their own good and to teach them the lessons that have made them such wonderful, upstanding citizens today, a guy who really had a heart of gold beneath his gruff exterior,

God-fearing, honest, and, unless a mean drinker or marital escapee, someone who worked to support his family as no man ever had.

This is your basic set piece. The thread of truth running through it is this: There does seem to be a preponderance of distinctively type A, superdetermined parents—mother or father or both—behind the people who achieve prominence in Washington, and fairly frequently a clear-cut weak-parent–strong-parent combination.

Just as our presidents bring to national attention with them an atypical abundance of troublemaking siblings, for example, so they seem also to hark back to an atypical collection of ambitious, strong-willed, and from time to time truly eccentric parents, especially mothers—from the imperial Sara Delano Roosevelt to the unpredictable "Miz Lillian" Carter and to a battalion of others.

Harry Truman wrote his mother ("Dear Mama . . . ") almost every day while he was president. Rebekah Johnson is generally credited with having assiduously propelled her son Lyndon up the ladder to making himself a public somebody. George Bush's* well-born mother was known for a streak of independence in the conventional wisdom of the world she lived in, though his senator father is the one generally credited with imbuing the son with what he saw as the better-off person's duty to participate in public life. There were other driving dads, albeit fewer than driving moms. The hurricane-force determination of John F. Kennedy's father, Joseph P. Kennedy Sr., is notorious.

A high proportion of others besides presidents, in every sector of capital activity, are said similarly to have been launched on their careers in childhood by preternaturally attentive, driving parents, the stage mothers of civic life, who intended that their young should leave their mark. When you take this aspect of their lineage along with the fact that so many prominent Washington figures have re-

*The forty-first president.—Ed.

tained into middle age and beyond the psychic makeup of successful children, it is no wonder that the hearkening to parental voices is so pronounced.

I don't count such responsiveness as something totally exotic or peculiar to Washington. Rather, it strikes me as being more like an exceptionally intense form of a phenomenon we all know. After all, the ability of doddering parents everywhere—across class, culture, and kind—to reduce even their *aged* offspring to a kidlike anxiety about being chided or found out and to enforce an often irrational, senile will on them is universally understood and, to most of us, a matter of rueful amusement.

Of this common variety is that part of Washington officialdom's traffic with its mums and dads that is not either fictional political contrivance or something truly conscience-wracking in relation to the way the offspring are doing their jobs. I remember witnessing one such classic encounter in Washington between Rose Kennedy, then well into her nineties, and her fifty- or sixty-something children Edward Kennedy and Eunice Shriver. It took place during the annual visit she paid them on her way home from Palm Beach to Hyannisport in the spring, which was the occasion every year of frantic housecleaning and filial apprehension as to what denunciation would be leveled at them this time concerning their inadequacy as household managers.

After the dessert at a large, fancy dinner party Senator Kennedy gave for his mother during one of these visits, when Eunice Shriver had already made an affectionate, lighthearted toast, referring to her mother's undiminished ability to terrorize them on such matters, and while her son, the Senate committee chairman, was still on his feet delivering his speech of welcome, Rose Kennedy, apparently provoked beyond endurance by what she considered yet another lapse, interrupted him in midsentence to hiss in reproving tones heard by all, *"Teddy, the coffee should have been served by now."*

I remember too an interview I was conducting one day with the formidable, elder army general Edward Rowny, whom the Pentagon had regularly dispatched to strategic arms talks with the Soviet Union over the years to protect its tough position against both the Soviets and what the Pentagon considered the wobbly unreliability of the State Department and White House. Rowny was being considered for another administration post at the time, and we were discussing the newly rigorous disclosure laws for federal appointees and how people going into such jobs in government were now running into trouble with relatives who didn't like the reach of these new laws into their own financial affairs—spouses, siblings, parents, and children.

To my astonishment, Rowny, then around seventy, told of how his father, still a very active man in Baltimore business and politics, had been making his life a living hell, alternately insulting and stiffing the FBI agents and finance snoops who sought to question him. What I remember best is General Rowny himself—not exactly a kid, after all, or a man you would think of as being readily pushed around—emotionally reduced to dependent boyhood in the mere telling of this story. He would earnestly explain to me: "So I said, 'But, Dad, wait a minute . . . *Please*, Dad, don't say that to them. *Please!*'"

"*Please*, Dad"? General Rowny? The scourge of the disarmers, defender of the deterrent, designated thrower of the throw weight if it ever came to that? It was wonderful. It was also ludicrous, of course, and Rowny, shaking his head in disbelief at his own helplessness in the face of paternal displeasure, knew that too.

Most of us don't have regal parents dropping in for bunk inspection on their way from a winter spent in Palm Beach or jobs that bring the feds in for a second look at daddy's tax returns. But it is a rare adult who has not had the experience of being rendered summarily childlike by the parental imperium, the pick-up-your-room voice in which the elders can flatten "children" not all that many years short of Medicare themselves.

What is distinctive for the Washington public person is not this. It is that the abiding parental claim to be principal guide, authoritative instructor, and moral court of last appeal extends into critical realms of professional life, not just matters of housekeeping or intrafamily dealings—and that it has so much more influence than that of other would-be judges and disciplinarians. My mind harks back to Oklahoma senator David Boren's genuine turmoil over his aged father's unhappiness with his dovish position on the Persian Gulf War. That position he had been able robustly to argue with others. His father's assault on his stand was the only one that seemed truly to trouble him.

The importance of this direct access to the public figures' feelings will become increasingly important as those figures become more important and more able to work their will on others. For when, in success, they begin to grow arrogant or isolated or indifferent to the opinion of most other critics, parental opinion will likely be the one opinion that can rattle them.

Recall the occasion when Republican senator Alan Simpson of Wyoming, coming out of a Reagan White House meeting, made some unusually nasty remarks about his opponents, causing a brief public hoo-ha. It ended when Simpson backed off and more or less apologized—as a consequence, he was to concede, of hearing from his ninety-something mother in Wyoming. Yes, she had called him, Simpson said, adding, "Order has been restored."

When things get really ugly, well beyond incidents like this, when public people are in big trouble for doing manifestly squalid things, you often get a sense that in some part of them, they fear above all else (as Nixon did) the parental reprimand, including that of parents long gone. To some extent, their entire careers will have been a fulfillment of their parents' expectations. These figures desperately crave parental approval in a way and for reasons that finally mean even more to them than all that highly prized and neurotically chased-after "rating" stuff—the Blob stuff—that the surveys and straw votes and focus groups and direct-mail initiatives yield.

In offhand remarks they have dropped over the years, I have heard many seemingly hardened, self-certain pols betray this unexpected vulnerability. And the spectral or actual presence of parents in their lives has one additional humbling effect on those whose egos are beginning to get out of hand. Of such a public person it may be noted that his parents above all others knew him "when"—knew him as a bawling, helpless, inarticulate, tiny thing.

Unlike everyone else he will know, including others from his pre-big-shot days, parents alone are *guaranteed* never to think of him as, say, "the senator" or "the White House correspondent" or whatever the grand title may be. When even he, in the gathering derangement that marks his ascent to public notice, has come to think of himself as synonymous with the title and the image, they will not.

They may boast to all their friends about his achievement and insist that others in their presence refer to him by his imposing title, but that won't alter their root understanding of his identity. Their moral influence, which is in so many cases huge, rests in large part on this unique perception of who he was and, never mind the bells and whistles, still is. Not even the public person's own offspring, whose approval is often of equal urgency to him, have this access to his conscience. Neither, as a rule, does his wife.

The Washington I came to in 1961 was known as "a man's town," and that's exactly what it was. Now, a generation later, thanks to epochal political and social upheavals, I believe it could be called a recovering man's town, but still a man's town.

The reason I have often used the male third-person pronoun in commenting on the habits of Washington public figures is that in the overwhelming majority of cases—way up in the 90-plus percent range in most categories—it *is* a he, not a she, one is talking about. And although I have made mention of the Washington "spouse" from time to time, I am going to drop the pretense of gender-blind generality now.

When we talk about the spouses of those who make the policy and the headlines and the trouble in Washington, we are still as a rule talking about wives. Yes, there is a growing collection of official husbands these days, men married to women who hold big-time jobs in government and around it. But their number is still inconsequential, far from constituting even a tiny statistical blip, and their folkways as a group, if they exist at all, are only beginning to be ready for the attentions of cultural anthropology.

The wives, in contrast, or, more inclusively, the women in the lives of Washington's dominant men, have been ready for such attentions since long before Margaret Mead ever set foot on Samoa. Too bad, I sometimes think, Margaret Mead didn't stop here first.

The marital and sexual mores of this Washington have been changing under pressure. What has changed most is the way the men who run the place are expected and/or commanded by protocol to relate to their female partners, as well as to the women at the outskirts of their lives. It has changed because the women's conception of themselves has changed. So the impact of all these relationships on the way the men do their actual jobs has been undergoing change too, as has the fundamental character of the claims made on their conscience, time, and professional behavior by the women with whom they are most intimately involved.

At one level the wives who are helping to compel the change may sometimes be seen as merely participating in a larger, familywide effort to bring back down to earth the one among them who is getting awfully self-important—exercising the invaluable "Oh, come off it" prerogative of close kin everywhere. This is not new or a product of the 1970s-and-after women's movement. It is as old as my time here.

"We are teaching Daddy how to dial his own telephone calls again and even drive his own car!" the wife of a former Johnson administration housing official once replied, in a murderously sarcastic Tinkerbell voice, when her husband was asked at a party, with a little too much awe for her taste, how his first days of retirement from the crushing burdens of office were going. You had a feeling that she had taken out just one load of sodden garbage too many on a chilly night, while the overburdened one was off participating in a symposium on Section Eight housing policy at a tropical resort somewhere.

VIPs' parents and children have always engaged in this worthy—I would even say nationally useful—deflation work too, and something like it no doubt occurs in other professions and parts of the country when a family member's head is turned. But there is a sense in which the Washington wife's claims on (and often against) the public life of her husband are very different from those of his parents and his kids and different from those of her counterparts elsewhere as well. Not always but very often they have to do with guilt and shaming and are shaped by the ever-dwindling but still considerable peculiarities of man's-town Washington, the only context in which the woman's changing role can be understood.

Washington in the Kennedy era, when I first saw it, was still home to a kind of demeaning, grown-up little-girl culture. Coming to it, as I did, from an independent, somewhat raunchy postcollege life in the Village in New York, this culture stunned and amused me, struck me, in fact, as encompassing everything I had left my conventional life at home to escape.

In my youthful self-assurance, I was right about the culture but dead wrong in supposing, as I did, that it took a committed nonconformer to its rules such as myself to see what was ridiculous about it. Only slowly and as a result of acquaintanceship with some of the women involved, did I come to realize the different truth. It was that the premises on which the wife culture was based were already being quietly, often sardonically questioned by many women who felt politically compelled to go along with it publicly, and that it had begun to be rejected outright by a handful of audacious others.

The world itself was one of flossy, party-favor luncheons (a lobbyist's gift of French perfume or pretty scarves or costume jewelry at every place setting), where pointless gab was expected. The occasional, quick stop-by of the hostess's public-personage husband would produce the requisite waves of appreciative tittering when he said something like: "Well, it looks to me like you ladies are really having a good time. I sure wish I could stay here with you instead of going back to the office. But then all your husbands would get jealous!"

The underlying premise was pretty clear. It was that these were mindless dollies with nothing much to occupy their afternoons except airhead chatter and tiny, glutinous mounds of chicken à la king, whereas their menfolk—the daddies—were *busy* and had *important* things to do at the office.

In this unperceptive reading of them, the only serious contributions such women could make to their husbands' professional lives were as hostesses (often laboring unthanked at full-time, semiofficial duties that went with the husband's post) or as attractive but prim adornment-adjuncts to their husbands' careers. They served as stage props, meant to be seen and not heard at certain office and social functions and to grace the platform at the departmental swearing-in or the late-night campaign rally.

The reward for their uncomplaining attendance at untold numbers of these events, forever beaming and wordless, would be an acknowledgment from the podium by their husbands, with the traditional chuckle about how they had married "above" themselves. "My wife is too good for me," these guys used to love to say, tribute to the durable, Washington set-piece notion of the wife as better-born guardian of the family's table manners and enforcer of its occasional, recalcitrant forays into culture.

The single transcendentally important thing to be said about all these stilted tableaux is that they were based on false assumptions about the women involved and the lives they really led—even then, back before Gloria and Betty and Simone and Germaine had been heard from. Of course, there were always some who seemed to enjoy the baby-doll aura and were happy to busy themselves with what were essentially time-killer activities. And it is true that thirty years ago far fewer of these women were working at paying jobs outside the home than now.

But the number of real enthusiasts for the patronizing conception of themselves embodied in that grown-up little-girl social life was always pretty small, in my observation. And the affront to the rest had nothing to do with the irrelevancy of whether they worked at paying jobs or not. The affront was to the dignity, seriousness, and value of what they *were* doing as intelligent women, wise wives, conscientious parents, and very often tireless contributors to the well-being of the communities they lived in.

The prevailing contempt for them was summed up in the much-repeated bon mot of the Washington wit Alice Roosevelt Longworth that Washington was "a town of successful men and the women they married before they were successful." (Paradoxically, the same contempt for women who were fulfilling a conventional role in the family and the community was also strongly implied in the rhetoric of some who regarded themselves as true feminists, especially in the early days of the contemporary women's movement.) On the whole, Washington's wives put up with the put-down, but they neither deserved it nor especially relished the social and ceremonial obligations it imposed on them.

"Put up with" is the key phrase. On my fitful excursions as a reporter into the prevailing wife culture of those years—once for a fairly good stretch of time while I was doing a long magazine piece about the offstage political role of Lady Bird Johnson, and sometimes while covering campaigns on the road—I was repeatedly struck by how many of these women were actually working around or against that culture, which sought to segregate and trivialize them as a species. I will get around in a moment to the circumscribed, rule-ridden world of the exceptions—those women who successfully functioned politically and professionally in the capital under the prevailing inhibitions, doing what was still tacitly assumed by practically all to be "men's work."

What numerous of those wives were doing was far tougher, in my view, than what the rare professional woman had to bring off. I think of certain cabinet wives, congressional wives, wives of men who worked on the White House staff who over the years dutifully went along with the party-favor-lunch thing as bored good sports yet managed to keep their sanity and self-respect and to live lives of independence and influence.

Lady Bird Johnson would be a good example; it was what I found so interesting about her. So would Lindy Boggs, the savvy wife of Representative Hale Boggs of Louisiana (and mother of ABC and NPR correspondent Cokie Roberts), who before her husband's death and her own election to his seat was a model congressional missus who doubled as one of the smartest women in town.

Another was Barbara Laird, the late first wife of Melvin Laird of Wisconsin, who was a Republican congressman and Nixon defense secretary. Although Laird's protracted career as a Washington big hitter may have made his wife the champ participant in these command-performance events, she always exuded a seriousness, wisdom, and sly wit (including about some of the policies he was promoting) that made it plain that Barbara Laird was miscast as a mainstay of the ladies-luncheon circuit.

The same was self-evidently true of Pauline Gore, wife of a senator and mother of a vice-president, whose family I knew when we both lived in Washington's Fairfax Hotel. Gore, a lawyer by training at a time when female lawyers were rare, and a truly bright woman who had an enormous impact on the careers of both her husband and her son, was also a faithful, publicly uncomplaining attendee at the time-devouring, mind-numbing social ceremonies of wifedom.

Such women were just a few of the many who, though they might quietly confide their own impatience with these ceremonies, were at pains to give no offense and commit no heresy—starting with the major heresy of not turning up—that would call unfavorable attention to themselves and by extension do some damage to their husbands' standing in the political/governmental community.

The conventions were the conventions, and they were controlling. If you think this sort of thing went out with the bundling board and the bed warmer and Ye Olde Antique Shoppe, you need to know that in the mid-1960s, after Robert Kennedy had been elected senator from New York, it was considered a very big deal in circles where the protocol lingered whether Ethel Kennedy would participate in the weekly sessions, mandated by ladies-auxiliary-type custom, wherein the Senate wives got together and rolled bandages for the Red Cross in the old-fashioned, World War II way.

This they were doing years after modern medical science and industry had rendered their handiwork obsolete, so the more or less compulsory bandage-rolling bees were ridiculous, and the answer was that at first she didn't turn up. But in time, under pressure she did—even Ethel Kennedy, touch-football and practical-joke-playing, famously modernist, I'll-do-it-my-way Ethel Kennedy. That was the force of the prevailing myth. Women were always having to recertify that they were who the long outgrown culture said they were, even when they knew it was not true and when they were living lives that daily refuted it.

The same held true until fairly recently for professional women in Washington; whether wives or not, they made comparable concessions to the unwritten rules. There had always been a few women in the picture, of course, who were simply too big or smart or willful or well connected or unflagging in what they did to be ignored, let alone put in their place, wherever that was. I'm thinking of women as unalike in most other respects as publishing powers Agnes Meyer and Cissy Patterson; cabinet officials Frances Perkins, and Oveta Culp Hobby; Maine senator Margaret Chase Smith; and a handful of others.

Each of these was much too much of an independent power to be called a "token." They weren't chosen by anyone to "represent" women. All became, in different ways, forces to be reckoned with in the capital's affairs. Not quite in their class, yet still a kind of outsized exception to the rule in her time was the durable, dogged journalist May Craig, correspondent for a number of papers in Maine and one of the relatively few women in journalism, in my early days in Washington, who were not writing for what were then known as either the "women's" or "society" pages. Her split-screen public persona nearly perfectly illustrates the ambivalence people still had well into the 1960s and 1970s about women's working in traditionally male jobs, as well as the concessions such women reflexively made and the snickering they routinely accepted as part of the deal.

On one half of the screen was the May Craig who was famous for her tea-party-style hats, who seemed not to mind being habitually made fun of and treated as a harmless crank whenever she got journalistically as tough as the guys did. She was a woman who appeared easily to countenance being regarded as a somewhat comic, freaky phenomenon precisely because she was (by then) an elder female in what was thought of as a wisecracking, middle-aged guy's job.

On the other half of the screen, this woman, who went along with the dotty-old-lady gag and sometimes seemed even to play to it, was a hard-driving reporter who frequently turned up on the TV interview shows of the day and was known for her obduracy in asking hard questions. (She used to pull her chair up until she was right under the nose of Everett Dirksen at his crowded, nontelevised weekly Q-and-A sessions in the Senate Press Gallery, and she would never release him from her fixed, accusing stare, except when she took notes. "Does that answer your question, May dear?" Dirksen invariably asked, with mock solicitude, at the end of his remarks, to which, with a disgusted shake of her hat, she would just as invariably reply, "No.")

Craig is actually credited by many with getting language into the 1964 Civil Rights Act that extends its coverage in certain key areas to women. Her campaign to enlarge that law's scope was much guffawed about at the time, as Craig made a sort of holy mission of it at press conferences and elsewhere. The relevant proviso was (and still is) sometimes referred to as the "May Craig Amendment." Some believe it was adopted only with the help of anti-civil-rights legislators who thought it so preposterous that it would help them kill the whole bill.

But if that's true, the joke's on them. The point is that May Craig embodied the yes and no of women's role as professionals in Washington at that time. Like so many others—wives at home as well as women with daily jobs—she worked with, through, and around the reigning beliefs about the limited capacities and the proper pastimes of women and seemed sometimes to defy them, sometimes craftily to exploit them for her journalistic purposes, and sometimes even to believe them herself.

This was more or less what all of us did. Although I might have fancied myself some kind of daring rebel, it is clear to me, surveying those times from the vantage point of the 1990s, that I still knew my place and that I abided by most of the rules. These rules were about much more than what was suitable and perhaps even required for the wives of important officials to do in their spare time. They also covered mixed social events I would attend, when all the women were dispatched as a group from the dinner table after dessert and sent to powder their noses and wait while the gents stayed on in the dining room to engage in the only good political conversation likely to go on that evening—exchanges it was presumably felt the women would not have much interest in and would divert or otherwise wreck by their presence anyway.

When the now fairly famous uprising against this custom finally came in the 1970s, I was expected to be among the women who declined to evacuate to the parlor so the fellows could chat. I played my expected part but was always kind of uncomfortable about it. This was not because of any grief I might be causing the men on whose sanctuary I was encroaching but because so long as most of the other, nonprofessional women did go off and gather, I thought it looked as if I thought I was too good to be with them. An overly tortured consideration, maybe, but it did bother me.

More important, the man/woman rules also covered—and inhibited in different ways—our actual ability to do our jobs. Clubs routinely excluded females, for example, and not just social, old-geezer clubs either, but clubs that were nearer to being professional associations from which exclusion could carry a price for a woman in that line of work.

I had such an experience as a brand-new Washington correspondent for the *Reporter* in 1961. I was taken upstairs from the offices of the magazine's bureau in the National Press Building to the top-floor National Press Club, there to be shown where the wire-service ticker was. I would need to consult it to keep abreast of late-breaking news as our publication neared its closing deadline every two weeks. This was a normal, safety-net practice followed by our bureau and dozens of others and was one of the principal services the ticker was there to provide.

I was taken there by Douglass Cater, the man I had been sent to town to replace while he took a brief leave from his job as the magazine's Washington editor. But the club official on duty, seeing me there in the hallway with Doug, looked shocked and at once informed him that I could not set foot in the place for any purpose that did not come under the strict rules that provided for "ladies' presence" at certain social events—and then only in certain prescribed areas of the club. Women were not permitted to be members (they are now), and, contrary to Doug's expectation, a woman subbing for a bureau chief would not be allowed to walk the ten or so feet of sacred club ground from the door to the ticker to check the late news for five minutes on her magazine's closing day. Period. Doug, incensed, argued, but to no avail.

I do not regard this episode as one of the great human rights violations of our time, nor myself as some pitiable victim. Nor, when I reconsider it, do I even try to figure out how on earth such silly rules could still have been in force in our trade at that late date. They simply reflected the regressive professional and social ambience of the city as a whole.

What I do find startling all these years later is my own wimpish *"que sera, sera"* reaction at the time. For it was Doug, not I, who did the only complaining either then or later. Sore as I felt to have to accept this exclusion, it did not even cross my mind that I could or should do anything to try to get the rule reversed. I felt only that I needed to make up for it by getting access to another wire in some less handy place, regarding the outcome as just one more unreasonable inconvenience that called for extra effort on my part, not an inequity that I needed to challenge and fix. And so I set about finding out how I could get a last-minute check on the news some other way, not even remembering to feel annoyed about the circumstance for long.

It is plain to me in retrospect that in this and countless other small questions of conduct and privilege, I had become, like most of my female counterparts working in Washington at that time, highly adept at the fine art of mixed maneuvering that I could spot, with some amusement, in the redoubtable, quirky, period-piece May. I may have thought of myself as quite different from her in generation, outlook, and practically everything else. Hey, I was a modern, serious, no-hat reporter, wasn't I?

Yet each of the elements apparent in her approach to her professional circumstances was, in slightly different form, apparent in mine: defiance of the rules of who should be in this particular workplace to begin with, combined with exploitation of the female stereotype for my own purposes and—yes—tacit acceptance of the legitimacy of limitations imposed on the way I, as a young woman, might go about my business. This triple-headed way of operating wasn't something I even thought about much or can remember thinking up at all. It was just something I did.

The defiance had nothing to do with boycotts or bills of particulars or political organization or anything like that. It lay solely in the nature of the work I had chosen to do. That was the defiance. There was at that time a thriving journalistic subculture of females, always described as "women reporters," who were hired to cover, in a gushy way not allowed on page one, what was accounted strictly women's business. They gave much attention to what they called the "doings" of the wifely lunch bunch, of which their own group was a kind of journalistic offshoot.

Some among them were pretty tough and skillful, not to say ruthless, reporters who could wring real political news out of a half dozen indiscreet remarks that might have been dropped along the way by the wife of this big shot or that by the time the chestnut parfait was served; others were an embarrassment to their press cards. But all were essentially ghettoized.

Whether they got nuggets of political news or not and whether they brought a subversive, satiric eye to the proceedings or not, their product appeared amid the recipes and bulletins on fall hemline lengths out of Paris. That was the law. It was seen almost as natural law in the old medieval sense, a way of behaving that had been ordained and instilled in the human breast by divine will. Women reporters wrote women stories about women and household or fashion, the only things women could be counted on really to read about anyway. It was the way life was meant to be. Not to abide by this law was to challenge the God-given order of things.

Though our numbers were not great, there were still quite a few of us out of compliance, as there had been in journalism for years before us. Many had backgrounds that were for one reason or another good training for our anomalous role. I most certainly did. Reflecting on my own elder female relatives, for instance, it occurs to me that it would be misguided to believe that the power-suited young woman with the MBA and the running shoes was in the 1970s and 1980s the pathbreaker for her sex so far as hard work outside of the household was concerned. Women performed plenty of unglamorous, nondomestic labor before that. I think of the aunts on the first-generation side of our family who, along with their brothers, worked long hours at wearing jobs in the family produce store, and my aunt on the other side who was sent on the road as a saleswoman with a line of embroidered hankies when her father lost everything in the Great Depression.

Some of the other elder female relations on both sides had worked in their husbands' businesses or taught school in addition to fulfilling traditional roles as wives and mothers. These were not women who rejected leisure and sought to validate themselves in the workplace; they were women who had to work, and many of them aspired to leisure with their every fiber. I think too of my maternal grandmother, an intellectual and deeply involved volunteer worker in the arts in Chicago, a voice teacher and onetime opera singer (all of which contributed to her stormy breakup with my grandfather).

I had been raised in a family where as much was expected—actually, demanded—intellectually of females as males, educated from ninth grade through college in the kind of all-female private schools that, whatever their shortcomings, are known to impart to their young charges a feeling of I-can-do-anything self-assurance.

Finally, I had been brought along in my first years in journalism in New York by a famously good and even more famously autocratic male editor, Max Ascoli of the *Reporter,* an equal-opportunity oppressor who believed that all of us on the staff—men and women alike—could do anything he suggested, and damned well better.

Ascoli embodied preregulation America. He was an erratic, irrational, brilliant, whimsical, sadistic Italian humanist Jew, who spotted and spoiled me, the youngest and last of the staff writers he brought along. I had gone to see him about my long-term prospects, scared to death after having written a few articles. He was amused and had seen what was coming: "You start now. Monday." What? "How much money do you want?" I said I didn't know. He told me what it would be, less than the salary for any guy: I had "no family to support."

Ascoli said things to everyone for which an employer would fry today. He said that I would be an interesting, perhaps even successful experiment for him. He told me to sit with Maria, calling us the "big bitch" and the "little bitch" in praise of what he took to be our mean and useful skills: "And darling . . ." Darling? Back to court so soon. We just got the "bitch" thing settled. "Darling, I do hope it works and you do well because if you don't, I'm going to have to fire you."

Max threw copy on the floor when he didn't like it. My contribution to his taming was to be the one person who wouldn't pick it up.

But for all of his faults, he had a genius in editing. He put women in jobs as no one else did without self-consciousness or contrived good purpose. He didn't see why he should not. He was totally arbitrary and often outrageous.

I came up with the idea, outline, and research material for a big political-year article but was an utter novice at writing such a thing and had no byline. My male betters among the correspondents told him that I could never do it (and I did have an awfully hard time) and, besides, coming with my unknown name on it, it would have less authority. He just shut them off: "She thought of it. She writes it. If you're so smart, you would have come up with it yourself."

When Ascoli and I had a final blowout in 1968, I went to the *Washington Post*. He tried to make some mischief for me with the deal. We didn't speak or communicate and stayed mad for more than ten years. One day I got a letter from him about some piece in *Newsweek* or the *Post* he admired. It was a pretext for resuming contact. I wrote back right away that I appreciated his note and would like to visit him when I was in New York.

When Max died, I was one of those who went to the funeral, which was not the most well-attended event. He had become a Catholic. None of his Jewish mourners knew when to get up and sit down. He was instinctive, imaginative, impossible, not fair or perfect or modulated, but he had shown me what life was like, how to get along, when to draw the line, the infuriating and endlessly engaging inconsistencies of people. By today's standards, Ascoli was a walking human rights violation. I never wish I'd sued him. I even miss him.

Experiences like this probably helped point me toward where I was inevitably to wind up. And I suspect that something roughly similar was true of many women like me in Washington in that period who had been granted passes to function outside the female compound. Not that we were universally accepted as equals. Even when women got normal, non-women's-page jobs in those days, there were certain areas to which most editors still thought it prudent and hormonally appropriate to assign them.

Welfare and related subjects that had some connection with children seemed natural—not politics or defense policy or agriculture or economics or the police or sports. And where foreign coverage was concerned, though there were some female war correspondents and other exceptions, it was oddly believed that Latin America was especially suited to those few women who perversely insisted on going overseas. I think that was because the whole continent was deemed at once safer and less important—and thus less exacting— than other continents and perhaps also less distant from home and hearth if a guerrilla army or the vapors became a problem. I should add that whatever the thinking had been that created this tradition, an impressive collection of women journalists over the years provided first-class coverage of Latin America and managed repeatedly to get in danger's way. Our *Washington Post* correspondent Joanne Omang earned the professional compliment of having the Argentine secret police burst in to search her place and interrogate and harass her for various impertinences in her reporting while she was on the phone filing yet another offending story with the foreign desk.

For my own part, by the time I had been in Washington a while, my interests had led me to specializing, with the encouragement of my roughneck boss, in defense and nuclear arms policy. There could hardly have been a more flagrant breach of the natural order. I grew accustomed to little jokes about this and to tiresome exclamations about how amazing and wonderful it was, as if I had heroically overcome a congenital disability. A defense official once introduced me at a private gathering this way: "*Look at her.* Would you *believe* she writes on nuclear policy?" We all chuckled—including me, I am sorry to say—at the outlandishness of it.

Years later, when I was made a deputy editor at the *Post*, there was a similar combination of wonderment and smiling, small barbs.

They were accompanied by anxiety that it was going to be mighty awkward at those times when I had to be in charge of a meeting and eight guys would be arrayed around my desk, presumably taking direction.

The most revealing aspect of this anxiety is that I shared it. Powerfully. I even worriedly discussed my potential predicament with a small group of close male and female friends before I got started on the job. What we arrived at, after much mulling, was that I could handle this inversion of normal practice, but only if I were scrupulously careful not to say or do anything that might be perceived as *threatening* to the editorial-page men's—well, you know.

That's how I thought then. Most of us did. It was as condescending to the terrific guys who sat on that editorial board as the general ethos was toward women in Washington, and a measure of how thoroughly self-conscious and unintegrated the workplace was at that time so far as men and women were concerned. We are talking 1971.

I will be frank to say that it also never occurred to me to blow my stack or even take a mild, verbal swipe at the more egregious news sources who patronized or made fun. I sat still when such officials leaned back in their leather chairs and managed to suggest in a dozen different ways that, as a woman, I might be having trouble comprehending the very complicated subject they were expostulating on, but—and this part was always explicit—it sure was a nice surprise to have such a lovely little lady come in for an interview on such a serious subject.

Again, like many of my female counterparts, I suspect, I would just sort of smile and look vague, fuss with my notebook and, as the guy rattled on unimpeded, speculate silently as to what fiendish thing I might do with the string of ignorant and potentially self-immolating quotes he was handing me on a subject he believed he understood and I didn't.

What I am saying is that I and others like me who did the same thing had intuitively adopted a kind of Vietcong mentality: complaisant nods, private thoughts. It edged over from craftiness to duplicity to at least passive exploitation of what we could fairly assume they assumed about us. You didn't pretend to be a "dumb broad." You didn't do your Adelaide impersonation from *Guys and Dolls*. But neither did you go out of your way to disabuse them of the conclusion to which so many had freely leapt on their own the minute you entered the room.

For me, there is one crystal clear recollection of such a moment. It was when I was ushered into the office of Indiana Democratic senator Vance Hartke, a force at the time in the convoluted, secret manipulations within the Finance Committee, which I desperately wished to know more about for the piece I was working on that week. "Sit down, sweetheart," said the senator, whom I had never met before, motioning to a chair by his desk. "I have something in my drawer here for you." Whereupon he drew from a supply in his top left-hand drawer a tiny, plump, heart-shaped vial of perfume with a little purple bow on it.

People of the 1990s to whom I tell this story ask at this point with happy anticipation, "What did you say to him?"—expecting to hear that at the very least I threatened a citizen's arrest. I am obliged to reply that I don't remember but probably it was something along the lines of, "Oh, gosh, no, thank you *so much*, but I really can't take that." And that then I let him "help" me understand, for over an hour's invaluable blab, what was going on in the byzantine crevices of that committee, his words inadvertently filling some important gaps in my knowledge, precisely the part of the story I was looking to complete.

I sat in a lot of rooms in those years quietly getting the good of such misunderstandings and wondering what would happen when they read the piece. I'm not especially proud of it. It's not that I think

I should have raised hell and charged him with some sort of affront to my personal or professional dignity, a reaction that I, for better or for worse, am constitutionally incapable of in any case.

It's that the pose, or at least my acquiescence in the man's pre-conception of me, seems demeaning and, worse, sneaky. But then I wasn't proud of it at the time, either. I thought of it as a borderline vice, a cost of getting my job done, at least not an outright imper-sonation or active lie about who I was and what I was coming to see him for, only a way around the abiding, medium-size problem that confronted me in so many of those rooms.

But there were also rooms I could only deal with by walking out of them, not in protest but in uneasiness about being there at all. That is because in addition to the sly, exploitative aspects of the way I handled working in man's-town Washington, there was finally my ultimate acceptance of the validity of the claim that we didn't quite belong. I think of how I once behaved, for instance, after I had been asked if I wanted to be part of an established, informal interviewing group made up of four male reporters covering the Senate during a prolonged period when this was my beat.

They were guys I had come to pal around with, and I was awfully pleased to have been invited to become a regular in their weekly off-the-record sessions with some knowledgeable, well-placed senators who were willing to talk freely and a lot with them. What I observed when I turned up a few minutes into their session on the appointed first day was that upon my entry into the room, feet came down off the senator's desk, around which they all had been slouching in their chairs. My reporter friends and the host senator himself all sat up and straightened their neckties and—it could not have been clearer—the group as a whole drastically tidied up its language, al-tered its tone, and completely lost its ease and its purpose.

They were very nice, very courtly. The conversation was mildly interesting but pretty stiff. Despite my standing invitation, I never came back. As in the matter of the denied access to the Press Club wire, so, at the other end of the scale, with the matter of the freely proffered favor: I figured I would compensate for the forfeited information some other way.

In some part of me, I obviously accepted the premise that there was a male world that deserved to be respected in Washington, whether or not that might cost me a little something in my work. That it should be free to operate under the rules and in the atmosphere it had established for itself, and that I ought not to intrude or do anything to disrupt it—fit in where I could, yes; but intrude where I couldn't or where, even if I could, my mere presence would make the guys uncomfortable, no. And so I left them to it.

I have gone on at length about all this not because I think the particular impediments or put-downs I experienced strictly on account of being a woman are particularly earthshaking or that they were not offset for me by plenty of professional good fortune and the unexceptionable, collegial treatment I received all along the way from most of the men I worked with and many I covered. Indeed, even to recount the grievances now, which is, after all, to admit remembering them, embarrasses me a little because it sounds so whiny.

The reason I have summarized this history is simply that to me it represents the ethos in which we were all living in the capital then. This can by extension provide an idea of what confronted the average Washington official wife who sought access to the privileged world of man's business. If that world was so inhospitable to those of us who had professional reason to be there, you can only surmise how inhospitable it was to those who did not.

The access these women wished was not as players, for the most part. Judging from the full-fledged complaints I would sometimes hear and the cryptic, resigned gibes that regularly punctuated their conversation, they wanted only access to information, and even then, not much. They wanted some awareness of the interminable dramas that seized their husbands' offices, kept them there at all hours at the expense of so much else, accounted for the summonses away from dinner and the continuously ringing phone, and finally commandeered the men's energies, thoughts, and attention like an occupying army.

As they were sometimes compelled on painful occasions to witness their mates being publicly humiliated for some action, they felt bitter about having been so thoroughly excluded from any understanding of what it was, why it came about, what it meant, even whether it was true or not. They felt even more bitter upon being told, in the worst cases, just to console, divert, or otherwise deal with any alarm on the part of the children and not worry their pretty little heads about how it all had happened or was likely to turn out. Staff would take care of everything, they were assured. Staff would tell them where to sit at the hearing, what not to say if approached by a stray journalist, and so forth.

There *were* marriages in Washington public life in which the wife was, to a far greater extent than most, a clued-in participant in the joys and sorrows and political near-death experiences of her husband's career, in which they actually worked pretty closely together on his job. But so far as I could tell then, except for the very rarest few of these, the basic rules stayed in place: The job and the man himself who became its living embodiment and had hardly any existence at all apart from it took precedence over all else.

I'm not just thinking about staying late at the office or canceling some dinner at the last minute or even not turning up as promised at the kid's softball game. I'm thinking of the fact that after-hours life itself, the companionship of friends and family, the time available for recreation or relaxing with out-of-office others, was also taken over and transmuted into something else by the career imperative. For such so-called private or family life became in fact little more than a Clausewitzian pursuit of career by other means—career around a glittering dinner table, career on the tennis court or the golf links. The couple were expected to go to social gatherings not because they liked the company or because the wife even knew these people, as often she did not, but because it was politically or bureaucratically beneficial; there would be people there who needed to be mixed with—helpful people, indispensable people.

Yes, this happens with "the firm" in many other cities and occupations, but surely only on selected occasions, not in the same day in, day out way it so frequently did in Washington, swallowing up entirely the couple's so-called off-duty life. Worse, the wives of public figures and of other holders of notable jobs often were (and this still happens) rudely shunted aside and neglected at these events once they got there. It was the husband who was the party-giver's prized guest, whereas the wife, who hadn't wanted to come in the first place and did so only because she felt she must, would be conspicuously regarded as a necessary add-on, a cross not just to be borne but, even more troublesome, to be creatively fitted into the seating plan wherever she could do the least conversational harm.

Mean and unwarranted as such assumptions were, the wives who were so treated had to put up with much more than these indignities of forced-march social life. For in that Washington of days gone by, the wife of a public person—and this category always included the wives of people outside government who had big, sensitive, visible jobs in the private sector—was allowed zero independence politically, intellectually, or professionally if what she might do or say could constitute any potential hindrance to her husband's career. It was not just where she went of an evening; it was, perhaps more important, what she was thought free to say when she got there—that is, if the people she was so ingeniously seated near even bothered to include her in the conversation.

I confess I have overstated, overgeneralized, and thus in some respects caricatured the situation. It wasn't, even in the old days, *all* like that, and the impact of exclusion obviously was different for different women—just as prevailing customs were adhered to more strictly or less from family to family. But overall this was how it worked.

For the truth is that political/governmental Washington had and continues to have something of a dog-pack instinct so far as the organization of the den is concerned. Head dog rules; all other dogs spend their days, as dogs will, faithfully, even obsessively trying to please. The man worked in an office, especially in that era, where he was head dog, and this was frequently true even if he wasn't boss of the whole operation but only of some part of it. He was head dog *somewhere.*

And gradually but inexorably, the demands of his office-based head-dogship would be extended into the family and the home, often ruinously. Even so, people largely accepted that this was the way it had to be. For many Washington wives, then, their husbands' careers became not the fulfillment of family ambition or a signpost of success but the enemy.

You used to hear it said that in the marriage of a busy, driven public person in Washington, the mistress who threatened the wife— the *real* "other woman"—was the man's career. This should not be taken to mean that there are not also *other* other women of an unmetaphorical kind. Of these, two utterly different main variants recur. What they have in common is that as "other woman," each is perfectly suited to the world into which the preoccupied man may have all but vanished from his wife and family by then.

That is because the role each plays fits in so well with the concept of the man as paramount leader, ruler over the all-important office (or subdivision or even tiny unit of the office), whose every whim needs to be foreseen and catered to, the better to free him to fulfill his awesome professional mission before which all else must yield.

One of these variants is the devoted, platonic, worshipful, close-in, self-sacrificing, female assistant/alter ego. The other is the bimbo, as the roster of twenty-minute dalliances followed by much more prolonged periods of public hee-hawing and mortification has lengthened.

The assistant/alter-ego women are by far the more important of the two. World War II–era Washington is said to have witnessed a migration to town of single women who never married, stayed on, and became some of the most quietly influential people in the post-war capital. They were secretaries and in time, perhaps, executive assistants or staff aides; but whatever they were titled, many of them were the person to see or at least know the name of if you wanted to do any business with Senator Glotz or Commissioner Plotz. "Call Angie" was the invaluable guidance a person in the know might give a friend. "Call June. Use my name." "Call Roberta; she'll know the answer to that." "Call Lillian. Lillian will handle it."

Not all the Angies and Junes and Robertas and Lillians (whose last names were often unknown to those who had been chatting them up on the phone with a kind of false familiarity for years) had arrived in wartime Washington, of course. And not all of the women who held such jobs ascended to positions of confidante, woman to see, and keeper of the gate. But more than a few did, and many from a later generation are still there.

They knew and know not just more than the wife does about what's going on in the husband's professional life and mind; they know more about those matters than do all the other people who work in the office, people who (not incidentally) tend to curry their favor. Their dedication to the boss is full-time, unconditional, relentless. To the extent that the job and its considerations have supplanted most other elements of the boss's life—and also of theirs—the office becomes in its way a kind of proxy home and its staff a kind of proxy family, and these women become for sure the proxy wives.

I don't suggest there is something sexual going on in these relationships, though in some offices there might be. What there is, indisputably, however, is adoration and total, selfless commitment of a kind that cannot be replicated in any other setting in the boss's life. And there is frequently as well a strong component of intellectual intimacy, borne of wholly shared knowledge, carefully guarded professional secrets, and a big base of joint workaday experience and history that absolutely closes out, just plain ices other people.

The boss has confidence in this woman above all others, entrusts his professional well-being to her judgment and discretion every day—"Lillian will handle it." And the intimacy of all this, while not personal or sexual, may in fact be much more intense and much more a threat to his wife than any foolings around with the memoir-writing bimbo who has newly hired a publicity agent.

The smart assistant knows that she is a natural, potential source of jealousy, by her very existence a kind of rebuke to the wife. The wise and humane ones among them are, in the lingo many would doubtless use themselves, ladies, and as ladies they take care to be thoughtful with the family and never perform a gratuitous muscle flex or chest thump in their presence just to show who's who and what's what.

But there are others. A few, one suspects, are themselves resentful of the fact that at some point in his day or week Mr. Head Dog does in fact go home to another woman. And some just have a classic case of the Washington power-mads. In any event, the fact is that in enough of these situations to be noticed, the assistant/alter ego/proxy wife ends up unceremoniously instructing the church-vow wife on the phone about where to be and when for the rally, telling her with whom she is to have dinner next Tuesday night, and, worse, talking to her husband in her presence in ostentatiously codelike circumlocutions, all powerfully indicating, as if there were any doubt, that there are serious, *man's-world* subjects to which the assistant is privy that are far too weighty and/or confidential to be shared with Bubbles.

It is a culture jolt of fasten-your-seat-belt proportions to go from this first loose grouping of "other women"—these largely reliable-looking, middle-aged and older female assistants, in their unobtrusive, perfectly cared-for clothes and simple pearl earrings—to the bimbos, the broads.

The most insistent thought I have on the adulterous sexual hijinks of prominent public figures in Washington is that they probably should have gone in the chapter on high school. Truly, there is something irredeemably adolescent about the public sex scandals in the nation's capital in recent decades. Think about it. We've had Congressman Wilbur Mills, the august Ways and Means Committee chairman, and his honey, the stripper Miss Fanne Fox, leaping into the Tidal Basin one night. We've had the Kennedy brothers' teen-party-type escapades. We've had Gary Hart on an illicit, college-break-playtime weekend aboard the *Monkey Business,* hanging out with a fun bunch of singles who could have been his children. We've had Carter White House officials' notorious *Animal House* partying. We've had other U.S. senators in trouble for grabbing and groping their way around town. We've had the Beowulf-length sagas of hit-and-run sex alleged by the Bill Clinton accusers, culminating in the Year of Monica Lewinsky. And the (literal) body count goes on.

I do not know why the pop sociology scribes, who like to analyze and catalogue patterns of behavior, have not long since turned their attention to this gruesome aspect of life in Washington: the awful biff-bam, backseat-of-your-father's-Chevy quality of what passes for adult sexual scandal. These episodes turn out to be either pitiful, eye-averter, instant-gratification stories or accounts of secret attendance at frat-house-on-Friday-night parties of the kind most men their age—including those who live full, rich, extramarital sex lives—left behind decades before.

Again and again in this city, grown men of public standing will be found to have put their careers and marriages at risk for a pattern of hopelessly kidlike sexual fooling around, jackrabbit proceedings that unfailingly turn out to have been rather more scandal than sex. In this connection it remained for the unrequited but indefatigable Oregon senator Bob Packwood to achieve the ultimate Washington breakthrough: the four-star sex scandal more or less without any sex at all, only a lot of unpleasant lunging.

Pathetic though it all may have been, it was in keeping with the reigning disorder of the place: the increasingly regal isolation of the big shot within his own castle of convenience, surrounded not just by self-important male courtiers but also by obsequious or at least subdued females—the wife who was expected to know and accept her politically ordained station; the adoring secretary/assistant who put his smallest need before all else, however large, and saw to it that others did as well; and finally and fittingly, the bimbo who serviced and flattered and exacted absolutely nothing of him in the way of attention, recognition, or even recollection. That is, until she went public with her ghastly, lucrative story.

I don't mean to suggest that there haven't been in the past and aren't going on at this very moment intense, grown-up sexual relationships between Washington public men and women they aren't supposed to be involved with. I do mean to suggest that when you leaf through the thickening national scrapbook of the trouble our public figures keep getting into by reason of their marital strayings, you almost never find yourself in the presence of anything adult like this, not even minimal emotion or, more to the point, any discernible sexual passion at all. You read of nothing that would warrant the use of words like "mistress" or "girlfriend" or "affair," for example. You read of nothing that Edith Piaf, by any stretch of the imagination, would have been prompted to sing about, except perhaps to roll her eyes to heaven and exclaim, "My God! That is disgusting!"

For these men's lives had long since become too narrow and driven and self-focused even to allow for the kind of sexual engagements that might be worth risking a scandal for. From the wives' point of view, when their husbands were caught in this type of frenzied, teenage-throwback infidelity, the humiliation was all the worse because it was so degrading to everyone. Once, in such circumstances, the wives were expected to be ordered about by staff, to be snubbed by hosts and hostesses, and to keep such opinions as they might have to themselves. But fewer and fewer of them will sit still for any of it anymore.

It was an odd fact: The Washington culture that existed when the women's movement became a force in American politics in the 1970s was at once singularly disposed to resist its arguments and singularly ripe to respond to them. This was true of both women who worked outside the home and women who worked in it.

On the resistance side, most female jobholders seemed not to have yet connected the peculiarities and disadvantages of their own status in Washington with the broader charges being made. And for those who were fulfilling the traditional role of Washington official's wife, there looked to be as much fresh insult as sympathy or support in the movement's assertions about the role of homemakers, which could be seen as expressing contempt for who they were and what they did. In addition, as with all movements of this general kind, there was, especially at the beginning, a certain amount of extreme, off-the-wall, attention-grabbing political gesture, and this was bound to put off a population of women so thoroughly enmeshed in establishment ways and thought.

On the other side—the receptivity side—was the fact that increasing numbers of women in both categories were beginning to chafe under the restraints of man's-town Washington. As you would suppose, when the politics of the women's movement really heated up, some Washington women thought the enterprise was great; others thought it misbegotten. But at least as common were the large number of women who harbored some part of *all* the responses at the same time, being half pro and half con, adamantly resistant one day and unexpectedly receptive the next.

I was surprised, for instance, at how much resonance some of the message turned out to have for recalcitrant old fuds like me and many of my associates and friends, women who had long since accommodated to the culture of Washington and found their own way to work in it. This was although we were skittish about, if not downright hostile to, any number of the movement's objectives, tactics, and attitudes. But establishment working women I knew, Republicans as well as Democrats, conservatives as well as liberals, started bringing up stories about the latest women's campaign or a court case that was being brought.

These tended to be women who held high positions in and around government and were thought of by everyone, including themselves, as the least likely on earth to traffic in radicalism. Yet I cannot tell you how many times, after we had ritually made plain to one another all our innumerable reservations about what was going on in the movement, we would end up saying, "But you know, there *is* something" to this or that claim. And then we would fall into spirited conversation about all those female-unfriendly assumptions and habits that were the mood music of our workday and to which we all had learned cheerfully to hum along.

I ask myself now whether this might have been pity-poor-us, victim stuff being indulged by women who were, relatively speaking, awfully well-off in their jobs and anything but suitable objects of tearful sympathy. But I don't think it was. It was always a pretty shy, tentative critique so far as each person's complaint on her own behalf was concerned, and it had something of the quality of discovery of an unexpected new feeling of solidarity with other women.

These were Washington jobholders ranging politically from Democrat Alice Rivlin, director of the Congressional Budget Office (and subsequently Clinton's budget director), to conservative Jeane Kirkpatrick, American ambassador to the UN. There were others who, though publicly less well known, also held down heavy jobs, such as Margaret Tutwiler, who was a top adviser to James Baker in the Reagan and Bush administrations, and Faith Whittlesley, a very conservative Reagan White House political aide.

I was struck by how many of the women who made up this relatively thin slice of Washington professional life conceded being stirred by the fact of Geraldine Ferraro's nomination for vice president in 1984, although many were on the other political side or outspoken nonfans of Ferraro personally. Even some of those who considered her nomination a big mistake saw it as a kind of vindication of themselves. For these were women, one learned as it all began to be hashed over, who had grown used to being talked down to in a hundred different ways by men who were often their workplace subordinates—and also, very often, by the big boss's female secretary/assistant, who took only guys seriously and had a terrible time according equal respect to another female.

They were also women who had learned that any discipline they sought to impose on that section of the workplace for which they were responsible or any dissatisfaction they might express with an employee's defective product—however cool and professional they might be—ran the risk nevertheless of being at once automatically reconfigured as a charge against them, the "woman" charge. This was that they were temperamentally unfit as managers, disorganized, mercurial, hysterical. The identical actions taken by a man and in considerably hotter fashion, they had observed, often as not would generate grudging admiration ("The old man's really on a tear").

From time to time it was evidently even thought acceptable to invent a crazed-female personality when the real female personality wouldn't oblige. I once was in a room with my boss and great pal the *Washington Post* publisher Katharine Graham when she was on the phone getting some very disappointing news about a business deal that had fallen through. She was utterly composed and businesslike about it. I was later to read in a magazine article about the collapse of that deal that she had become desperate and emotional during the call, shouting and sobbing hysterically into the phone.

Finally, their own contributions to the program or bureau or campaign they worked for would frequently be appropriated and claimed by others or left off the list of bossly notice, just as they themselves were so often left out of the motorcade or meeting.

Not each of the women I knew had all of these experiences—I did not—but most were familiar with enough of them to subscribe to the basic critique. Their beef was strictly professional: that they and women like them were patronized and misused in a kind of mindless, inadvertent way, or subtly excised from full participation.

Most of us had been, as individuals, pretty lukewarm to the movement from the beginning. As a result it was said that this was because we were reluctant to share our rare positions inside the male citadel with others of our kind. I suppose I am not a trustworthy deponent here, but I truly believe it was something quite different—in addition to the fact that some part of both the agenda and the outlook seemed wrong to many of us, as some of it still does to me.

It was that we had all become so thoroughly acclimated to the peculiar unspoken rules and inhibitions governing the working life of women in Washington that we honest-to-God took a lot of prodding to recognize them for what they were and arrive at the astounding conclusion that they could and should be changed. I think most of us were where I was when, with little more than a shrug, I had accepted being kept out of the Press Club hallway or when, in what now strike me as hilarious deliberations, I gravely conferred with friends about how to work as boss of the men on the *Post* editorial board without threatening their manhood.

I don't think the women who were prominent in the movement would regard our change of heart or attitude as much more than a two-centimeter move of a two-hundred-ton glacier over, say, two million years. But their political agitation did affect us, caused us to talk of these things with one another as we had never done before and reflect on our own odd situation in Washington as well as that of other women. Relatively few plunged into the politics of the women's movement, but we were increasingly lost to man's-town Washington as tacit allies.

We were women who could be cited as proof that there were no male-imposed barriers to hiring and promotion, never mind our suspiciously small numbers. Much more important, we were women who could be supposed, by our passivity, to be on the company's or agency's side when any individual female employee or group of them came forward with complaints.

That was what changed. For whether we had previously been thought of as collaborators, tokens, exceptions, or, as my friend the columnist Joe Alsop once said in what he took to be a lavish compliment, "honorary men," we were now something else. As time went on, we were generally to be found using our influence vigorously to promote their side in the office disputes.

What was the impact of the change going on at home? In the fright literature about the women's movement, you will read of monster mamas rising up; seizing all of poor dad's prerogatives, authority, and dignity; treating him like dirt; and on and on. The truth is that nothing that has taken place in the Washington domestic/marital upheaval of recent years even mildly reflects these mad scenarios.

But the disproportionate seismic impact of the change only affirms how fettered the wife in political/governmental Washington was meant to be in the first place. For the goals being sought were merely that these women be released from the archaic constraints the weird political culture of the capital imposed—constraints that had long since disappeared from comparable professional circles out-side Washington. The wives in question mainly aspired just to be credited with having lives worthy of respect.

More and more of them all across the political spectrum began insisting on having, for example, the final say on how many bunting-covered platforms and gold-painted ballroom chairs they had to adorn in the course of a week. When you hear people describing how a lot of Washington wives have let it be known that they are "not going to take it anymore," this virtual annihilation of their own separate selfhood is what they are saying they are not going to take. I have to tell you that it does not strike me, anyway, as the return of the Reign of Terror.

Once again I qualify as to the sweep of all this: It never was the case that every wife in political/governmental Washington was so thwarted. And it always was the case that some whom the guardians of the system believed *should* be thwarted (on account of their hus-bands' particular jobs) and whom they strove mightily to keep under behavioral house arrest got loose. I think of an independent, take-no-guff woman such as Lydia Katzenbach, artist, therapist, and wife of LBJ's attorney general and undersecretary of state, Nicholas Katzenbach. As far back as the early to mid-1960s, she had clearly established that she was not going to be the Invisible Woman so far as expressing her views or having a life of her own was concerned.

In present-day Washington the conduct that got Lydia Katzen-bach marked as a wild rebel has pretty much become standard oper-ating procedure among wives. They express opinions. They have calendars of their own. They have jobs, if they want them, and when they plead the press of prior commitments or other business—whether family or professional—no one clucks about how if they were loyal wives they would just pin on that pizza-sized corsage and get on down to the Washington Hilton ballroom where they belong.

So reluctant is everyone nowadays even to *seem* to be casting doubt, in the old way, on a woman's entitlement to pursue her interests that when some wives of public officials enter into exploitative commercial or financial arrangements that are clearly conflicts of interest (intensely seeking the business patronage, say, of those who are regulated by or otherwise dependent on their husbands' decisions), no one generally says a thing. This is its own good-news–bad-news story, since you can always tell when a desirable Washington reform of any kind has finally taken hold by the way a substantial number of people will have figured out how to misuse it to their own financial benefit.

Betty Ford's couple of years in the White House had great influence on the change in the Washington official wife. She was not nearly so political as the outspoken Eleanor Roosevelt or the backstage power Lady Bird Johnson. Unlike Jacqueline Kennedy, who took her distance from much of the wife-culture social life (and got condemned as a snob rather than hailed as a liberated woman for her behavior), Mrs. Ford continued to take part in these rituals.

In fact, I would guess that over the years, as the wife of House minority leader Gerald Ford, she had put in as many I-wish-I-were-someplace-else hours as any woman alive. Yet she was wholly different from those who had seen their role in far more traditional terms, like Bess Truman, say, or Mamie Eisenhower or (though to a lesser degree) Pat Nixon. By much that she said and did, she seemed intentionally to be putting in place a new set of assumptions not just about what was allowed but about what was desirable in the role.

The uniqueness of her particular assertion of independence and expression of her own individuality lay in that she seemed to be doing these things as a wife and not as a suppressed or aspiring job-holder. She no doubt agreed that those married women in Washington who had their own career interests should be allowed to pursue them, a proposition that already had its proponents. But that was not the main message she conveyed. She endorsed the idea that the Washington wife need no longer be counted on as a silent, smiling, nonvoting partner in everything her husband did.

You could already in those days hear plenty of wives taking a discreet, private distance from their husbands on certain issues—the wisdom of further pursuing the war in Vietnam as a prime example. But Betty Ford's engagement of people in the story of her breast cancer, her willingness to talk about the strains on family of a nonstop-campaigning, political-fishbowl, home-alone life—all this was new. It fascinated the press. Moreover, it helped innumerable Washington women to become much bolder.

By the mid-1980s, a city long accustomed to the wife as good soldier was finding that more and more of these soldiers had gone AWOL. That didn't mean—except in the context of high-strung divorce cases and comparable marital meltdowns—that the wives had turned on the husbands, gone state's evidence in the corruption cases, endorsed the opponent, or done other end-of-the-world things like that. It meant they had acted on that continually lurking and potentially cataclysmic issue that probably underlies all human relationships: They were not going to be taken for granted.

It has been in these respects—far more, I would argue, than in the higher incidence of women's taking jobs themselves—that the upheaval has occurred. For a great deal is different now in your basic Washington household. It is no longer a safe assumption that the wife's views are considered something to be privately dismissed or publicly suppressed.

Nor is it safe to assume any longer that the family is a career accessory to be put on display at strategic moments. These days, when a Washington public figure says he is leaving his job because "I want to spend more time with my family," you may no longer take it as prima facie evidence that federal agents have subpoenaed his books. He may actually be telling the truth.

Ignored, scorned, and/or panoramically cheated-on wives were now going over the side and speaking out in unprecedented ways, which they knew would prove a public relations nuclear holocaust. But aside from such dramatic acts of fury and revenge, there was a much quieter and steelier resistance to these and lesser provocations taking place among Washington women.

The American public has repeatedly witnessed the sorrowful, sunken-eyed wife with the wan, unconvincing smile, trotting along on the campaign trail in the company of her candidate-husband, gamely there to demonstrate (which no one believes) that all is well between them. Unlike in other marriages, all of this couple's travails must be played out on a public stage, and she has heretofore been expected, good-soldierwise, to be on twenty-four-hour campaign call, no matter what.

Maybe her candidate-husband has been caught hanging out with Miss Teenage Sex. Maybe it's a matter of his having been discovered in some other, nonsexual variety of hanky-panky. Or maybe it's just that he has had virtually no time for or interest in her and their children between campaigns at all, until now. Whatever the trouble may have been, Americans have also become utterly familiar with the classic damage-control shot: those absolutely chilling family portraits on TV, filmed after Dad was compelled to own up to a series of crimes or depredations or personal kinkinesses that cause you to cringe in their mere contemplation.

There, dressed as if for Sunday night dinner at the club, stand the whole bunch: Mom and Sis and Junior. And right before Dad tells the assembled reporters that he is now cooperating with the Justice Department authorities or turning himself over to a rehab center, he confides, with tearful eye and husky voice, that he just wants to say how much he appreciates the total understanding and support everyone in his family has given him in this difficult hour. The supportive, understanding family, peering out through their fixed expressions, all look as if they had recently been immersed in formaldehyde.

It is this kind of willing self-mortification on the part of their families that few public officeholders or private-enterprise big shots in Washington life can absolutely count on anymore. A wise, funny woman in Washington, Julia Taft, nailed down this notion for me one day, shortly after her husband, Will, had been appointed Reagan's deputy secretary of defense. She was being facetious and well knew that given her husband's nature she was in as little danger of such a fate as any spouse in town.

She asked her husband whether he had ever noticed that when a public figure had to confess to misconduct, the wife and kids were always in the picture looking miserable. Well, she said, she knew that nothing like that was going to happen to them, but just *in case* it ever did, there was something Will ought to know: "We are not going to be in that picture."

I think we all have stared at the likeness of that twelve-year-old girl or fourteen-year-old boy standing behind an errant father at a confessional press conference, their stricken faces lit by flashbulbs. It is painful to fathom how a child of that age can possibly accommodate the horror of the proceedings or—and this is at least as confounding—how such a child can be asked to participate in such a scene:

Oh, by the way, Junior and Sis, another change of plans for today. Dad has been caught in an act of sexual bestiality, trying to take his mind off all those wicked charges that he stole money from the poverty program. So put on something nice. We're going to go down to the Capitol to have our picture taken offering him our understanding and support.

All right, I know this is not exactly what happens or how it happens. But at an age when many ordinary kids consider the mere idea of having parents an insupportable embarrassment, what can it be like to learn of the gross sexual squalors and/or felonious activities of someone who is Dad?

And not only that. What can it be like when all this is played out on the nightly news and in the papers and in the expressions on the faces—if not in the remarks—of schoolmates and neighborhood kids? Are you supposed to smile? To look solemn? To look as if you don't care? To look as sickened as you really are?

It's not as if the parent who brought his children to this unthinkable pass is unaware or unconcerned by it. On the contrary, there is likely to be no more complex, turbulent, guilt-producing, and often tortured relationship in the Washington public figure's life than that with his children. And this is not only true of those dads who get into newsworthy, highly photogenic trouble—the adulterers and thieves and found-out addicts of one sort and another. It is frequently true as well of your run-of-the-mill politician and non-elected Washington hotshot. Even if they have not consciously exploited their children for political or career purposes or subjected them to terrible anguish by their deeds, almost unavoidably the public careers of many of them will still have had the effect of a great, heedless mastodon lumbering through those children's lives.

The disturbance in the relationship is usually about much more than missed sports events or the kids' having to change schools and leave friends behind. It is often about kids being severely punished for the parent's career, to a degree not balanced out by any of the small-beer, transient privileges that accrue to them—the special tours and tickets and seats at the parade.

The children of those who have been in elective politics for years will likely have learned a lot of tricks to deal with the difficulties that arise. They probably also will have found a little society of similarly situated kids to commiserate with. The ones whose families just suddenly get catapulted into the high-visibility, high-vulnerability life will have more motion sickness. Without warning or preparation, they will find themselves with a parent who is being ripped to shreds and sneered at on TV night after night, or blamed for some tragic bloodletting on this continent or another, or held accountable for the economic misery of millions of poor people.

Well before the controversy that enveloped his appointment as attorney general, while Edwin Meese was still a White House aide to Reagan, he and his wife, Ursula, spoke with great feeling on this subject in connection with their young college-age son, Scott, a very promising, widely liked boy, deeply involved in volunteer social work, who was only months later to be killed in a car accident. The Meeses talked about this with a group of people chatting between speeches at a public event one night. They had been on the phone with Scott, who had called them from New Haven that day, they said, discussing the assaults he was drawing for every unpopular thing the administration did, as if these actions were somehow both his doing and his fault. He was also constantly being told what a bad guy his father was. He was just a kid having to find a way to cope with all that.

You don't have to be a soulmate of Ed Meese to understand how wrenching this was for both parents. And unlike other kids who have only the school or the family or, conceivably, the cops to answer to when they get into classic trouble, the children of public figures may find their own missteps suddenly in the public domain, lighted up like a Hollywood supermarket opening, with bullhorns blaring out a version of the story for all to hear. This is another source of political-parent guilt. Parents in public life have always risen up in special, protective wrath when they suspected their child was being made to pay an extra price because of the parent's own embroilment in public controversy—as Harry Truman did in his famously direct, pugnacious response to the *Washington Post* music critic's slam of his daughter Margaret's singing. This is a condition, after all, that violates every shielding parental instinct and actually reverses the norm: Papa is supposed to go to work each day to make life better and safer, not worse and less secure for his young.

The chagrin for public figures who have kids in the most vulnerable age zones has deepened in recent years. For nowadays, with so much more attention focused on the needs and sensitivities and newly presumed entitlements of children, as well as on the obligations of their parents, even the most conscientious of public dads who have the most psychologically sturdy of children may fret that his office duties are depriving those kids of their birthright—the time and closeness and priority—he cannot or at least does not give them.

I measure the change that has occurred in the way people think about this subject by contrasting two events. Thirty years ago many of us considered it (as I still would) a sign of selflessness and dedication to public service that Hubert Humphrey, wracked by anxiety over a cancer operation his young son was undergoing in Minnesota, nonetheless stayed in Washington to make absolutely certain that the final vote for passage of the big Civil Rights Bill of 1964—which was by then in practically no doubt at all—did not somehow come undone. (He left as soon as the vote had been taken.)

I thought of that episode when, a couple of years ago, a pro football player was being handsomely complimented in the national press for having passed up a crucial game, infuriating the rest of his team, in order to be with his wife at the birth of their child. Would Humphrey today be praised for what he did? Or would his choice be regarded as self-important, callous, typical Beltway behavior, a bad-values, bad-dad performance?

The younger generation may often have another strong impact on the older that generally goes unnoted. Children may be resident representatives of all sorts of tastes and ideas and opinions that are at best unfamiliar to their elders—and sometimes anathema to them. What the ambitious, fawning staff aide can't or won't say, the kid will.

I think of the teenage grandchild of the Soviet Union's longtime ambassador to the United States, Anatoly Dobrynin, who, with his wife, was raising the girl in Washington. The Dobrynins were absolutely gone on this child, who became an Americanized, Big-Mac-eating, awful-music-playing, mall-magnetized adolescent during the years she grew up here (the fate of many diplomats' kids in Washington). When Dobrynin would report on this with sympathetic wonder and an unmistakable hint of grandfatherly pride, I could not help thinking that for all the Dobrynins' sophistication about this country, their granddaughter had shown them things about it that they could not have seen without her.

In one of his clumsier remarks, Jimmy Carter allowed in his 1980 televised debate with Ronald Reagan that his young daughter, Amy, had made a contribution to his thinking on nuclear weaponry. He got what he asked for: Stand-up comics transformed his comment into an admission that the twelve-year-old was making U.S. nuclear policy.

Kids may be a rare source of dissident lore and insight and feeling, a kind of window on a world the official has increasingly rejected and distanced himself from. And this can be pretty important if it is a really hot and contentious issue, one with which the parent has become totally identified.

Virtually everyone else who thinks what the dissident child thinks is likely to have been kept safely on the other side of the moat, there to mutter threateningly about maybe scaling the wall some day. But the child is inside the gate, and the child tends to matter to even the most seemingly cold-blooded public parent, and the child will be heard. It was one thing in the old days to get a wife to surrender the prime of her life. But no one ever got a fifteen-year-old to forgo adolescence.

Vietnam was one spectacular example. However many official wives expressed antiwar sentiments during the later years of U.S. involvement, I suspect it was nothing compared to the number of their unhappy, demonstrating kids. I frequented plenty such homes in those years and saw the sad, soulful children (whose dress and grooming were exactly like those their parents were ridiculing and denouncing in public speeches) argue with their parents, the people responsible for the policy they so hated. They seemed to be deeply sincere and respectful and desperate at the same time, which made it all the more poignant.

These kids didn't convert many of their parents, at least not so far as causing a U-turn in Vietnam policy was concerned. But many had some impact on how the parents thought, even if only to persuade them of the reach of the dissent or open them somewhat to argument.

Something much more complicated is involved than exists in normal, turbulent parent-teen struggles. A kind of inversion occurs. All that is embarrassing in the parent-child relationship does not come from the parent: It is a busy, two-way thoroughfare. It is one thing, after all, to say, "I do not want you to go to that party if there are not going to be any parents at home," quite another to say, "I do not want you to march in the protest that is planning to pour a pail of chicken blood on my car in the VIP parking lot." It is one thing to say, "Don't disobey me," another to say, "Don't embarrass me politically."

There have been various instances of financial exploitation of their fathers' political position by grown children of well-known public figures. But more often we are talking about a kid—an underage one—who will have gone out in a kid way and done something or turned into someone that flies in the face of all Dad's most florid, oft-stated public pieties. The annals of capital life in the years that I have lived here are replete with item after item of this kind: the drug warrior's child who is found to be on drugs, the homophobe's child who professes to be gay, the law-and-order zealot's child who gets picked up for a violent crime.

Far and away the most stunning, moving account of a family's prolonged wrestle with all this—both the parents' and the child's— was the *New York Times Magazine* article by Peter Haldeman, the grown son of H. R. Haldeman, who was Nixon's White House chief of staff. The father whose affectionate attentions the son recalls ("I learned how to tune a uke from my father. . . . He signed the lines in my Cub Scout handbook certifying that I'd tied a slide knot") was publicly known, as he says, as "Nixon's son of a bitch," pictured with fangs, when young Haldeman was a teenager in the Nixon years, attending Sidwell Friends, the same progressive, Quaker school that Chelsea Clinton later attended.

Peter Haldeman wrote of what it was like in a politically liberal environment to be the son of a man widely denounced as an unfeeling, arrogant martinet, all prior to his serving a jail sentence for Watergate crimes. He talked of his own dalliance with drugs and his isolation as he came to perceive himself to be gay, his suicide attempts, his being kicked out of school at roughly the same time his dad was being kicked out of government, and how his own troubles at school had hit the news, depicted in *Time* as "an anguished reaction to Watergate."

And most affectingly, he talked of his continuing engagement on all of this with a father he loved and who loved him, even as the two of them (the crew-cut Nixon-loyalist dad, the hippie kid) were embarrassing and offending each other—and how they finally reached equilibrium and understanding. The humanness of the father, his susceptibility to his son, and the enhancement of his sensibilities under the son's prodding—all this seemed to me the important story. It is a story that occurs again and again in Washington in the conflict between the sacred abstractions to which the parent, in his political life, has wed himself and the reality of his child's unabstract life.

Whenever there is the disclosure of some politically explosive fact about a public person's kid that fits this category, we in the press tend to dither about where and how to play the story, while the political or career antagonists of the kid's parent try to figure out how to get the good of the situation without seeming even to have noticed it, let alone to have tried to capitalize on it. These reactions of both media and political antagonist are premised on the idea that the fabricated, unreal image-person—the great Blob's love slave, the public relations construct—is the one who has taken the hit and is responding.

So both immediately begin to speculate on what Mr. Phony's tactical response will be or how badly he has been hurt. Once again, we have become so inured to the idea of these people as unreal and so utterly absorbed in the world the unreal inhabit that we very often fail to see that it isn't Mr. Phony who's taking the call from the kid—the call that says the kid has done something or become someone that flies in the face of everything the parent in his political/career persona was identified with. It's the vulnerable dad, the real one, who responds. For as it apparently was with Haldeman, the parents I have had knowledge of in every comparable instance have been humbled and rendered helpless—as distinct from angry or combative or distant or scandalized or even consumed with the exigencies of getting their political message or career persona repaired and back on track.

Whatever else the driven public figure may have put on hold for the sake of his career, whatever other normal human feelings he may have trouble activating again, his residual feelings of responsibility for his children, his elementary concern for them, and his powerful impulse to maintain the confidence and trust of a child who once worshiped him without qualification will again and again reassert themselves in these parent-kid crises. The kids can sometimes instruct by becoming an open channel to dissent, even if it is often only a marginal, naive, and unimpressive dissent.

But more important, the kid *can* humble the parent and render him helpless; he *can* humanize a parent who has otherwise appeared to leave Planet Earth for some isolated, arid reach where life is only and always about the rigors of ambition. It is the ultimate power of the kid. Not always, but often enough, unlike all the others in his family and inner circle who have their strong claims on the public person's life and who can temper his power and confound his plans, the kid alone has the Bomb.

CHAPTER SIX

The News Business

*J*OURNALISM WAS WHAT began to make me finish my sentences and take the heat for a completed thought. Once in a while, when I encounter the exasperation with which so many people nowadays view our business—its waywardness and its seemingly unencumbered ways—I think of this. For me, it was a step into, not away from responsibility.

Actually, I couldn't have gotten much farther away from responsibility at the time, at least by the now archaic standards of the 1950s, so there was no place else to go. I had been out of college, dabbling my way through Western Europe for three years and then for a few more in Greenwich Village, growing up (or at least trying out for the role of grown-up) in all the unoriginal, chaotic, and—as we used to say—bohemian ways.

To the extent that I had decided anything, it was only that I didn't want to be an English literature professor after all, any more than I wanted to go back to Seattle and follow what I understood to be the educated young matron's trajectory or any other trajectory I had been prepared for. So I just kind of drifted into the trade.

I hooked up with the *Reporter* magazine as a part-time news-clip filer in the library, explaining that this was all the time I could spare from a very important novel I was about to write. I probably thought I was telling the truth, but of course no novel ever materialized or even began to.

Instead, I just kept inching along at the magazine, near paralytically deadline-shy and ambivalent about making a commitment to the job, the business, the boyfriend of the moment, or anything else. I moved gradually to full-time research in the library, news-summary writing for the exacting boss, beginning steps at political reporting, and startlingly, in Kennedy's first year in office, a sudden dispatch to the magazine's Washington, D.C., office to substitute for Douglass Cater during his three-month leave from the editor's desk.

This assignment came at a time when I had written a mere five articles, two of them book reviews of novels and poetry by authors I loved and had asked to review mainly so I could get the free reviewers' copies of their work. I knew nothing of Washington except what I had seen as a benumbed twelve-year-old tourist in the summer of 1943, when my dad was trying to distract my brother and me after my mother's unexpected death. My boss said later that one reason he had sent me was to challenge my political ideas, which were as weakly based as they were adamantly held. He thought it would be amusing to see what happened to them.

So summarily I was in Washington and a reporter, and so it turned out to be for the rest of my life. I hated the city at first, as did everyone I knew who had been sent there from New York. We liked nothing more than to gather at night at the house of our mentor and fellow exile Murray Kempton to ridicule the incorrigible unhipness of the place and grieve. After two years of camping in a residential hotel while I waited vainly to be reassigned to New York and managed to be on the shuttle to La Guardia every Friday night at six, I realized what my employer had in mind. I began looking for somewhere to live in the capital and reluctantly gave up my beloved studio apartment in the Village.

What you should see in this brief sketch is a very big difference from what often happens now. Although we younger reporters were dazzled by the feats of the great World War II correspondents, whose dispatches had loomed so large in our lives when we were growing up, journalism itself was no big deal.

We didn't even routinely refer to what we were doing all day as "journalism" or call ourselves "journalists," terms that to me still exude a touch of the grand as self-definition. We worked for newspapers and magazines and TV and radio stations or networks, as we saw it. We were reporters, and that was no glamorous big deal or topic over which you anguished concerning its ethics, duties, rights, and the rest. I was grateful—resolutely unhatted creature that I was—not to be called a "lady reporter." But that was about as far as my aspirations concerning my job description went.

There were a very few among us who had been to graduate school in journalism. And there were a handful who had long aspired to work one day for the *New York Times.* But for the majority this was a line of work you just happened into or chose because it looked like fun. Or if you were female, you went into journalism because you didn't want to be the typist-secretary in a publishing house for some guy who had graduated the same year as you—a job that college placement counselors of the era tended to view as your optimum professional destiny if you also had been good at literary studies but didn't want to teach and had the misfortune of being a girl.

The reporting trade occasionally got the second-born, noninheriting sons of some elite families, sort of à la the church in medieval times; increasingly after the war it also got an infusion of young Jewish men and women who were attracted to writing and habituated by upbringing to a somewhat on-the-outskirts observer's role in society. But in fact, unlike today, with all the proffered academic preparation for it, being a reporter back then tended simply to be what you did while you were still deciding what you were going to do.

And then you looked up and you were thirty-six or thirty-eight and—what the hell—you supposed it *was* what you were going to do. For me, as a fallen-away English major, there was even one small, additional, negative ping: In the world I was leaving behind, "journalism" was in fact a term of dismissal, verging on contempt. "It is merely journalism," we would say of some effort at serious writing that we judged a total failure, and we had to say no more.

The kind of sentences my new job was to make me finish were

pretty much alike, the prodigious output of a newly politically minded young woman who could shake her head, roll her eyes to heaven, and sigh sardonically but who regularly failed to provide any predicates for her subjects and was unaware of a need to do so. It would sound somewhat like this, for example, when I might be offering my view of Eisenhower's secretary of state: "Oh, *Dulles* . . . I mean, what a . . . I mean, God, . . . you *know?*"

That was my idea of a perfectly cogent political observation, and a lot of the people with whom I kept company would take it as such and respond in balloony kind. I should tell you we were very pleased with these conversations, which we believed marked us as being in the dissenting vanguard of 1950s American political life.

Getting from there to sentences that could at least in principle be diagrammed, however extravagantly long they were (and, I fear, remain), was what the early days of reporting were about. The sentences had to have endings, and with endings you venture publicly to assert a reality that at least some other people have also witnessed and are qualified to judge, thus making you fair game for their critique.

So you are hanging out there for inspection and, surely as important, you've got your boss and publication hanging out there too. For you have said not, "How *pathetic!* How *disgraceful!*" but rather: "This is what they are doing"; "This is as far as they got in the agreement yesterday"; "This is what the final legislation requires."

You have been obliged to work, in other words, with something beside your own biases and fantasies and clevernesses and put what you think out there for all to see. Elementary as it seems, the procedure was transforming. For the objective necessarily went from *being* right in one's own estimation and that of like-minded friends to *getting it* right. And that implies a whole different trip. Often as not it will take you to some unexpected, end-of-the-line station where you've never been before and abruptly put you off the train—politically stranded, as it so regularly turned out for me in the years to come, when what I had found could not be made to conform, at least not fairly by my lights, with the lovingly held, prior point of view.

There is nothing especially worthy, let alone sacrificial about this. It is merely what we are supposed to do and what we get paid to do. Invest it with no special virtue. And *never* confuse the procedure and outcome with the superficial "contrarian" pose so trendy today, which is just another phony, self-promoting, look-at-me thing: "Hey—is this unpredictable or what? I'm defending the attack on Pearl Harbor!"

On the contrary, the model for proper conduct of our business is George Orwell, the incomparable journalist of our century, who followed his inquiries into all the unanticipated, uncomfortable, and illuminating places they led him. And one more thing: If we are competitive and take personal pride in our product, then trying to get it right, far from being an exercise in self-effacement, can be at least as self-interested a pursuit as all the shallow, show-off stuff ever was.

For our egos want us to be the ones who got it right, and if we beat out the opposition in the process and, luckier yet, they actually get it wrong, all the better. I concede that the ungraciousness of this attitude, which is supposed to mellow with age, has proved maturity-resistant in me. Even as public-spirited colleagues have risen above it and worked to improve the quality of journalism as a whole, I still am only very reluctantly shamed into participating in such efforts and remain incapable of abstractly rejoicing for either journalism or the advancement of public knowledge when another paper prints something I think is awfully good and wish we had printed on the editorial or op-ed page. It drives me crazy and propels me to yet new levels of dog-eat-dog competitiveness that, I am told—and I believe—are singularly unattractive in one my age.

So don't think I am talking about any particular rectitude here or public service mission or constitutional burden we have uncomplainingly assumed. I am merely enunciating the abiding, core function of the newsman and newswoman—what they will do right if they are any good and the standard by which they should be judged. When instead of performing this function we abandon both our curiosity and our drive to satisfy it and either start trying to get the story to justify our assumptions or conclude that we don't need to ask or look or even wonder, because we're so smart we already know, we have walked off the job.

When we are on the job and doing it right, however, I would say we are, in some respects anyway, among the *most* accountable of players, not the least, as the contemporary lamentation has it. The grossly defective widget you worked on in the factory or whose specs you approved at the meeting may be what caused my car to plunge into the scenic canyon and me to come to an untimely end in a tangle of indignant mountain goats. But chances are it will take a long time for your mucking about with the widget to catch up with you, if it ever does. We, in contrast, are out there naked for all to see every day of our lives, compelled to admit by the very nature of our visible product: "Well, here it is; it was the best I could do by deadline."

You may not be able to haul us into court or get us defrocked as journalists or get our publication enjoined. And you can't vaporize the story that appeared. But you are able to look at that product, know who we are, and respond, either in our publication or another media setting, to all within earshot or directly to us: "What a crock. *None* of that's right, never mind *fair*. Cancel my subscription—call the ombudsman—tell the publisher we're going to pull all our ads; *that'll* get his attention," which, however he finally responds to it, be assured it will.

It turned out that the unaccustomed respect to be paid to a reality existing outside the confines of my own brain was only step one. For this, as I learned, pulls you at once beyond the relatively straightforward concept of "accurate" into the far soupier realm of "fair." Nothing is easier, after all, than being meticulously factual and egregiously crooked at the same time if you want to, and sometimes if you don't want to but let yourself become unconscionably sloppy: "President Kennedy, in a ringing appeal to self-interest yesterday, called on Americans to 'ask . . . what your country can do for you.'"

It's the extreme bad-faith case, to be sure, but technically still "factual," complete with the three fastidiously placed dots acknowledging that the sentence has been abridged. My introduction to all this was the work of the personally pleasant but professionally implacable checking staff at the *Reporter,* whose job it was to aggressively challenge every assertion a writer made that was susceptible of proof.

They had final say on what checked out sufficiently to get into the magazine, and no one among their editor/bosses, let alone those of us whose articles they were clearing, could override them. You spent as long retrieving and reading to them the full original quotes you had taken or copied from a transcript, arguing about implications and left-out material that might have skewed the meaning, as you did reporting and writing the article—or at least so it seemed to me and some of the other writers when we were in mid-grapple with the checkers. But they saved us from ourselves a thousand times over.

Of this discipline in the news business, the following may be said. First, it was then and still is essential, although it isn't nearly as rigorously practiced by most editors as it should be anymore. Second, you have to live with the fact that even at best it only partially works; something not just a little "off" but occasionally humiliatingly wrong will slip through despite your honest efforts—it just will.

Third, though it is essential, it is only a modest part of the story. For those of us reporting in a place like Washington are not cameras, nor are we meant to be; we are not merely trying to serve up a likeness of some tangible phenomenon, like a huge rock formation, whose dimensions and chemical composition can be precisely described. There are a lot of facts you have an obligation to get right, but there is no big, single factual truth in most political stories, just sitting out there waiting to be discovered and about which reporters will, if they are objective, send identical accounts back to base camp.

Life isn't like that in any other setting; why would it be like it in a working community where the elements of ambition, belief, value, and personality are constantly in play and usually in conflict? Washington stories present the reporter (or editorialist or commentator) not with a checklist to complete so much as a "situation," one that is less ideologically neat than capriciously human most of the time.

Often as not, with the tacit and mutually beneficial cooperation of all the warring parties, it also publicly pretends to be something it most assuredly isn't, something far more rational and respectable and virtue-driven. In crucial respects, in other words, it pretty much replicates life in the workplace, the family, or any other collectivity of people with minds and purposes of their own that daily absorbs your attention.

Uncle Earl and his justly aggrieved, soon-to-be-former-wife, Mary Ann, and everyone else who was at the table would probably tell a slightly different story about what actually happened at that disastrous Thanksgiving dinner last year, for instance, each version making the one who narrates it look blameless. In response, you would do a little discreet nosing around among the rest of the relatives, trying to correct for what you knew to be the biases of each; you'd reconstruct the sequence of events as best you could; and finally you'd come up with what struck you as the most plausible version of what caused the terminal blow-up after all these years. In some unadorned way you'd be performing "journalism." You'd be doing what we do much of the time. It's the point at which the messiest, most unavoidably subjective, and far and away most controversial part of our work begins.

I see I have now introduced what was to me at the time, so far as my new reporting job was concerned, the essentially alien concept of human life. Confusing, disruptive, and wholly unforeseen as playing any part whatever in what I was being sent to Washington to do, it more or less met me at the airport and has remained an unrelenting professional snare and vexation ever since.

By this I mean that although I did have at least a hint of what was to come, thanks to a brief period of reporting on the personal politics of self-righteous reform versus shameless old hack in New York, I still wasn't prepared for the fact that living, breathing, willful people—not "issues"—were at the center of what was involved in the capital. For I had persisted in seeing the Tammany landscape as a kind of *Guys and Dolls* reprise, not so much about people as comic stereotypes. Honest-to-God people—as distinct from positions, policies, statutes, rulings, and other unfleshly particulars we were meant to ponder—didn't make their first major appearance as a political factor until my Washington time. The effect was as close to electric shock as anything that befell me in my job.

There was first the caption and then the capsule. The caption expressed a peculiar Washington inversion of proverbial wisdom: Seeing was not believing. On the contrary, seeing was, if anything, immediately to cease believing much of anything you believed before you came to Washington, head stuffed full of politically bolstering images and certitudes.

Here is the capsule version of what I saw almost from day one, as Doug Cater wheeled me hastily around town before he left, explained stuff to me, set up some helpful contacts, made his vain effort to get me access to the working facilities of the National Press Club—and left me to it: Some of the politicians to whom I had been sympathetic and who I had thought were doing serious work were not, and they were jerks into the bargain, utterly ineffective and either unaware of it or, worse, aware and not caring that their posturing hurt their cause so long as it pleased the folks back home.

Some were world-class practicing hypocrites who sold out their loudly broadcast beliefs every day or lived lives that amounted to systematic violations of them. Certain of those I considered the bad guys on the other side were doing the same number on their constituents and struck me up-close as being even stupider and/or meaner than I had imagined.

But others of them, alas, had many more redeeming features than I was prepared for, let alone prepared to be intellectually comfortable with. Easy personal friendships and working relationships that were incomprehensible to me existed between people I'd assumed to be sworn enemies for life and were a reason that some important things came about and some truly awful things did not. There's another way of putting this: Without the dimmest idea of what was coming, on September 21, 1961, I was dropped overnight into existential Washington.

My first befuddlement was that just about everyone I encountered seemed already aware of what so startled me and to have chosen to be somewhere between bemused and mildly entertained by it. My second was the dawning realization that I didn't speak the language, which was what I was later to master as two-track. More than being unable to converse in it, I had a hard time even picking up the signal. Were these people—the politicians and fellow reporters and handful of elder permanent residents to whom I had letters of introduction—being ignorant or ironic or intellectually confused or terminally duplicitous or what?

I didn't know. I knew only that they and everyone else I subsequently met seemed long since to have adapted to the moral and political ambiguities on which the action of the place turned and also to the fact that the picture journalistic and governmental Washington was routinely transmitting to the rest of the country often bore only the most tenuous resemblance to the less edifying reality they talked about among themselves as a matter of course. They took for granted the little and somewhat larger than little fraudulences, seemed unperturbed by them, and serenely wove them into their assumptions, wisecracks, and other chatter.

For me, the challenge in those first days and months was figuring out how I was supposed to accommodate all this in my job as reporter, what part of it I was meant to share with the magazine's readers, and above all what I was to make of the apparently endemic, bipartisan, and universally shrugged-off level of deception that marked the place.

Reflecting on what had taken me by surprise at the outset, and on so much like it that I observed in Washington and politics generally over the years, I was eventually to conclude that there is a two-part truth that just about every one of us knows and has always known but that practically none of us will admit for fear of being seen as an accomplice. It is, first, that the basic linguistic unit of speech in politics—all politics, not just the Washington kind—is a statement that is already somewhere between one-eighth and one-fourth of the way to being a lie. (I will leave it to others to decide whether this is any different from the basic speech of either commerce or love and, if so, in what degree and with what moral difference.)

The other part of the proposition is that such deception appears to be built into the process, a function of what we demand and expect and what they feel is required to stay alive and get anything whatever to happen. Politics, in other words—and not just politics practiced by people you don't like, but politics across the board—pretty much rests on a foundation of fractional lies, justified by some commonly shared if rarely acknowledged presumption of necessity. The phenomenon, after all, has long been copiously in evidence from the White House briefing room to the debate among candidates for city council and every other office to the solemn pronouncements of State Department spokesmen to the ocean of near parody gibbledy-gabble that daily engulfs the pages of the *Congressional Record*.

Our preferred way of dealing with this discomfiting truth seems to be to add one more smallish-to-medium lie of our own. We grouse or look the other way or pretend to be shocked, even though at some level we have known all along that what is being asserted as truth didn't really happen that way and never was going to.

We knew that our elected representatives were not acting out of the unalloyed high purpose they solemnly claimed. And we knew that likely as not when they promised tireless, strong, conclusive action on something we cared about deeply, the odds were that more than a few of them were already shopping around for a respectable-looking cop-out in which to take shelter and pretend they had done their utmost but that the bad guys had stopped them or, even more contemptuous of our intelligence, that the cop-out *was* the great deal they had promised.

Yet whenever one of these implausible fictions that we never took seriously to begin with hits the news for some reason and is exposed for what it is, we manage to project heart-wrenching disillusion all over again. More reckless, in my opinion, we leap to endorse and thus encourage what must be the most tiresome strain of commentary running through the nation's op-ed pages—and that is saying something—namely, that if the politicians don't cut it out, we the people will become *cynical*. Yes, we say, you are making us cynical, awful you—ignoring the fact that America and Americans were born cynical, or at least profoundly skeptical, about politicians, which is perhaps why we have survived as long as we have.

Two fairly common expressions of misplaced indignation that have always fascinated me are relevant here. One is: *"Are you calling me a liar?"* I have heard this question asked only by outraged people who didn't need to ask it because they well knew they had just been called a liar and, rather more the point, had just lied. Still, it seems always enough to chase off the most justified of accusers, who retreat into some half-apologetic mush-up of the issue, when the proper response would be, "Yes." From this and our other numerous dancings around, it seems obvious to me that we are collectively chicken on the subject, terminally embarrassed by it, and finally unwilling to confront it.

The other expression of misplaced indignation comes in response to one who has tried to make a practical case for doing something not so good but well this side of demonic because it's the only way of achieving something else that is highly desirable. *"Are you saying the end justifies the means?"* the professedly shocked one will ask, as if this were not a calculation each of us makes over and over in our daily lives, concerning everything from disciplining a child to driving way over the speed limit to get to some truly urgent appointment to telling a lie ourselves to ease a nasty situation or help a friend or get out of an embarrassing bind—and that's all before you get to the larger matters of personal self-defense or fighting a war or compromising a traditional test of some kind in order to alter the composition of the group likely to pass it. Still, people will almost always retreat in disarray from this one too, saying heavens no, they never meant to suggest any such unprincipled, philosophically discredited thing.

What makes these two strange affectations relevant is that each goes to the apparently indigestible but undeniable fact that in politics in general and Washington public life in particular, lying is habitually put in the service of policy and political self-preservation. It sounds squalid, and of course much of the time it is: sycophantic flattery of people the politicians not only do not admire but actually detest; inflation to the point of unrecognizability of the public figures' own virtues, purity of motive, and vast influence in making things happen, some of which they had nothing to do with; Scout's-honor declarations of commitment to programs and ideas in which they have next to no interest and which they certainly have no intention of supporting if doing so would entail the tiniest element of electoral risk; outrageous lies told to cover up outrageous behavior.

Virtually all public, official, political discourse has a fairly constant water-to-meat ratio of falsehood like this, more or less on a par with your average supermarket canned ham. The people who engage in the falsehood tend to think of it as something else and rationalize it to their own satisfaction on grounds that it is required for survival in office. And if they're pitched out of office, they ask as a kind of corollary what earthly good they can do for the causes that mean so much to the folks who object to their trifling with the truth.

If the squalor level doesn't rise too high, I think there is often something to be said for this argument. But as we have seen, it is of course terribly abused when public people cite the worth of their policy positions as a free pass to lying about personally extremely sordid or corrupt behavior—"How can you begrudge me this, after all I've done to fight the deficit?"

They have a much better case when they leave the suspect ground of deceptions purportedly required to ward off career death, a standard that can end up sanctioning almost anything to defend against an all but nonexistent risk, and enter the realm of the lie as "cover," the lie as sole means to a desirable policy end. For it is at least arguable that the federal government as a whole, the U.S. Congress, and probably our diplomacy, among other instrumentalities, could not function at all without routine exercise of this form of duplicity.

A commonplace, workaday example would be an opponent's agreeing to help with a particularly important vote, not necessarily out of the goodness of his heart but perhaps because he figures, say, that he is going to need a return favor next week on something those asking for his help don't like but that matters greatly to him. He is given "cover," by which is meant that the side he is helping out will pretend he has been faithful to his constituency and is dead set against their bill but has managed by being tough to extract large

and painful concessions from them and so now supports the measure and blah and blah and blah—none of it true.

This kind of informally agreed-to dissembling, understood by all
involved though rarely openly acknowledged, is woven into the very
fabric of Washington public life. Most of the newly published transcripts of taped conversations within the government contain yards
of explicit acknowledgment of the practice. It is probably what keeps
the place chugging along, with all its well-known shortfalls, defects,
and disasters, rather than settling into a terminal paralysis of fixed,
by-the-numbers, partisan ayes and nays on every issue that comes
along, as is the case in more ideologically rigid political systems. And
just as important, it has the advantage of allowing politically vulnerable people to do something they genuinely consider worthy and in
the best interest of the country without *seeming* to do the good thing
they are doing, which their following happens to think is not good
at all but rank and traitorous.

This is lying as "cover." The most dramatic example I remember—highly controversial at the time, but I think absolutely required—was the pretense in May 1960 that President Eisenhower
had not authorized or known of the U-2 spy planes' flights over the
Soviet Union, when the famous one crashed, tore up the planned
U.S.-Soviet summit, and threatened the whole structure of the two
countries' slowly evolving relationship. Later the story was amended,
in an ambiguous, fuzzy, and not entirely plausible way, to suggest
that although he knew of the program, he had not known of or
specifically authorized this particular flight, which was regarded as
provocative and embarrassing on the eve of a summit. These were
prudent lies and of course especially interesting ones because virtually everyone on both sides knew they were lies and also knew that
they must tell another and pretend not to know these were lies, for
reasons of policy and "face."

A different kind of real-life illustration would be the consistently belligerent rhetoric of Nixon's first defense secretary, Melvin Laird, during the Vietnam War. It earned him a reputation for ferocious commitment to American combat engagement, which was at once what he wished it to do and profoundly misleading. For Laird, as Washington-wired and crafty a person as ever lived, had two over-riding political purposes concerning the war, beyond the physical protection of the troops for which he was responsible.

The main one was getting U.S. forces out of combat there. He had concluded that their military involvement in Vietnam was a lost cause and an ever more destructive one, which, if it weren't closed down before the 1972 election, would wreck both the Nixon presi-dency and the Republican Party. He favored achieving this with-drawal by so-called Vietnamization, which meant replacing U.S. troops with South Vietnamese troops. This was a disengagement tactic many people supported, but not at the incredibly souped-up, Indianapolis 500 speed that Laird did, with its implication that get-ting us out pronto was the sole point and, as for the South Viet-namese client state, well, that was ultimately their problem, not ours.

His other purpose was, by means of the very tough verbal line, to head off any talk of Republican martial wobble or sellout or any un-derstanding at all of what he was really doing. The verbal line was the "cover," a.k.a. the untruth that, in Washington terms anyway, made it politically possible for him to turn his energies backstage to "getting us the hell out," as he would sometimes put it. He was nat-urally a source of distress to the true believers in administration pol-icy, who were in control and against whom he was conducting an underground war the only way he figured he could: by adopting a policy they had endorsed and trying to set it into fast-forward.

When you have pondered where you would put this exercise on the eccentric Washington moral scale, consider one more illustration of the falsehood as "cover" that I think can actually be characterized as borderline valiant and that certainly implied more virtue in the man who told the lie—and told it repeatedly—than telling the truth would have done. He was Robert McCloskey, then State Department spokesman for Dean Rusk, and on the morning of the outbreak of the Six-Day War in the Middle East in June 1967, he told his packed briefing room in effect that the U.S. government intended to do nothing that would betray a preference as to the war's outcome. On the contrary, he explained, the United States would "steer an even-handed course" throughout the conflict between the Arabs and the Israelis, famously adding, with a gratuitous literary flourish, "our position is neutral in thought, word, and deed."

The next sound you heard was the roof falling in. The Israelis, who had been attacked, and their supporters were irate. Almost immediately McCloskey retracted the statement and abjectly apologized. A little later I saw him at one of Rusk's backgrounder-and-whisky sessions for the press. When the query about the statement came up again, he stepped forward and apologized for it once more, reasserting that he had acted on his own as both wordsmith and policymaker and couldn't imagine what had got into him.

Those of us who knew McCloskey had no trouble at all imagining what had got into him. It was an instruction from the policy coaches on the seventh floor to say exactly what he had said, including the prescripted quote that turned out to have been uttered first by Woodrow Wilson and was thus thought to be historically resonant and very clever. McCloskey, in other words, had been following what is called "guidance," orders routinely sent down before the briefer briefs.

I would bet my life on it, for McCloskey, an old friend, was the kind of guy who was scrupulously, even obsessively, faithful to guidance. He was also the kind of guy who wouldn't have some Woodrow Wilson quotation like that just floating around in his head and, even if he did, would not have dreamed of improvising that way on the most boring, uneventful day, let alone on one of the most dicey diplomatically and politically charged occasions on which he had ever briefed a roomful of reporters.

To his credit, he didn't run out after hours either and contrive over drinks to signal that he hadn't done it, thereby getting himself off the hook with his friends. He provided continuing "cover" for the policy dingdongs on the seventh floor who had fashioned the statement—not, presumably, because he thought they were so wonderful but because letting the assertion be seen as a relatively low-level accident without meaning was, if I dare grandly say it, in the national interest. This is surely what Bob McCloskey concluded when he willingly donned the figurative "Kick Me" sign that he wore at the department and everywhere else in public for the next few days.

It's obvious that in the matter of all this tactical and strategic lying, there can be no one-size-fits-all ethical code to differentiate the serious breaches from the comparatively trivial little pride-sustaining fictions or the wholly unwarranted, self-serving whoppers from the arguably warranted cover stories (when Kennedy's "cold" took him back to Washington from a campaign trip before the Cuban missile crisis burst into public view). And surely such a code would be of no help in making the right choice on the toughest calls of all, which rarely concern small cheatings or huge, conspicuous ones but more often those in-between, medium-size, next-step corruptions that people can so easily graduate to in a world of this kind and justify to themselves. Still, this is the kind of set of instructions people in the capital never stop demanding be drawn up and put into effect to create a clear rule for every possible ethical contingency, leaving nothing to discretion, judgment, the invocation of exceptional circumstances, or the workings of common sense.

But how could such a compendium of regulations be strictly applied to or enforced against the denizens of a community that has built its very dwelling on a treacherous masonry mix of politics and

lies and then gone on to site the dubious thing on the side of a slip-
pery slope? It couldn't.

An ethics code is fine as a sort of overall guideline. But for those
who want to keep their foothold, however far down the slope they
may already have slid, what is required is the self-generated exercise
of restraint day in and day out, a search for the right boundaries and
an instinct for proportion, meaning an instinct for what might be
uncomfortably allowed and what regarded as impermissible and
abusive.

I know the likelihood of any of this happening will seem to others
as remote as it also does to me and thus no more a practical possibility than a dramatic change brought about by a literal adherence to
a highly specific, written code of conduct. The difference is that if a
self-regulating, shamed-into-it ethic were in time to assert itself and
prevail, it would have at least a fighting chance of changing the tenor
of ethical life in the capital.

A promulgation of rules by itself? Never. Just look at the way in
which bipartisan Washington managed to turn the very specific and
detailed prohibitions of the campaign financing laws to its money-
raising advantage in 1996 (and before) and to justify every corrupt
breach with a barrage of legal argument and political sophistry.

No, the needed attributes can be achieved only by the establishment of a dominant culture that propounds—and *lives*—the message about boundaries and distinctions and makes it socially and
politically advantageous to do so. Such a culture has been notori-
ously missing from the capital in recent decades. Except in anything
but extremely imperfect form, it was probably never here.

But when I look around at the personal-hustle ethic by which so
much of political Washington lives—a community that is now far
more unembarrassed, unapologetic, and aggressive about its corruptions than was the case in those long gone days when I was still

trying to figure out what was going on—I am ready to settle for the most imperfect and pitiful form of voluntary constraints that existed in the past, based on a generally accepted idea of what was too much.

Today there seems to be no travesty of decent behavior revealed in the press that is too revolting to be emotionally, even belligerently defended and rationalized on TV by nightfall by the one who committed it. If all else fails, he will tell you his mother sexually abused him as he lay, innocent babe, in the bassinet. Political propriety in Washington was always going to be officially unregulated.

But Washington has become personally unregulated as well, in fact morally anarchic. This is all the worse because, fatuous as it sounds, the only way abuses can be controlled and standards established is by a kind of self-imposed honor code, and I don't think anyone here is waiting up late, like the proprietor of some political Motel Six, for that to happen.

If the politicians and officials of Washington have an infinite number of chances to cheat every day (and an equal number of chances to decide not to), they have nothing on us in the press, who are their neighbors, just one precarious house down the slope. This inescapable circumstance of journalistic life in Washington was what I began to be educated into, in a no-frills crash course, more or less the day I arrived.

I did not have the luxury of focusing on the surprising gap between what the people we were covering purported to be and what they really were. For the press had some of the same problem and presented some of the same perplexities as the politicians, and these I had to deal with, not just marvel at or condemn. At the heart of our problem was the invariable difference between what we knew, in all its maddening refusal to come out morally or ideologically neat, and what we publicly said or printed. Omission may not be an active lie, but it can be a knowing distortion of truth.

How each journalist calibrated the right relationship between the two would be slightly different in most cases, but such variations amounted only to minor distinctions in an unambiguously prevailing custom. You weren't going to blow the whistle on every discrepancy you saw between the posturing pol and the facts of the matter. And you were expected to agree not to report certain information in order to get some indispensable sources to fill you in at all. So we were always making the same kind of ends-and-means calls as the politicians and, like them, I surmise, resolving most of them on the basis of what we wanted to do anyway.

For all its cut corners and withheld revelations and subtle, high-pitched whistles that no one can hear but other Washington dogs, the exercise doesn't represent some kind of sharp-edged conspiracy or concerted effort to deceive, however. That would be far easier to deal with: Blow the cover, win a prize.

But our daily slipping and slopping around is very much like that of the Washington politicians. Our issues and our temptations and our lapses may concern different matters, but like them, every day of our lives we are presented innumerable golden opportunities to get away with cheating on the fairly flexible, vague rules and professional understandings that we informally accept to guide us.

Consider the accepted practices: We don't say everything we know, even when it is highly relevant and also pretty hot. We decide which part to make public. We—yes—knowingly suppress information on a regular basis and essentially lie or at least paint a picture that we know in some important respects is misleading in its incompleteness.

When you put it this way, journalists protest and retreat into the euphemism that such suppression and sometimes plain untruthfulness is merely conforming to the "ground rules." But by the under-the-ground rules, it is institutional custom to let public officials and others we are covering deceive, insofar as pretending they weren't the ones who said what they said may be called a deception, and I don't see why this shouldn't be.

They escape responsibility for their statements, which are attributed to vague, unknown, anonymous others, although we know perfectly well who said what—we just don't tell our viewers or readers. How many such background briefings, starting back then with Rusk and going on to countless others, have I attended over the years, invariably abiding by the stated constraints?

We take a further step into uncomfortable collusion when we agree to their request to go "completely off the record." This amounts to permission to tell us things that would really rattle the political china if we revealed them but that we are duty bound not to say they or anyone else (for instance, mysterious "high officials" or "well-placed sources") even said.

A nice example of where these practices can take you comes from a *New York Times* article in the summer of 1997, although I'm sure if I'd bothered to search I could have found a comparable one from the *Washington Post:* "A spokesman for the tobacco companies involved in the agreement, who *spoke on the condition of anonymity,* said the companies *had no comment* on the cancer society's stance." (I have added the italics.) We have reached the point where you can't even disclose the identity of someone of whom you have asked a question and who has said he prefers not to answer it—and this from a "spokesman," no less.

The fact is that we in the news business are generally walking around with a headful of information we have agreed voluntarily to withhold, each us of making our separate contract with the sources, unless the rules are set and agreed to in a group briefing. If our subjects get too brazen about manipulating our discretion or do things we think take unfair advantage of it, we frequently find some way to expose them, as we sometimes also do with a story that is just too newsy or too urgently cries out to be known by the public for us to obediently sit on it. Usually, we will also come up with some acrobatic justification to cover our breach of the informal contract.

The sorts of things I have been talking about here represent only the relatively above-board part of our little trimmings and shadings, the part that is openly blessed by professional consensus and custom. As a novice I soon learned that such consensus and custom didn't begin to cover the choices and calculations I daily made.

Like the old-timers, I quickly found that I might know things that were juicy or squalid about the national hero of the moment, but were they relevant to the story? Wasn't it the bill that had been enacted and its prospective impact on American life that mattered, rather than that its sponsors were cynical about it and probably neither expected nor even hoped it would ever really go into effect? And in any case, how could you document their attitude? Wouldn't mere assertion of your sense of it involve going into off-limits speculation about low motives—as much too much traditionally does, the glancing shots, the little hit-and-run asides in passing?

Well, yes, but wait a minute: It probably *was* something you should at least signal in some subtle fashion, even if only so other Washington initiates would pick up on it when they read your story. (This would only in part be out of a sense of responsibility for having created the illusion of the pols' good faith in the first place. It would in equal part probably be a self-interested ploy to keep press pals from jeering that you had been taken in, a Washington journalist's idea of a fate worse than dismemberment by ax.) And when you got through with all this, you probably found yourself asking something like: "By the way, how did we all get snookered into protecting the anonymity of that guy who is now out when he lied so egregiously about what he had done, confident that we had all been silenced by our acceptance of the ground rules?"

I have made the internal deliberations involved sound too tortured, too like the ordeal of some flayed saint undergoing a dark night of the soul, when the point is actually the opposite. The point is how routine and unremarkable and almost automatic such calculations and considerations become for people in our business, how readily we incorporate them into our workaday life. What is relevant? What is dirty? What is fair? What is just ever so *slightly* cheap, and you know it? What is conventional wisdom and pack-pressure leading you someplace you don't really want to go but don't quite have the guts or self-assurance not to? You're fiddling with this stuff all day long and making snap judgments on it.

Well before my two years of Washington hotel living were up, I believe I had acquired the same "doesn't everybody?" attitude and bearing that had baffled me in the early days. The best illustration of my journalistic learning curve in those years concerned civil rights. For long before I had figured out much of anything about the elaborate workings of the Southern Directorate, I could not help becoming aware of the following fact: So far as who was doing what at the start of the 1960s to dismantle what was still official, government-authorized and government-enforced discrimination against blacks—discrimination that practically everyone today would find not just abhorrent but unbelievable—I seemed to have the lineup of players just about completely wrong.

Yes, northern liberal Democrats tended to take a strong stand. But for an awful lot of them it was a wall-poster-only stand, accompanied by neither effort nor particular interest in whether anything happened, which for a couple of years it did not. Some actually seemed to benefit politically from their pose as valiant, thwarted warriors and to find that a suitable substitute for lifting a finger to get anything done.

This didn't cover them all, but it covered far too many of them for me, even in my initial naiveté, not to notice. True, in Congress and the Kennedy White House both, there were some making strenuous, sincere efforts to get administration support for at least a little action, and some heroic young people were preparing to risk (and lose) their lives for the cause in the South. But far more liberal Democrats in Washington seemed to buy the pragmatic wisdom that any move at all to give meaning just yet to those stirring things they and Kennedy had promised while campaigning would be politically suicidal.

The argument was that the president was operating on such a slim margin of support that he had to cool it with the southern leaders of Congress or else he would lose a lot of other things he justly held dear. So I pondered this, a novel thought to me, but one I supposed worth seriously considering, and I came to respect it, in a kind of uneasy, provisional way.

But that wore off after a while, or the position became suspect to me as I eventually looked around and saw how convenient it had become over time for all who had so readily settled into it. I got to wondering about where the end point on a position like that might be in the basic Washington weighing of self-interest against principle. Would there never come a time when you would say: "Yes, this is a politically practical and defensible stance. But I'm getting a little too comfortable in it. We're all getting too comfortable. Is it a reason, or has it become just a rationalization? Doesn't this garden party need a couple of skunks?"

I think you can't understand the underground, rumbling, volcanic moral force this issue had unless you understand what the argument was about and how utterly different from now were the government-countenanced practices still existing at the time. We are not talking about an exchange of complex propositions on the meaning of affirmative action. It was only three decades ago or so, but in political and cultural time it could have been the ice age.

As an example, I am talking about an era in which black Americans were not allowed to enter any roadside restaurant on Maryland's Route 40. This became an issue mainly because the exclusion was creating dread "diplomatic incidents" when black ambassadors from newly independent African states who were traveling between Washington and the UN would be rudely ejected from the various establishments they tried to enter. The administration's response was for the State Department to seek special waivers for these foreign blacks so they could patronize the greasy spoons and rest stops if they wished. Officialdom explained that it had taken this tiny step to avoid "diplomatic embarrassment" to the United States. I thought it a truly amazing conception of what the U.S. government should find embarrassing about the situation.

Trying to sort out the plausibility of the various explanations for putting the civil rights agenda on indefinite hold in such times, as well as the relative sincerity of those espousing or at least going along with the move, became part of the story in my view, and it consumed my interest for a time. It was not an attempt to arrive at a political position but an attempt to answer a baseline reportorial question: What are these guys doing anyway? Lying? Being practical and responsible? Copping out? I noticed that I had become progressively more interested than indignant, a sign that, for better or for worse, I was adapting in some Darwinian way—a feather here, a claw there—to my new habitat and job.

Yet none of this essentially intellectualized effort to puzzle out the political tactics of the thing had anywhere near the impact of a developing realization: At that moment the principal force truly committed to taking *immediate* action against the kinds of crude racial repression still officially in place seemed to be, of all things, a bunch of Republicans, many of them nationally unknown.

They weren't all northeasterners and Californians with sizable liberal or black or urban constituencies either, although senators like New York's Jacob Javits, New Jersey's Clifford Case, California's Tom Kuchel, and others were a part of the group. Far more intriguing and, frankly, at first incredible to me, was that the effort's most tireless organizers and/or communicants were a few generally conservative midwestern House members, notably Tom Curtis of Missouri and Bill McCullough, a white-haired, conventional Republican in his sixties, from the small town of Piqua, Ohio.

You could go and talk to these men. You could plumb what in a few of them—especially Curtis—seemed to be an obsession with the subject. You could learn of the kind of continuous internal communication that went on within this unexpected, loosely organized little community of conviction. Its elders were staffed by young men who were subsequently to take off in wildly different ideological directions and make their own names in public affairs and Republican politics—Bruce Chapman and Stephen Horn and Lee Auspitz and George Gilder.

But then they were mere kids with a cause. They were equally zealous about busting the system of legally sanctioned exclusion that was such an anachronism and an offense by then. They didn't believe the whole bipartisan, pro-civil-rights collectivity in the capital, so much more vast than their tiny group, had to fall silent and immobile for an indeterminate time to appease those autocratic southern committee chairman. They believed with an exertion of will something could and should be accomplished or at least started now.

So my boss in New York had been right: As the proprietress of a whole collection of weakly based but adamantly held ideas, I was utterly unprepared for the existence of such a group and felt as if I had happened on some political Brigadoon.

I don't doubt that they relished the taunting of the recalcitrant and somewhat embarrassed liberal Democrats—why shouldn't they have? And of course they didn't manage to reverse the combined will of the Democratic administration and a majority of their own party in Congress to hold off change as long as possible.

But their unrelenting pressure was wonderful—an invaluable help in keeping the subject alive and keeping some of those who should have been helping but weren't at least fairly nervous; this small band of gung-ho Republicans did finally shame some of their Democratic colleagues into support; and, decisively, when the tableaux of Alabama fire hoses being turned on peaceful demonstrators changed the political landscape and civil rights legislation finally stood a chance, they were there and ready.

Bill McCullough was then ranking Republican on the Judiciary Committee. The morning after he had played a critical part in sending the civil rights bill to the House floor for action—defying the will of many of his colleagues—he came to the chamber to find lying across his desk, and the desks of all those Republicans who supported him, tightly furled black umbrellas. They were meant to cast McCullough and the others as Neville Chamberlains, weaklings and betrayers of their own.

The stunt simply sounds silly now, but it had an eerie, sinister feel to it at the time. I was struck with how much more McCullough had paid in than had all those congressmen from districts where, unlike his, it was to their political advantage to support the bill and who, having acquiesced in no action for all that time, were now sighing, "At last!" and pretending it was their handiwork.

The Senate, where the big showdown on the House bill was to come, was a kind of advanced seminar in gradations of Washington dissembling and political trickery for me, a study in the sliding-scale lie and its uses. The most absorbing aspect of it was the continuous effort to tease along and placate minority leader Dirksen, whose support was (1) critical and (2) clearly available—provided he was dealt with right.

Hubert Humphrey, then Senate Democratic whip and a man totally and disruptively committed to civil rights action since anyone could remember, was in charge of placating Dirksen and anticipating his every political need. He was, during that period, forever giving Dirksen credit for things that he, Humphrey, had actually done and, as important, seeming to take seriously the endless fake objections Dirksen would raise by way of appearing to be fighting for drastic modification and softening of the bill's provisions.

This was a classic "cover" operation. There were a lot of Republicans already committed to some form of the bill. But there were not enough to get it past a southern filibuster. The greasing of Dirksen and his pretense of effecting many changes in the legislation more to his reluctant colleagues' liking enabled the Illinoisan to bring a critical number of additional Republicans along—this in a year when his party was cranking up to nominate Barry Goldwater for president at a convention that would reek of hostility to a civil rights bill.

I remember Dirksen's summoning us to the press gallery one day well before the convention to announce that he just finished reading the bill's Title II very carefully. It was the title that banned discrimination in public accommodations (such as was happening on Maryland's Route 40 and all over the South and in not a few places in the North).

Dirksen said ominously that he had something like 121 objections to it that would absolutely have to be fixed for him to support the bill. We all knew this was bunk but reported it because it was his stated position and because we couldn't prove it was bunk. As expected, the 121 objections began to sheer off like vast sheets of ice from a mountainside—sixty suddenly crashing into the abyss here, twenty-three more a day or two later there—until only a few items that he really wanted negotiated were left.

Dirksen's performance was artful, disingenuous, and immensely constructive. Taken with the supporting roles of Humphrey and others in making it work, it allowed the enactment of that legislation. The minority leader performed this maneuver because he believed, among other things, that it was a highly worthy effort that would bring him a smile from history and credit to his party for the fact that a higher proportion of Senate Republicans than Democrats had in the end also voted for it.

He was enraged when it became a target of attack at the convention that summer, in particular by candidate Goldwater. Shortly after the convention Dirksen professed to have been overcome by some physical ailment none of us had heard of before and abruptly checked into Passavant Hospital in Chicago. His prolonged stay there prevented his campaigning for the Goldwater ticket. I'm in no position to gainsay whatever may have been going on medically. But at the time a lot of us thought that it wasn't what it seemed, either.

The continuing professional calculation of the job I was settling into concerned finding the right boundary lines myself. They represented determinations you made over and over, all but reflexively after a while. First, how much should the Washington journalist buy into the two-track, wink-at-the-little-lies, know-more-than-you-ever-tell system? It has to be mastered. You have to be at least fluent in its language and aware of its major hypocrisies and badly kept secrets to know what is going on.

A retiring press spokesman at the State Department once facetiously warned his successor that the most unpleasant mistake he ever made in the job was not a foreign policy mistake but the mistake of leaving me out of a background briefing. He reported, accurately, that upon reading the unsourced stories in the morning, I surmised where they had come from—no great feat of deduction—and called him at dawn and bayed and howled until he promised never to do such a thing again.

If you are writing political essays and critiques that are actually improved by a measure of distance from all this activity, it is one thing. But if you are reporting and trying to analyze a news situation that requires you to have the major elements of what is happening right and on deadline, you are going to have to take advantage of that system and get a little smudged up by it insofar as under the conditions it imposes, you will not be leveling with the reader.

There has been an enormous revision of the unstated standards for the press in this regard, a cleaning up of the act. An older generation of famous journalists was much more obliging to its government sources, much more willing to keep its secrets, and much more involved in its actual policymaking than it ever should have been—and than the successor generation in Washington today would dream of being.

I think their falling into camp was largely an unconscious after-effect of the close cooperation and feeling of common purpose that developed between many of these men and the U.S. government during the war and then almost immediately afterward, when an unfamiliar cold war was at its most ominous. Correspondents had grown accustomed to letting officials alone so far as their secrets were concerned or keeping the secrets when they knew them, especially any that bore the holy insignia of "national security." And as journalists as different as Jack Anderson and Joe Alsop have written, they also had no reservations about jumping in with privately offered policy advice or even offers of active engagement in government business while they were still reporting and writing.

I'm glad we broke with that tradition, but I sometimes think we are unjustifiably smug about it, in that in much more insidious, uninspected ways journalists nowadays are often working well within the news and political parameters that government sets and doing its bidding, all the while boasting of our newfound independence. We almost unconsciously accept and parrot the PR framework the government constructs, establishing the outlines of an issue, the terms of what will be considered "winning" and "losing," and so forth. Our concept of what is news, of what is important, is made to conform to the government's terms. We far too rarely go outside those terms and report a universe we see, as distinct from the world they press on us, a world in which small victories and impermanent defeats are made to loom much larger than they have any right to. To me the irony is that many of those who are most thoroughly captive to this palmed-off perspective—merely another form of "spin"—have adopted a kind of surly swagger in their pressroom dealings with officialdom, as if they were really unreachable, unpersuadable troublemakers.

But whether people are in the tank in this odd respect or working truly independently, if you compare the postwar and Kennedy years with now, what you will see are two starkly different landscapes. The happy-go-lucky, semiacknowledged element of the collaboration is gone. On the contrary, we have become bristly, correct, and much more exacting in the formal arrangements we are generally willing to sign off on.

This is largely a consequence of our having to admit how badly gulled we had been over the years by officials' taking ever larger advantage of journalists' postwar complaisance in accepting the prescribed silences and collusions of the two-track system. But even in the years well before the government-versus-press turmoil began to heat up, as a novice journalist I would routinely calculate how far I should wander into that web of consensual deception.

The other continuing calculation was how much to incorporate the human dimension of these political dramas into a purportedly political story. How much did such considerations matter? Often they were decisive to the outcome. Did they therefore have a place in my account? Or were they irrelevant to the details of the bill? Did it matter to the ultimate worth of the legislation what *anyone's* motive was?

Well, no—and yet reporting a saga such as that of the civil rights bill along conventional lines of who was for it (at the moment) and who against was to perpetuate a political cliché and falsehood. It was to give an unwarranted break to some politicians who were cheating and deceiving their constituents.

All right: what business is that of ours? If the voters are dumb enough to elect the guy, that's their problem, and we overstep when we get into the mode of punishers and sentence passers. Except of course that we *are* the ones reporting the misleading story in the first place and have that aforementioned obligation to put some of these things into it.

How deep do you vanish, then, into such extrapolitical, human comedy dimensions of what you report? As always, there was no fixed or generally applicable standard beyond: look out. You had to decide each time what part of the personality and behavior stuff was relevant and at what point you were losing the signal and in danger of turning a political piece about legislation or executive branch policy into *All My Children.*

It was somewhere in the course of trying to sort out these things in JFK's Washington that I became engrossed in what I was doing and realized I had stopped pining for my lost life in the Village. I figured that was a pretty good thing for me and a wonderful thing for the future of the novel.

For my imagination was now fully engaged in deciphering the intentions and handiwork of people who were neither quite fully human nor quite disembodied abstractions and agents of policy to me. They were Washington hybrid life forms, part person and part political/professional caption or label, the way so many of us in the capital see others and lament that we ourselves are seen. Their personal stories were relevant, but finally only in a limited way, and every assertion you made about them was subject to verification. I had thrown myself enthusiastically into this pursuit, which surely unfit my imagination totally for the incompatible pursuit of fiction.

Sometimes I would divert myself by speculating how the great novels of the ages might have begun if this strange new journalistic me had written them: "Stately, plump Buck Mulligan (not his real name) . . . "; "Happy families are all alike; every unhappy family is unhappy in its own way, according to data released this week by the University of Michigan Social Science Research Center."

What follows is a memo I sent to *Washington Post* publisher Don Graham, executive editor Ben Bradlee, and ombudsman Dick Harwood in the spring of 1984. Don, Ben, and Dick had asked my opinion of a set of ethics guidelines they were drawing up that would cover all news employees on the paper. They wanted to know whether, as editorial page editor (which I by now was), I thought it should cover editorial department staff too, since we were considered a separate and independent part of the paper. I did.

The memo shows what a long distance the media (as we were now universally and unaffectionately known) had traversed from relative anonymity as pressies to center-stage prominence as a national player. The Washington press had mutated into a much more densely populated and self-conscious institution that was now routinely reviled on the national bullhorn—and glorified and worried about as a destructive, unaccountable force in American politics.

It was also now increasingly reported on in the manner that we reported on others who, fairly enough, found our own discomfort at being so covered inexpressibly funny. But the memo also shows that despite these really big changes, which had occurred over a couple of decades, the fundamental pitfalls, dilemmas, and temptations the Washington journalist daily faced had not noticeably changed from those one-horse days to the later era of post-Watergate glory and glitz. It was just that a lot more people were involved in news coverage and a lot more people were watching them.

The memo also suggests that, as always, the questions being raised could not be resolved by managerial promulgation and enforcement of guidelines. It all came down in the end to individual good-faith efforts to interpret the code honestly and draw the right lines and resist a lot of temptations.

Dick/Ben/Don:

Here are a few thoughts on the material that went out on a proposed new code of ethics. First, at the end of the memo the question is put whether the paper should prohibit acceptance of honoraria for speaking before special interest groups as it does fees from governmental agencies. I think the answer is yes. We are currently very vulnerable on this. It sits ill with the rest of our policies.

Second, I think we need to be very careful about that part that says, "We want employees to understand that gossiping with outsiders—and particularly with employees of other news organizations—about events at the *Post* is discouraged." I think employees already understand that, it's just that some of them don't especially care; and I believe there is nothing that the paper can or should try to do about it: we, who live off the willingness of employees of other organizations, public and private, to tell us things, can't be in the position of leaning on our own for doing the same thing.

Third, the section on entanglements and relationships in general with people about whom we write is interesting and important. There is an age-old journalistic problem here, but the solution is not for the writer to cut himself off from any but the formal, office-hour encounter with those in the news. We need to see them more and know them better. The hard, but absolutely essential part is to maintain strict journalistic standards in writing about such persons—whatever discomfort that may entail. This is what someone such as Chal [the *Post*'s longtime national correspondent Chalmers Roberts] was a genius at— you'd see everyone in government at his home, he was their friend and their continual interrogator and frequent nemesis. He would serve them a drink today and belt hell out of them tomorrow. I remember [editorial writer Alan] Barth calling [Supreme Court justice] Abe Fortas when the *Life* story [on Fortas's financial malfeasance] came out—Abe was his very close friend—and interviewing him as to what happened with a toughness that would have made you think they hardly knew each other. This, as I say, is the hard solution, but in my view, the only practical and productive one.

On this same subject—the relationship with objects of our attention—there is another problem worth mentioning. From time to time we here in editorial get calls from reporters on the staff urging us to write editorials denouncing something or other or stopping some bill from going through, and some of these calls are very agitated, betraying a commitment that isn't supposed to be in there. Most of the calls are negative. They want us to help stop something that is about to happen or to call for some investigation or indictment or electrocution . . . well, not quite, but they want us to help them "get" someone. This suggests to me that in addition to the problem of the journalist who likes the people he is covering too much, there is the problem of the one that dislikes them too much or gets a personal vendetta going or is merely (and unethically and maybe unconsciously) committed to seeing his own journalistic stories vindicated in the downfall of the unbeloved one. "Emotional relations with public figures" [a phrase from Dick, Ben, and Don's memo] can include negative emotions, and I think we have to be on the lookout for reporters and editorialists indulging them to the detriment of fair comment.

More on relationships: I think somewhere it should be put in the code that members of the staff are not to give [private] ad-

vice to public people. I find there is a constant effort of politicians and other titans of our time to get us to advise or tell them
what we "would think" if they did this or that, etc. I tell them to
get lost, or that they should go ahead and do it and read what
we think about in the next days' Blat. But this is a constant pressure on journalists and, I expect, a seductive pressure on some,
and it seems to me a word on it should be included in the code.

Fourth, we editors can check a lot and question a lot and use
our own knowledge and resources to make sure that what
people write for which we are responsible is fair and straight-
arrow. But day by day we must depend on them and have confidence in what they say. We are at their mercy on this one big
thing: when they have goofed, even in the face of a complaint
from a credible person about whom they wrote, they are in a
position to snow us as to what happened or what the facts or
circumstances were or what they were told or what is going on
generally.

There is, I think, no rule we can apply and enforce here, no
foolproof way to ensure that we are not so snowed. And the
human temptation to cover it up and not to look bad is ancient
and often overpowering and, since we ourselves look better if
the flaw is not revealed, there is a kind of silent incentive to
accept the version of events that holds the reporter or editorialist (and thus his editors) blameless. But what we have to do is to
make utterly plain that honor around this place and respect and
admiration go to the person who has the character and guts to
be fair and to let error be publicly admitted—and fast. Somehow that has to be acknowledged and articulated as a big ethical
issue of our business, and one that people on our staff violate at
their peril.

These are my thoughts on reading the ethics package. The

only one I haven't expressed is that I think the proposals are very good, and I would expect those who labor back here in the Bermuda Triangle to abide by them, too.

Meg

Among journalists the most hotly—and often hypocritically—argued of the questions raised in the memo concern degrees of acquaintanceship, cordiality, and familiarity with the objects of our coverage. The thought is that knowing these people, spending time in their company that is not strictly along such professional lines as asking them questions in the office or on the phone or at a press briefing, is inevitably corrupting, if not already evidence of corruption. This is the absolutist version, and people always seem willing to make exceptions for themselves and their own relationships, which they understand have grown out of adventitious circumstances or are of a nature that is not in any sense corrupt.

The problem is that the critics of others rarely make distinctions as to how the social relationship came about and how it affects the journalist's work, if it does. It is true that there are cases of people in our business who are far too cozy with the people they cover and unashamedly do their bidding. This happens all along the spectrum from liberal to conservative.

Columnist George Will became the object of much criticism for helping Ronald Reagan prepare for his 1980 debate with Jimmy Carter and then commenting on Reagan's performance. Other contributions, consisting of general advice and actual help with speechwriting for politicians by sympathetic journalists—in particular Bobby Kennedy and to some extent Bill Clinton—have remained secret and/or gone unnoted. Michael Beschloss's book on the LBJ tapes, *Taking Charge,* provides other instances.

I used to work with one such cat's-paw who, when he was about to spout the official line that he had got over drinks the night before from his dear friend and next-door neighbor, would invariably begin, "It is felt . . ." There was never any acknowledgment of who it was who "felt" these things. Nor was there ever any doubt in our minds who it was.

By contrast, played straight professionally, there can also be benefits in some of these relationships with people you are covering. There are times when they will level with you and provide an insight (not always or necessarily flattering to them) that you did not have and could not have gotten in formal questioning of a stranger.

The association may familiarize you with the real but hidden internal bashings and jealousies and ambitions that are wracking their side in a hot political dispute but rarely publicly acknowledged and more often denied. There is to many of these relationships an opportune, superficial, misleading sense of old-buddyness; one participant or the other, usually the government person, will be shocked at the speed and cold-bloodedness with which he is dropped when he has left office.

There is another kind of amiability that develops between professional journalists and people they cover that is a function of the need for civility among people who live together professionally in the small enclave of political Washington and, no matter how sharp their conflict today, are going to have to do business with again tomorrow—on the committee, on the phone, on the chamber floor, in the office, at a press conference. A conflict does not end their dealings with each other. It would be unnatural for everyone to go personally icy and aggrieved on everyone else on the basis of their disagreements, although they may refight them on the phone; and it would be unnatural if a certain saving companionability did not develop among them as well. They thus maintain a veneer of politeness even when they are likely feeling anything but friendly.

Such an old and practiced hand as Lyndon Johnson apparently didn't always understand this. Beschloss cites a tape of LBJ talking

in private that perfectly sums up the way the thing so often works:
"The *New York Times* called up down here and said they wanted us
to please come by and meet their editorial board. . . . I spent two and
a half hours and we had a wonderful meeting. . . . Then the next
morning, they showed their independence by saying I was a son of
a bitch."

Encountering people at social occasions the night after we may
have blasted them on the *Post*'s morning editorial page, I adopted a
personal policy of being the first to go over to them and start a conversation that gives the aggrieved one a fair chance to total me. I suspect I am usually wearing what Stephen Potter, the author of *The
Theory and Practice of Gamesmanship,* called "the V-shaped smile"
(there is no tighter, more unconvincing smile).

Usually the person responds with a V-shaped smile of his own
and a few strained jocularities, which aren't very convincing either,
and I respond in phony kind. The exception is if the spouse is standing right there; then you can get loudly denounced to hell and back,
and that has happened too. I still cringe when I recall my first such
public dressing-down in the 1960s by the enraged and voluble wife
of a postmaster general. It stopped conversation throughout the
room. But usually the conventional, dissembling decorum prevails.

It would be inaccurate, however, and a cop-out to say that all the
apparent friendly relationships between members of the press and
people in government, or among people in one line of work or the
other who represent starkly opposing points of view, are merely an
expedient façade or a phony construct that is a means of getting the
job done. Many are real.

I was once at a party in New York with a bunch of politically involved conservative writers, about half of whom lived in New York,
while the rest of the guests—a more politically mixed bunch—had
come up from Washington. The room split just about evenly down
the middle when the conversation turned to the seeming affability

that marked the relationships of political and institutional adversaries in the capital, people who were continually savaging one another in the press or thwarting one another's most deeply desired programs and yet were seen having a drink and a little chuckle over an unrelated matter later in the day.

The people from outside Washington kept saying two things. One was that they couldn't believe their conservative friends from Washington when they said, as they had that night, that they actually personally really *liked* some of the liberal writers with whom they so deeply disagreed; the other was that if they did, they were not, as one phrased it, "serious people." You could have reversed the political roles from conservative to liberal, I suspect, and had the same conversation, divided the same way along Washington-versus-elsewhere lines.

The incredulous, and occasionally horrified, reaction to all this apparent good fellowship in the capital had of course been my own when I first arrived in town. I too had felt it must either have a politically and professionally neutering effect or be evidence of a lack of seriousness on the part of the participants. Over time I was to observe the distinctions within the apparent bonhomie I've been trying to enumerate, in particular that large part of it that was entirely superficial, the V-shaped smile kind of thing. I also observed that another part of it was not superficial but could be called communal and inevitable. It's not just that people in Washington, no matter which side of the political or institutional divide they are on, have to work with each other day in and day out. They also have to live with each other.

In addition to people, whether adversary or not, whom they see and work with every day, people in Washington have families, neighbors, fellow congregants in churches, and kids in the same schools, Scout troops, and bands and on the same teams. Political and professional barriers are transcended by the familiarity and common purpose that result from all this. It's not just that people may get to know and appreciate each other in such a nonworking context but that they may find themselves allies on a whole different realm of nonworking issues as well—such as trying to get the laggard municipal authorities to pick up the mass of wet leaves that are blighting the road they all live on or finding out where their teenage children are late at night.

During some of the roughest of the hostilities between the Nixon administration and the *Washington Post* in the early 1970s, when our managing editor Gene Patterson's daughter and her high school classmate, Bob Haldeman's son, were out together one night well after their announced curfews, the two sets of parents were frantically consulting each other, trying to figure out where they were, bonding in the way that only parents in such circumstances can—and undeterred, as you would suppose, by their contemporaneous dispute over our publication of the Pentagon Papers.

Finally, there is another distinctive class of relationship with high government officials: those that have developed over a long period of time and date from well before the principals ended up in their current fancy jobs. At any given time in the capital, there is a core of people who more or less grew up together, not from childhood but from their professional youth in Washington, who were beginning-worker kids together. When I was new in town, one of my friends was Nancy Gore, who lived with her family in the same residential hotel where I had been stashed, the Fairfax, and I well remember my acquaintanceship with her much younger brother Al.

There were others I knew along the way who were, when I first knew them, academics in think tanks or assistants to the assistant to the assistant in various government offices—Joe Califano, James Schlesinger, James Woolsey, Tom Foley, Dick Darman, Alice Rivlin—who were later to have cabinet jobs or, in Foley's case, become Speaker of the House. There was Pat Moynihan, who as a young academic wrote articles for the *Reporter,* as did Henry

Kissinger from Harvard. There was Madeleine Albright, then married to a journalist colleague, Joe Albright. There was Leon Panetta, who was, when I met him, a young civil rights assistant in the Nixon administration who lost his job and left his party over what he considered its failure to act on the issue.

These were among the many contemporaries who at different times were friends and went in and out of office during the many years we knew each other, often from think tank or press to government, from opposition or detachment to incumbency, from junior drone status to big-shot title. In the case of some reporters who periodically crossed over to work in government, who went from outside to inside and back again, there seemed to be a need for constant readjustment of the rules of engagement.

Were we colleagues in the press this week or combatants in the ring? The first call I got from Doug Cater, when he eventually went to work in Lyndon Johnson's White House, was to berate me for writing an item that was a "base canard" about the White House appointment process, which he insisted was false and I insisted was true. (It was the puzzling appointment of Meredith Wilson, famous for *The Music Man,* to the National Endowment for the Humanities, not even the arts. This was a mistaken-identity snafu: The Meredith Wilson who was supposed to be asked was a humanities professor at the University of Minnesota and a close friend and mentor of Vice President Humphrey.)

In any event, the new, reconditioned status of our relationship had been established. We now represented different and often incompatible interests. But the prior friendship could hardly be made not to have existed nor been summarily cut off, although Doug declined my smart-aleck suggestion that we argue out the issue over a lunch of base canard à l'orange at the Sans Souci.

What it required, as is generally true in all these ambiguous relationships, was to be managed with integrity and care—and not to be allowed to become an impediment to straight, clear, honest, and if need be extremely unfriendly treatment of the government friend by the journalist when the occasion arose. Nor, I suppose, from the point of view of the one who goes into government, could it honestly be allowed to become a license to treat the old friend with rank favoritism or tell him anything he wanted to know or exempt him generally from the constraints on others.

Still, it must be acknowledged that the journalist does have an advantage in the ease of the old-time relationship, which does not entirely vanish even under new, mutually wary and cautious behavior and sometimes outright warfare. In the midst of the chaos created by the Clinton administration's first health care proposal, which seemed to a lot of us impractical, overreaching, and premised on suspect figures to boot, and when it was near impossible to get anyone in the administration to answer, without a load of spin, questions that had been raised by the opposition or by our own reading of the provisions, we took advantage of such friendships.

I invited Alice Rivlin, then at the Office of Management and Budget, a specialist on health care reform, once briefly a writer for the *Post,* and a woman known to have some misgivings about the bill, to a small dinner. It was attended by *Post* people—David Broder, Peter Milius, John Anderson, Jodie Allen—who wrote about the subject, knew a lot about it, knew Alice as a friend and former colleague, and had plenty of reservations of their own about the bill. She was asked and agreed to answer our questions and give the best case for the bill that she could. We knew she would be frank and plausible. She was anything but starry-eyed about the bill, which made her defense of various aspects of it far more credible than the hooey being dished up to us by defenders and attackers up until then.

All this is about how it works when things are going relatively well. Now a story of how it works, when it works, in the worst case.

It is an elaboration of the allusion to Alan Barth and Justice Fortas that I made in my memo to Don, Ben, and Dick.

On a Monday morning early in May 1969, the capital was obsessed with talk about a story that had appeared in *Life* magazine over the weekend. It said that Justice Fortas had been found to have accepted a $20,000 fee from a convicted stock manipulator's family foundation three years before, when Fortas was already a sitting member of the high court.

He had returned the money, but only eleven months later. Understandably, there was a huge uproar. And although it was later to be revealed that the story had been leaked to *Life* by minority leader Gerald Ford and other Republicans on the Hill, with the assistance of Attorney General John Mitchell (who himself was to end up in prison), none of that, if it had been known, would have made a sitting justice's taking money in the fashion Fortas did any prettier—or less disqualifying.

For us on the editorial page of the *Post*, this was an especially tough one—painful and, in truth, embarrassing. For years, we had been on the record as admirers of Fortas's decisions and basic approach to civil rights and civil liberties, as reflected both in his years as a justice and his decades before that as a lawyer, when he was willing to take politically radioactive cases and work pro bono for indigent defendants others also didn't want to bother with.

He had been subjected to a deluge of assaults over the years for this record, and we had been among his most unfailing, noisy, indignant, fervent champions. But this action, as reported by *Life*, could not, in our opinion, even be justified, never mind championed. Fortas had offered what struck all of us as a very weak explanation of his taking of the funds, and we all agreed that if he didn't have a better accounting to make, the offense was serious enough that he should leave the Court. We decided we would see if we could get in touch with him that day and ask him if that statement in fact represented the last word he had to say in explaining what he had done.

What made all of this particularly poignant was the presence in the room of the greatly distinguished and beloved senior editorial writer Alan Barth, a gentle, entertaining man of fierce devotion to his principles, who was one of Abe Fortas's closest friends. It was a classic example of the friendship between journalist and government player that has its beginning a long way back and grows over the years as each moves on to new positions.

Theirs was a longtime Washington relationship that had begun in the 1940s when Fortas, not long out of Harvard, was a young New Dealer in FDR's administration, and Barth, himself not that long out of Yale, had just come to the *Post*. They continued to be friends in the years that followed, when Fortas, gone into private practice, became involved in the litigation of political cases and Barth was asking and writing about them.

They also shared a passion for classical violin (Fortas played; Barth did not) and were both part of a little fraternity of amateur and virtuoso professional "fiddlers," as it was said, and spent many evenings either listening to or playing in homegrown string quartets. Barth, who wrote about civil liberties and civil rights, had other close friends on the Supreme Court with whom he had also more or less grown up in Washington over the years. He never hesitated to clop them editorially when they had ruled in some fashion he didn't approve of.

But the Fortas episode went way beyond that. It was not about a friend's being wrongheaded and making what you considered a very bad policy judgment or legal interpretation. It was about a friend's being personally corrupt.

Knowing Alan, none of us was surprised when the conversation was ending to hear him volunteer to be the one who took on the project. And knowing him, there was also no hint of feeling that there was a conflict of interest here: He was not volunteering to do the job so he could do it in a way that would contain the damage to his friend. On the contrary, more than anyone in the room Alan would feel bound to blur no edges, cut no corners. He would call Fortas, he then said, and ask if there were a less feeble, more convincing explanation. He completely shared the analysis of the rest of the group, he said.

When he made the call, he immediately explained to whoever answered the phone (Fortas was of course being scarce) that he was calling in his professional capacity, so as not to slide through the screening on a deception. He put his friend Fortas through some very hard questioning and reported to us that Fortas, in his view, had no better explanation than the inadequate one he had made earlier, which in fact got worse the longer Fortas elaborated on it. Alan believed we should call on him to step down. He would write the editorial himself.

Alan well knew—we all knew—that although there are plenty of areas in which *Washington Post* editorials have virtually no influence, zilch, this was one that would be relatively earthshaking: Fortas's longtime, most stubborn champions and ideological soulmates calling on him to quit the Court. Fortas would of course know Barth had written it. And although the authorship of an editorial is meant to be anonymous when it appears, as it represents the consensus of the group, Barth and his style and his area of expertise were well enough known around town to mean that everyone else who was interested would know too. This could only strengthen its impact.

These are the first two paragraphs of the editorial that Barth wrote, which appeared the following morning:

The public explanation given by Mr. Justice Fortas of his relations with the Wolfson Family Foundation is not good enough. It does not deal candidly or precisely with the allegations made by *Life* Magazine and these are quite precise allegations, having to do with a particular sum of money, $20,000, held by Justice Fortas for a particular period of time, 11 months, before it was returned. It begins with something that sounds like a denial and ends as something like a confirmation of *Life*'s story. And because it thus raises more questions than it answers about the facts in this matter, the statement succeeds, in the end, only in raising the fundamental question of whether the Justice adequately appreciates the great obligations imposed by his high public office upon his private life.

Unless Justice Fortas can provide a more compelling explanation, publicly and in some reasonable detail, he can best serve himself, the Court on which he sits and his country by stepping down.

Barth wrote that about one of his close friends. We work in a business so weird that it is a badge of honor to be prepared to set aside normal, friendly impulses to defend a friend in trouble; instead, the ethical obligation is to inspect the cause of the trouble dispassionately and, if the friend is found to be at fault, to report unsparingly on what he did wrong or, in the case of editorial writers, to give no special breaks in assessing and (usually) denouncing that wrongdoing.

That is the nonnegotiable condition of friendship between journalists and the people they write about. It is often hard to honor, and there are people in our business who don't even try; it also bespeaks a certain arrogance and coldness. But none of that changes what is rightly required of us in these uncomfortable situations.

A couple of decades after the Fortas affair, long after I had become editor of the page, I faced a somewhat similar situation, and I thought of Barth as I was getting ready to take it on. I tried to follow his lead, although my language was a lot less temperate than his had been. He had written out of deep disappointment; I wrote out of anger.

The situation concerned Alan Simpson, the Republican senator and minority whip from Wyoming. Our friendship had developed through all the classic Washington phases. Simpson wrote me a note about a *Newsweek* column I had written.

I didn't know him or any of the other relatively newly elected conservative Republican senators from the West. I wanted to meet him and see what he was about, although I already had a cliché notion of him imprinted in my head and even flaunted this going down the editorial hallway en route to the appointment we set up. I don't remember exactly what I said so flippantly to my colleagues as I sauntered by, but it was no doubt something like: "I'm going out to meet one of those new, creepy right-wing senators today!" I can only imagine what he said to his staff on the way out to meet me. The odd couple.

But he turned out to be Alan Simpson—funny; irreverent about the political behavior of Democrats and Republicans alike; no stranger to the Washington complex, as his father was a senator before him; and given, over the years, to staking out and unflaggingly pursuing some very important legislation that was not necessarily approved of by either his Wyoming constituents or his national party colleagues.

He was the lead, practically the only voice challenging the financially profitable and intimidating lobby of the American Association of Retired Persons (AARP). He was a rare zealot pressing for humane immigration reform. There were other such campaigns. He was a conservative Republican with a penchant for humor and civility and one willing to break out from the pack on issues he cared about if he thought his side was wrong. You could exchange very tough language and appraisals of each other's handiwork without coming to personal blows—until he suddenly seemed to have acquired a sharper, meaner, more personal edge, especially in any matter concerning the dread media.

Then, during the Gulf War, when Peter Arnett of CNN stayed

on in Baghdad, made plain he was limited in what he could cover and say, but rightly thought it would be of value to be there with cameras and the opportunity to report even in an acknowledgedly censored fashion, Simpson let it fly.

George Bush's* press secretary Marlin Fitzwater and others had already criticized Arnett for showing film of bombed residential neighborhoods (where, Arnett made clear, he had been taken by authorities and was not allowed to roam freely). But Simpson ratcheted the attack up about a hundred rungs to an entirely new place. The *Post* story that morning, under the headline "Sen. Simpson Calls Arnett 'Sympathizer,'" read in part as follows:

> Sen. Alan Simpson (R-Wyo.) charged yesterday that CNN correspondent Peter Arnett is "a sympathizer" with Iraq, that his reporting during the Vietnam War was biased and that he has a brother-in-law who was "active in the Viet Cong." At a Capital Hill luncheon with reporters, the Senate minority whip assailed Arnett for his censored television reports from Baghdad. He said the reporter is "what we used to call a sympathizer. . . . He was active in the Vietnam War and he won a Pulitzer Prize largely because of his anti-government material. And he was married to a Vietnamese whose brother was active in the Viet Cong." . . . An Arnett family member, who asked not to be identified, said the Viet Cong allegation is "completely untrue."
>
> The family member said Arnett's wife, Nina, from whom he has been separated for several years, had two brothers—a heart doctor who was forced into early retirement by the Viet Cong and died in the 1960s, and a math professor in Hanoi who was not politically active during the war and has not been allowed to

---

*The forty-first president.—Ed.

leave the country. . . . Author David Halberstam, who also won a Pulitzer for his Vietnam coverage, said yesterday he was "stunned by the ugliness" of Simpson's remarks about Arnett. "I like Alan Simpson. I think he's smart as hell, funny as hell," Halberstam said. "But the ugliness of him even mentioning someone like Nina, and connecting Peter's extraordinary coverage, as if that made him a sympathizer to the other side. . . . He's dead wrong. I know the family and that charge is particularly painful to them."

There was a bit of a buzz when I arrived at the office that morning. Everyone on the editorial staff had read the article; everyone thought it deserved an immediate and very rough response from us, an editorial protest that Simpson would have more than ample reason to notice; and everyone knew that I had become not a close friend but something of a pal of Simpson and his wife, Ann. They wondered how this palship would play out in what we wrote—if we wrote anything.

My feelings mirrored David Halberstam's. Simpson and I had been on the same side and on opposing sides of arguments before. But although it had seemed to some of us that lately he was displaying an uncharacteristically testy edge in some of his remarks, nothing like this personal smear had ever happened. "The Viet Cong"? A Saddam "sympathizer," with its implications of disloyalty and wartime treachery?

My 1950s liberal nerve had not been jammed by a dentist's drill like that since the actual 1950s. I also knew that I had to write the editorial myself. That was partly because I was so mad and partly because I figured that in deference to my presumed sensibilities concerning Simpson, the others might mouse around the "on the one hand/on the other" bush if they were to write it.

So I said I intended to do the editorial myself and would show it to them for their reaction as soon as it was done. Leaving them to wonder whether this was an effort to modulate the tone and limit the damage to a friend, I went into my office, closed the door, and proceeded to write as intemperate a gut-punch editorial as I had ever written. I mean, I don't know if it was over the name-calling edge, but it was certainly right out there *at* the edge.

There had been reports of an interview that Simpson and two other senators, Bob Dole of Kansas and Howard Metzenbaum of Ohio, had had in Iraq with Saddam Hussein less than a year before Saddam invaded Kuwait in 1991. My editorial characterized Simpson's remarks to Saddam in that interview as "bootlicky" and "obsequious" and said that "any journalist who greased around as Sen. Simpson & Co. did last April with a figure such as Saddam—or any other object of his coverage, for that matter—might deserve the title of sympathizer." It went on:

> But Mr. Arnett, who tries to say only what he has seen and regularly reminds viewers that both what he may say and what he may see is controlled by the Iraqis, has been doing a respectable, forthright job under what must be hideous circumstances. Nevertheless he has become an object of hysterical hatred to a lot of people who, so far as we know, never made the mildest objection to the kowtowing to Saddam that went on in the Republican administration before Aug. 2 or to the performance of the famous traveling troupe of senators in April. . . .
>
> [Senator Simpson] got into the sleaziest charges yet—reaching back to some relatives of Mr. Arnett's ex-wife as the basis of charges that the CNN correspondent had some connection with the Viet Cong and, by implication, was disloyal then and now. Peter Arnett is standing up straight over there in Baghdad. Here at home, Alan Simpson has dipped into the slime.

My recollection is that my colleagues said the editorial represented their views but suggested a few tonings down, such as substituting what they took to be the somewhat more decorous "dipped into the slime" for my original, piglike image of "wallowing in slime." I complied.

This was an odd kind of breach of the peace, a breach of the informal political and personal rules. It had been generated on both sides—I must suppose on his; I know for sure on ours—by genuine emotions. It was not professional wrestling, where you seem to be pounding the other guy on the head with a metal folding chair (but aren't), and he affects to be in excruciating pain (but isn't).

People knew the argument had stepped outside the controlled bounds of conventional dispute in Washington. Many who were common friends of the senator's and mine were rattled. I would get these calls from would-be "intermediaries" offering to help "work this out." I found them at once funny and irritating, since there wasn't anything that I could see to "work out." The editorial had said what we thought, no more, no less; that was it. A couple of Simpson's friends called me and said they and other of our friends were baffled: What was the meaning of that editorial? I thought: How could the meaning have been any clearer?

A year or so later, when Simpson and I encountered each other somewhere, we did not merely nod and pass each other by but stopped and chatted; it was one of those stilted, V-shaped-smile conversations, as we worked our halting way back to civility. We said—oh, most trusted of Washington standbys—that we must have lunch one day soon.

But contrary to both practice and expectation, not too long afterward, we actually did. It was only a slightly less stilted encounter. That would eventually change. In time when we saw each other we both relaxed, got our shoulders down from around our ears. But the dispute was never "talked out" or "mediated." It's not front and center, but it's up there in the attic somewhere, and we both know it is, part of the permanent furnishing of our resumed relationship.

Sometimes knowing a person about whom the paper is reporting and editorializing does lead to small, special considerations for them, but nothing, I should think, that even the most aggressive journalistic Rambos among us would find objectionable. There was the time, for example, when we on the *Post* editorial page were about to come out with a very tough assault on former FBI director William Webster's handling of the bureau's investigation of some of its own past misconduct.

I learned that Webster's wife, who had been very sick and, by choice, out of sight, was now in the last agony of her dying. The choice was simple: The guns were lowered for a decent interval. The only relevance here of my knowing Webster was that I thereby knew of his wife's condition; we would certainly have refrained from directly attacking anyone at such a deathbed moment if we knew about it. A little common decency, of the kind one would show to friends, family, and, for that matter, strangers in comparable circumstances, is hardly a threat to the independence of the press.

Nor is occasional sociability. Nancy Reagan was a friend of my friend *Washington Post* chairman Katharine Graham for years before the Reagans came to the White House. They began having lunch together every six or eight months or so, usually at Kay's house, shortly after the Reagans got to town. After a while they invited me to join them, which I did.

These were understood to be "not for quotation" conversations. But even with this precaution in place, Nancy Reagan was, to my surprise, amazingly loose-lipped about the recurrent turmoil in the administration and equally so in revealing her own strong views about the deficient ways of this and that White House player and her unambiguous feelings about how the numerous struggles should come out.

We know she was not shy about using her influence to achieve these results, so the conversation over lunch (and generally long into the afternoon) confirmed disputes that the White House had officially denied and provided a lot of information about and insight into the ways of the people running the Reagan administration. When it would be officially said that there was absolutely no truth to the rumors of some kind of animus between Donald Regan and Mrs. Reagan, for instance, or that stories that the two were battling to the death over some appointment or policy were nonsense, I knew better. We shared this kind of background corroboration with the *Post*'s national desk, although with reporter and Reagan biographer Lou Cannon on the case they didn't really need all that much help.

But you never get it completely right in these relationships. They have messy edges, and you need always to be attentive to the fact that either you or the other person will not see where they are or will forget or (generally the other person) will simply misread the relationship and expect something from it in times of trouble that they will not get.

I took a pounding when Nancy Reagan wrote exuberantly in her White House memoirs of her friendship with Kay and myself and made no distinction between us as to the degree of closeness. But it was dumb and careless of me to expect that anyone else would or even could notice the fine lines I was drawing in my own mind demarcating the social from the professional on these occasions, the propositions I refrained from agreeing or even nodding to, the conversations on certain subjects in which I did not participate.

In her book Nancy just sort of wheeled me in as a passenger in a sidecar, who shared credit for each of Kay's courtesies and kindnesses, whether I actually had anything to do with them or not.

There went my attempt to maintain a particular margin of distance in those luncheon conversations that I felt was required because I was responsible for an opinion section that covered the administration. When Nancy wrote of the friends who called to commiserate with her about the Irangate "problem" she and the White House were experiencing, she included Kay with a bunch of others like the Democratic elder Robert Strauss. And guess who else made a cameo appearance, riding along in her little sidecar?

I know I am sounding suspiciously defensive about this, and I don't want to suggest that my interest or my presence was merely exploitative: I liked Nancy. She did not seem like her ice-queen image. I was helped to understand the machinations and the tensions of her husband's White House by listening to her deeply engaged and, no doubt, one-sided version of them. And I was also helped to understand or at least strongly sense her indispensability to his political career as a motivator, an activator, and an energizer without whose constant presence he would not have got where he was or been able to function once he got there. She was the ignition and the battery of his whole political career, and I persist in thinking this essential relationship is the clue to Reagan.

But I can't imagine that I ever called her to express my sympathy with the White House's Irangate problem, since I and the editorial page over which I presided were very enthusiastic, open contributors to that problem and knowingly did a great deal to make it worse. I did initiate a call to her in roughly that period, however. It was to express my sympathy for a nightmare week in which her mother, to whom she had been exceptionally close, had died, and she herself had undergone a double mastectomy.

As a practical matter, I don't see anything in these casual, occasional mixings that is in and of itself bad or, by definition, harmful to journalistic values. Everything depends on the way in which the journalist behaves, on his or her ability to walk and chew gum at the same time. You can go to the houses of some of the most dogged, not-for-sale reporters I know—Chalmers Roberts; David Broder; Andrea Mitchell of NBC—and encounter guests from the upper reaches of Congress or the administration. The public officials will be warily exploring gossip and trading terrible jokes, all sharply aware of the limits and rules of such intermixing, none doubting that their gracious hosts of tonight would do them in tomorrow, if the occasion seemed to warrant it.

My point is that it's not the fact of the personal relationship in such situations; it's how the journalist handles the prospective pitfalls and temptations. Some *are* sycophantic and in the tank, though no more so than other journalists who, without any complicating personal relationship at all, are shamelessly trying to curry favor and special access and exclusive interviews for themselves and their news organizations by writing pieces about their government subjects that flatter them to the point of intellectual dishonesty.

But there is a still bigger defect to consider. I had written in my memo to Don, Ben, and Dick that I thought a much less well-tended and understood journalistic problem than that of personal affinity or political sympathy with some of our subjects and sources was the opposite. In some cases journalists harbor an abiding, close-minded, intractable antipathy to certain individuals and causes.

I'm not thinking about Hitler or Pol Pot here, but rather folks well within the conventional framework of American left-right politics. You can detest some of their causes and beliefs without detesting them and everything they say or do. But too often those whose political purposes we don't share and whose zeal in pursuing them we can't begin to comprehend don't get a fair shake from us; they will be picked on for statements that are fatuous or heartless but no more fatuous or heartless than statements by their opponents that we strain mightily to explain away.

For the unloved object of our attention, even the rare actions he takes with which we for once tend to agree will be presented in a context of grudging skepticism, embellished with plenty of speculative, undermining quotes. The quotes will likely be attributed to one of our most dependable if mysterious providers of deflation and doubt, an unidentified troublemaker who goes by the name of "Some Critics" and who generally makes his first subversive appearance about five paragraphs into a story and stays with it to the end, ultimately leaving it in ruins: "Some critics wonder, however, . . . They also question the claim that . . . And they point out that even if the congressman is being truthful in this case, there is no evidence that . . ." Our imaginations will simply have become incapable of entertaining the possibility that the guy may be sincere and honorably motivated in something he does.

Some things in Washington, of course, *are* what they seem, and there *are* reporters and commentators who go after their subjects in an unremittingly hostile way for distinctly unprofessional, bad-faith reasons. These include political bias, opportunism, and, all too often, a stake in the outcome of a story they wrote that subsequently seemed to be refuted and that they now desperately seek to vindicate.

But politicians and other public figures who automatically see unedifying motivations of this kind behind the hostility some columnists or reporters or news organizations chronically show toward them make a big mistake. For in my observation the fundamental source of what they are complaining about is rarely the journalists' political agenda, or their personal or professional agenda either.

The true wellspring is, rather, the journalists' ignorance of and self-satisfied indifference to the reality and particularity of the people they are writing about. I think the quality of journalistic output would not be compromised or endangered by a little more shoulder-rubbing with the objects of our reporting. On the contrary, it might be improved.

But instead, we in Washington have been moving in recent years toward a kind of effigy journalism. Those we write about we all too often project to the public as lifeless, one-dimensional representations of various political positions and cultural categories, each within his designated grouping being cookie-cutter identical to the rest.

They are effigies in that they are suitable only for sticking pins into or pasting over with little iridescent stickum hearts. For there is neither tolerance nor room in our concept of them for individuality or surprise or quirkiness or honest change of opinion, and no room for their espousing an eccentric, *unauthorized* mixture of views that whoever it is who decides these things has decreed do not belong together. If you've been badged by the press as an unreconstructed liberal, say, or a hard-line conservative, you're supposed always to act like our idea of one and not complicate our lives.

Thus, we tend to dismiss most divergence from the expected party line as trickery—temporary tactical maneuvers, presumptively politics-driven. Our effigy subjects have been defined entirely in terms of their "position" and are expected, in some sense even demanded, by us to live the lifestyle and vote the votes that we have associated with their badges: the left-wing this and the right-wing that, conservative Christians and secular humanists, pro-choice activists and pro-life demonstrators, hawks and doves, and so on.

As they emerge from the pages and airwaves of American journalism these days, they are, in my view, terminally boring because they are, as sketches of people, so monolithic, unconvincing, and implausible. Everyone knows real people are not like that. Loath to abandon their fixed idea of our views at the *Post* editorial page, many of our critics have a tag they use on the innumerable occasions when we are not faithful to it. At such times we are known, with reluctant, wary, and above all conditional approval as "Even the *Washington Post* . . . " It's like a temporary pass that runs out at midnight.

From my first days of observing Washington, the disappointments and the pleasant surprises—not to mention the continuing unpredictability of so many of the players—kept subverting my notions of a set, easily described, all but robotic struggle between these guys and those guys. It is sad but true that we are much more sophisticated and forgiving and aware of the ironies and idiosyncrasies and complexities and the balance of better and worse in our own and our friends' lives than we are in spotting or even looking for such qualities in the lives of our journalistic subjects—never mind crediting them as authentic when they turn up.

This tendency has bad consequences. One is that the credibility of our product is greatly diminished. For when we succumb to this stylized, board-game view of the people whose actions we are supposed to be trying to understand and report on, we cheat our readers and viewers, offering them a version of reality forced to fit a formula that may have little or no bearing on what is actually going on.

In addition, we are likely to be much harsher, in fact, often downright cruel, in our judgment of many of our subjects. That is not, I think, because journalists as a class are cruel. Rather, it is because they have in so many cases ceased thinking of the people they write about as people at all, thinking of them instead as opportune props and raw material for use in their stories and opinion pieces.

This insensitivity is apparently among the most maddening features of what we do. As one who has been the designated receiver of thousands upon thousands of letters to the paper each year, I know it also to be a continual source of complaint, exasperation, and sometimes despair among those whose lives we tromp through so heedlessly, oblivious of the gratuitous damage we may have left behind as we move on to the next story.

It is safe to say that for all our vanity and cockiness about our constitutionally protected role, few journalists have much appreciation of the enormous impact we have on the lives of those we write about. We don't recognize what a consequential, heavyweight presence we can be when we enter their communal lives, misunderstanding some project that is very important to them, ridiculing the decision they reached at some local council meeting, doing an exaggerated piece on the continuing, horrendous dangers of the neighborhood they have been working so hard to reclaim or a demoralizing report on the inadequacies of the school they believed had finally begun to turn around.

I'm not recommending that we become a bunch of civic boosters or soft-hearted sob sisters or spikers of stories that might hurt some politician's or civic reformer's feelings—only that we at least try to be aware of our effect on the lives of our subjects.

Here is an example of what I mean. It was the first time this question of impact really dawned on me and it has lingered ever since. I have come to believe there is an iron law of grammar correction on newspaper letters pages: If you write a letter to the editor indignantly correcting a grammar error in a previously published letter by someone else, you will invariably commit a grammatical error of your own; and this some malevolent, hawkeyed reader will spot, causing him or her promptly to submit yet another letter making *you* look like a fool.

One of these ridiculing letters of response turned up on a page proof I was reading early in my time as an editor at the *Post*. It was undoubtedly the least consequential item in any of the weekend pages I was going over, and yet I just kept going back to it; something about it bothered me.

I sent for a copy of the recently printed letter it was so mercilessly making fun of. It turned out to have been written by a grade school teacher in one of Washington's struggling public schools. I would guess that it was the first thing she had ever had published in the *Washington Post* or anywhere else and that it probably caused an admiring stir in her world at school.

Now she was going to be publicly humiliated. Would her students and fellow teachers laugh about it and mock her behind her back? Didn't matter—she would *think* they were. She would wake up in the morning feeling awful about it, wishing she hadn't written the original, rather haughty letter, wishing she now didn't have to show up in class.

Why were we printing this letter? Why were we doing this to her? "Well, I thought it was funny," said the young man who had put it on the proof. And I guess it was. But its publication would mean nothing to us and everything to the teacher. I killed the letter. It wasn't as if we were suppressing a story about Soviet spies in the CIA. A paper like the *Post* is a two-ton truck, and we run over a lot of people without even knowing it, and then we just roll on without even the most casual glance in the rearview mirror.

Years later, I, along with so many of my colleagues, had let myself get pretty smug and incurious in my approach to the people we were writing about. It didn't occur to me to wonder what had happened to them in the aftermath of our coverage or commentary. They were yesterday's obsession.

If we recollected them at all, it was as these vaguely preposterous figures from the past, the one-dimensional, stereotypical figures who had loomed large in some scandal or political uproar or heartstring-tugging story—and then were heard of no more, having taken up an incorporeal life in the paper's news-clipping files or as hard-to-remember answers in the game of Trivial Pursuit. They had only barely existed for us as people at the time of their maximum prominence in our pages. Now even their lives as journalistic depictions were over. They were no more.

Except that one of them, several years after her departure from the Washington stage, to my flabbergastion, came calling on me. I had just come out of that morning's editorial meeting and was chatting with editorial writer Pete Milius as we walked back to our offices. My secretary told me that a woman named Rita Lavelle was in the lobby and would like to talk with me. *Rita Lavelle?* You've got to be kidding. I had never met Rita Lavelle. Wasn't she the one who, a few years before, had gone to the clink for a brief spell, convicted in some kind of—what was it?—Environmental Protection Agency corruption case? Wasn't she a protégé of Ed Meese and a sworn enemy of her boss, Anne Gorsuch, who had also been under the gun in those hearings but got off?

This was pretty much the sum total of what I remembered about her, except for a couple of other things that began to float back into my memory as Pete and I, baffled, waited for her to come up the elevator. Rita Lavelle, a woman in her mid-thirties, had been the object of pervasive condescension and sexist put-downs during her stint on the national stage. Probably because she had been immediately pegged as an extremely conservative seller-out of public health to the chemical polluters, school was out so far as what people seemed to think they could say about her.

Journalists and others who rarely violated the new political decorum in such matters had taken to making fun of her on the basis of her physical appearance. She was short and plump, with curly blond hair, and so was repeatedly singled out for her Kewpie doll looks. Her conflict with her female boss was characterized as a "catfight."

Several in the press reveled in projecting her as a presumptive airhead as well, again, in part because of her politics and associations but in part as well because of her unsophisticated, un-Beltway-approved manner and appearance, which they just couldn't leave alone. She was, in this sense, the quintessential journalistic prop, treated as if she had been put on Earth by God only to confirm our ideas about corrupt corporate polluters and to amuse us and enable us to write witty copy that our friends would admire.

That she was a pretty reliable instrument of those she was theoretically meant to be regulating seems certain. The theory was that she was simply being used as a front by the big boys in the Reagan administration who were making secret deals offstage with corporate polluters in return for campaign funds and letting Rita Lavelle sashay around to fancy restaurants with a variety of chemical industry titans, all of them looking and feeling expense-account important as they ordered lavish meals for her as she laughed uproariously at their jokes.

She was hopelessly inexperienced in the ways of Washington, and she took her political and business sponsors at their word, believing they were all on the same side and that they would be as loyal to her as she was to them. So she covered for her principals and patrons (or at least tried to) when the investigation came and was on that account convicted of perjury and sentenced to six months in prison, which she served. As is so often the case in Washington scandals, she was the least influential player in the cast—and the only one to be convicted. They had sold her out.

And now here she was, walking into my office bearing a huge unbound manuscript, part memoir and part get-even screed, as Pete and I understood it. She was looking for a publisher and hoped we might have some tips for her on how you went about having a book published. We gave her what guidance we could, which wasn't much, since neither of us was very knowledgeable about book publishing.

We asked her about her life in prison and her life afterward; she was forthcoming and even funny at times on both subjects. But she hadn't come to see me, a total stranger, to discuss any of this. She had come, she said, to try to get her good name back. She had come because what we had said about her had been tormenting her. She wanted a chance to win Pete's and my good opinion, that was all.

She was a personable woman who then spent a little time telling us of her background: the eldest of seven children of a devoutly Catholic family in California, a source of great pride to her parents for learning about chemistry and getting a Ph.D. in it, an assistant in the Reagan gubernatorial administration, a woman who had created a life she was proud of and who had seen it trashed, first by what she took to be the treachery of Ms. Gorsuch and others in her agency and thereafter by the hazing of the press.

Periodically, in the course of all this, she would refer despairingly to what she called, without further elaboration, "that editorial"—how crushing it had been, how she was just asking for a chance to be heard by us and to make her case that our devastating characterization of her conduct had been untrue. She wasn't asking for another editorial or any kind of corrective story or statement by us all those years after the original squall, she said. She had taken her courage in her hands and risked "barging in" like this—which she hoped was all right—only because it was so important to her that we *know* she was not guilty of the terrible things we had accused her of, that her life added up to more than the worthless joke we had made it seem. She wanted to cease being an object of our contempt.

Now, nothing in this encounter affected either my understanding of what those hearings had been about or my opinion of the Reagan administration conduct that had triggered them. And nothing in it brought me any closer to Rita Lavelle's point of view on the subject. But I confess I had come to feel like a real heel.

This was not just because I realized that I had never taken her existence seriously or remembered that she had feelings or pride or vulnerabilities as we were all guffawing our way through her misery. It was something more revealing, which told worlds about the great discrepancy between the way the aggrieved objects of our commentary and reporting regard us and the way we regard them.

For it became plain through a series of quick, darting looks between Pete and me as she spoke, signaling our shared perplexity, that although Pete probably had written the piece (since it was his field), and I had undoubtedly authorized and approved it, neither of us had any recollection whatever of this editorial that loomed so large in Rita Lavelle's life. None. We had no recollection of what we may have said about her or the hearings in general in other editorials either.

I didn't want to say that because I thought it would be such a mortifying, dismissive thing for her to hear: "Oh, by the way, this thing that is so important to you and that you have been brooding about and feel misrepresented and trashed your accomplishments, don't sweat it! We can't even remember when we wrote that or anything much about it. No big deal."

I feared that she could only have perceived this as yet another put-down, a final, disdainful, wanton kick in the gut. So we asked her instead about which editorial it had been (as if we remembered any of them). She produced a piece that she had evidently been carrying around with her. It turned out, in fact, to be a relatively recent piece on pollution regulation that alluded only briefly to Lavelle.

Then came the next surprise. The part about Lavelle struck both Milius and me as awfully mild, so we remained at a loss as to the nature of our provocation. We asked her about it.

"Shenanigans," she finally said, pausing to let the full gravity of the charge sink in. *"Shenanigans,"* she repeated, as if she had just said "armed robbery" or "assault with intent to kill." "You continue to describe my activities at Superfund as *'shenanigans.'"* To Lavelle this was not only a degrading term of ridicule but implied all sorts of skulduggery and moral lapses as well. Of these she proceeded earnestly to proclaim her innocence while Pete and I respectfully listened.

"Shenanigans." I thought I was going to cry.

Afterword

By Michael Beschloss

MEG GREENFIELD BEGAN writing this book in the early 1990s. She worked on it during weekends at her slender brick row house on R Street in Georgetown and during summers at her 1960s-modern retreat on Bainbridge Island, Washington.

She told almost none of her friends that she was writing it. One reason for this may have been that, having never written a book before, she did not feel entirely sure of herself and wanted to keep the option of aborting the project, if necessary. But the main reason was probably something else. From the moment she came to Washington to live, in 1961, she was determined to preserve an inner chamber of her life that could not be touched or altered by the carnival going on around her.

That is a central theme of this book—how to live at the center of political and journalistic influence in Washington without losing your principles, detachment, or individual human qualities. Her scorn is reserved for those who don't manage that combination— men and women more concerned about their ideological purity than their effectiveness or, at the other extreme, hustling politicians and journalists who have long ago turned into caricatures of themselves. After reading this book for the first time, I realized much more than before that for Meg this was a battle she never felt she had the luxury to stop fighting.

Given her earlier life and her natural instincts, one might not have imagined that as editorial page editor of the *Washington Post* she could carry off one of the most influential positions in the country with such a supreme public sense of self-assurance and command. She grew up as something of an outsider by religion in Seattle, a lover of classical and English literature at Smith and Cambridge, a 1950s Greenwich Village semibohemian (by her lights, anyway), and a woman of strong, acerbic, sometimes idiosyncratic reactions to people. Still, she managed to operate at the heart of what used to be called the Eastern Establishment without letting her rabble-rousing streak interfere with her official role or letting her official duties and ambitions slowly extinguish her enthusiasms or moral sense.

Many who knew her presumed that this stance came easily to Meg. But by describing one Washington figure after another who succeeded or failed to maintain both public and private selves that they could be proud of, this book shows how much she kept the problem in mind. She seemed to worry that if she humored her private eccentricities, she might take the *Post* editorial page in some self-indulgent, William-Randolph-Hearst-like direction—or that if she took her formal responsibilities too gravely, her real self might disappear.

By keeping that inner core, Meg managed the rare feat of being a public person for thirty years without turning into one of the Washington creatures she depicts in this book. She always maintained the clear-eyed detachment about the people and events around her that informed her writing.

For her, the cost was often solitude. In notes for what would have been this book's final chapter, which she did not live to write, she said, "Wanting to be alone was a continuous and consistent impulse from as early as I can remember. I did want to be alone and need to be alone a large portion of the time." Even in a crowd, "I learned as a child to . . . arrange my psyche and my seeming presence so I was alone anyway."

She wrote that she "used to think" that her failure to marry was "Freudian," that she had been "spoiled" by the expectation of a "handsome man" to the point where she was "not able to love the ugly or imperfect." Perhaps it had been the "quarrels between my parents," she wrote, or her "self-consciousness" about being smarter than some of the men she met.

She wrote that late in her life, when she suffered through "deaths and traumas," including her own cancer, "being alone" made her more respectful of the "Stanley Kowalski"—the "inner animal." Thus by her last years, the woman known for her deliberation and reason was wondering whether the character in Tennessee Williams's *Streetcar Named Desire* who acted from his passions had something after all.

After exacting a small vow of secrecy, Meg told me in 1994 that she was working on this book. Over lunches at one or another Washington restaurant, she would ask nuts-and-bolts questions about book writing and book publishers. Once she was diagnosed with cancer, her commitment to the project grew more fierce.

On Independence Day weekend 1998, she invited my wife, Afsaneh, and myself, along with her dear friend and boss, Don Graham, and his wife, Mary, to stay with her on Bainbridge Island, where, in her impeccable garden exploding with color, she held her annual Fourth of July dinner and croquet tournament, with guests arriving by seaplane. She took me aside to report that she was working hard on the book.

Two months later, back in Washington, she asked me to lunch at the Bistrot Lepic, around the corner from her Georgetown house. Her health was failing, but she was, as ever, alert and decisive.

She asked me to be her literary executor, ensuring that the book would be published if she could not see it through to the end. She told me who should write the foreword and afterword, who should be the literary agent and publisher, and where her private papers should go (the Library of Congress). The book's existence should not be revealed until it was in the hands of its publisher.

I agreed, while insisting that she would bounce back and be able to do all of this herself. That winter she plunged even more deeply into the project.

In March 1999, after attending the annual dinner of the Gridiron Club in Washington, she collapsed. Friends and relatives gathered around her bed at Johns Hopkins Medical Center in Baltimore, with doctors murmuring that this was the end.

But it wasn't. Enforcing her will against the doctors' wishes, she had herself driven back to her house in Georgetown, where she enjoyed an Indian summer of almost two months. Friends and colleagues filed into the house to tell her good-bye without saying so. Bill Clinton, of whose presidency she had often been scathing, scrawled a kindly, jocular note thanking her for her encouragement during the *early* part of his career.

One day in late April or early May, looking up from the hospital bed installed in her upstairs bedroom, she asked me whether it was time to look at her manuscript. I took her by wheelchair into her home office. She pulled computer disks out from behind books and drawers and from under stacks of papers. With her craving for secrecy, she had labeled the disks with Greek-sounding code names.

I took them home, read the contents closely, and went to the R Street house on Wednesday afternoon, May 12. By now Meg was blind and unable to talk. I pledged that her book would be published. A solitary tear rolled out of one of her large, pale blue eyes. The next morning she died.

That summer, I asked Kate Lehrer (in whom she had also confided about her book) and Kate's husband, Jim, as well as Mary and Don Graham, to serve as informal advisers as I moved the book toward publication. These close friends of hers read manuscript and provided frequent counsel as I stitched the book together from the files on the computer disks. Amy McWethy helped to organize her private papers. The language of this book is a hundred percent

Meg's, except for normal editing and polishing. I had to use my own judgment in choosing which of her multiple drafts of each section to use—and in selecting the book's title.

During the last weeks of Meg's life, she described for me the final chapter that she had hoped to write but now knew she would never get to. She hoped that in this Afterword, drawing on her notes and this conversation, I would sketch out what she would have written.

Entitled "Friends and Family," that chapter would have been the most intimate of this book. She planned to "define the complicated relationships" in her life—"professional and engaged and personal." Among them were her close friendships with her two bosses, Katharine and Don Graham ("I learned from both"), and her *Washington Post* lieutenants Stephen Rosenfeld, Colbert King, and Peter Milius, noting that when she was ill, they were like "brothers" who "moved in and took over."

These people and others she thought of as "the family you create." She wanted to write of dealing with the Pentagon Papers controversy in 1971 while sitting next to the kidney-shaped pool of her *Post* predecessor, Philip Geyelin, of which the columnist Joseph Alsop, "the arbiter of all taste," had said, "Geyelin, this place will not be taken seriously until you get that pool straightened."

Traveling further into her past, she would have explored the childhood origins of her need for solitude. She noted that in Seattle, when her beloved older brother, Jimmy, was banished to his room, "he would protest until he got out." Not Meg. She loved to be alone, "trying to work some puzzle or just musing or conversing with myself."

She recalled that "when I was a very young kid, small for my age, and in the fashion of the time, dressed in puffed sleeves and organdy pinafores and equipped with an unnaturally low, basso voice which made it all weird, my parents used to get a kick out of having taught me to utter Greta Garbo's most famous sultry line. So when through with "Cock Robin," I would be asked to recite, 'I vahnt to be alone.' It wasn't child abuse. I enjoyed the laughing. And wanting to be alone made sense to me."

Comparing her Seattle childhood with her later eminence in Washington, D.C., she had planned to explore "my social pretensions, all my distance from the mainstream." Even as one of the most self-possessed people in America, she said she felt vaguely "frightened" when she attended one of "those White House hoo-has" or flew into Russia to interview Gorbachev, "with the voice of the grandparents I never knew coming out of the mud like *Fiddler on the Roof,* saying, 'What are *you* doing there?'"

Unlike "Rosebud" in Orson Welles's *Citizen Kane,* in real life there is usually not one single clue to what motivates people. But in Meg's notes and as she lay dying, she suggested one key (and asked me to jot down each detail).

It was Easter in the late 1930s. Her father, Lewis Greenfield, Seattle auctioneer and amateur performer, was taking the family to the prison at McNeill Island, where he would entertain the inmates.

The father was dressed in "what he took to be sportswear, years before we were persuaded that he wasn't wearing the jacket to one suit and the trousers to another." Her mother, Lorraine (who died just a few years later), looked "prim, smart, frail" in a "pastel plaid suit." Brother Jimmy wore a "white and navy jacket with Lord Byron shirt." Meg wore a "pink challis dress and white socks and Mary Janes."

As Meg's father performed onstage, she and her mother and brother watched as the "guys in gray prison issue" sat "slouched, hostile, with ankles crossed." Suddenly, one of the inmates cried, "Lew! Lewie!" Her father called out, "Hey, Blackie!"

As Meg recalled, she was unnerved by "shame and social embarrassment" that her father should know a criminal. But at the same time, she felt that "the place had been tamed, made familiar."

At the end of her life, she mused that the prison memory led to her adulthood in the East and in journalism. It led to her insistence on being in such stalwart command of herself—and, during her last three decades, her passion for helping a generation of *Washington Post* and *Newsweek* readers decipher the "endlessly engaging complexities and contradictions" of how human beings behave in Washington, and the politics of the United States and the world.

Just like on that long-ago day with her father in the prison, she explained, it was in her role as a journalist that she felt "enveloped and safe—just watching."

Index

PUBLICAFFAIRS is a publishing house founded in 1997. It is a tribute to the standards, values, and flair of three persons who have served as mentors to countless reporters, writers, editors, and book people of all kinds, including me.

I.F. STONE, proprietor of *I. F. Stone's Weekly*, combined a commitment to the First Amendment with entrepreneurial zeal and reporting skill and became one of the great independent journalists in American history. At the age of eighty, Izzy published *The Trial of Socrates*, which was a national bestseller. He wrote the book after he taught himself ancient Greek.

BENJAMIN C. BRADLEE was for nearly thirty years the charismatic editorial leader of *The Washington Post*. It was Ben who gave the *Post* the range and courage to pursue such historic issues as Watergate. He supported his reporters with a tenacity that made them fearless, and it is no accident that so many became authors of influential, best-selling books.

ROBERT L. BERNSTEIN, the chief executive of Random House for more than a quarter century, guided one of the nation's premier publishing houses. Bob was personally responsible for many books of political dissent and argument that challenged tyranny around the globe. He is also the founder and was the longtime chair of Human Rights Watch, one of the most respected human rights organizations in the world.

.   .   .

For fifty years, the banner of Public Affairs Press was carried by its owner Morris B. Schnapper, who published Gandhi, Nasser, Toynbee, Truman, and about 1,500 other authors. In 1983 Schnapper was described by *The Washington Post* as "a redoubtable gadfly." His legacy will endure in the books to come.

Peter Osnos, *Publisher*